BADFILM

Traditions in American Cinema
Series Editors Linda Badley and R. Barton Palmer

Titles in the series include:

The 'War on Terror' and American Film: 9/11 Frames Per Second
by Terence McSweeney

American Postfeminist Cinema: Women, Romance and Contemporary Culture
by Michele Schreiber

In Secrecy's Shadow: The OSS and CIA in Hollywood Cinema 1941–1979
by Simon Willmetts

Indie Reframed: Women's Filmmaking and Contemporary American Independent Cinema
by Linda Badley, Claire Perkins and Michele Schreiber (eds)

Vampires, Race and Transnational Hollywoods
by Dale Hudson

Who's in the Money? The Great Depression Musicals and Hollywood's New Deal
by Harvey G. Cohen

Engaging Dialogue: Cinematic Verbalism in American Independent Cinema
by Jennifer O'Meara

Cold War Film Genres
by Homer B. Pettey (ed)

The Style of Sleaze: The American Exploitation Film, 1959-1977
by Calum Waddell

The Franchise Era: Managing Media in the Digital Economy
by James Fleury, Stephen Mamber and Bryan Hartzheim (eds)

The Stillness of Solitude: Romanticism and Contemporary American Independent Film
by Michelle Deverereaux

The Other Hollywood Renaissance
by Dominic Lennard, R. Barton Palmer and Murray Pomerance (eds)

Contemporary Hollywood Animation: Style, Storytelling, Culture and Ideology Since the 1990s
by Noel Brown

www.edinburghuniversitypress.com/series/TIAC

BADFILM
Incompetence, Intention and Failure

Becky Bartlett

EDINBURGH
University Press

This book is dedicated to Adam

Edinburgh University Press is one of the leading university presses in the UK. We publish academic books and journals in our selected subject areas across the humanities and social sciences, combining cutting-edge scholarship with high editorial and production values to produce academic works of lasting importance. For more information visit our website: edinburghuniversitypress.com

© Becky Bartlett, 2021, 2023

Edinburgh University Press Ltd
The Tun – Holyrood Road
12(2f) Jackson's Entry
Edinburgh EH8 8PJ

First published in hardback by Edinburgh University Press 2021

Typeset in 10/12.5pt Sabon by
Servis Filmsetting Ltd, Stockport, Cheshire

A CIP record for this book is available from the British Library

ISBN 978 1 4744 5042 3 (hardback)
ISBN 978 1 4744 5043 0 (paperback)
ISBN 978 1 4744 5044 7 (webready PDF)
ISBN 978 1 4744 5045 4 (epub)

The right of Becky Bartlett to be identified as the author of this work has been asserted in accordance with the Copyright, Designs and Patents Act 1988, and the Copyright and Related Rights Regulations 2003 (SI No. 2498).

CONTENTS

List of Figures vi
Acknowledgements viii

1. Introduction: Bad Films and Badfilms 1
2. Investigating Intentions in Badfilms 20
3. The Disruptive Effects of Bad Voices 41
4. Recycled Footage, Plagiarism and Bad Art 70
5. Bad Acting and the Cultification of Bad Actors 102
6. The Potential Pleasures of Bad Editing 133
7. Conclusion: Taking Badfilms Seriously 162

Bibliography 175
Index 183

FIGURES

Figure 1.1	A T-Rex claims its victim in *One Million AC/DC* (de Priest, 1969); the same dinosaur also features in *The Mighty Gorga* (Hewitt, 1969)	2
Figure 2.1	The inanimate octopus prop, which was either borrowed or stolen from Republic Studios, *Bride of the Monster* (Wood, Jr, 1955)	30
Figure 2.2A, B	Jeff and his co-pilot encounter a UFO. Note the boom mike's shadow and the UFO's visible strings, *Plan 9 From Outer Space* (Wood, Jr, 1959)	32
Figure 2.3A, B	'Supernatural' activity, *Night of the Ghouls* (Wood, Jr, 1959)	34
Figure 3.1	Martin and his companions 'look at the rocket with utter amazement', *The Creeping Terror* (Nelson, 1964)	49
Figure 3.2	The space capsule, *Monster A-go Go* (Rebane, 1964)	52
Figure 3.3	The 'horribly mangled' corpse, *Monster A-go Go* (Rebane, 1964)	53
Figure 3.4	Mr and Mrs Radcliffe discuss their sons' whereabouts, *The Beast of Yucca Flats* (Francis, 1961)	63
Figure 4.1A, B	Glen and Barbara's conversation is interrupted by stampeding buffalo, *Glen or Glenda* (Wood, Jr, 1953)	86
Figure 4.2A–G	Joe and Jack's day, *Glen or Glenda* (Wood, Jr, 1953)	88
Figure 4.3A–F	Recycled scenes of spectacle as the Great Guidance	

	unleashes his fury, before Johnny wakes up from his dream, *Robot Monster* (Tucker, 1953)	97
Figure 4.4	Note the man holding the 'space platform', visible in the bottom right-hand corner, *Robot Monster* (Tucker, 1953)	98
Figure 5.1	Publicity shot of Bela Lugosi featured in *Bride of the Monster* (Wood, Jr, 1955)	115
Figure 5.2	Dr Vornoff declaring his intentions to 'conquer the world', *Bride of the Monster* (Wood, Jr, 1955)	116
Figure 5.3	Shirley (Pat Barringer) screaming, *Orgy of the Dead* (Apostolof, 1965)	121
Figure 5.4	Criswell rising from his coffin to introduce *Night of the Ghouls* (Wood, Jr, 1959)	125
Figure 5.5	Edward D. Wood, Jr, as Glenda, *Glen or Glenda* (Wood, Jr, 1953)	129
Figure 5.6	Jerry (Cash Flagg) as a mixed-up zombie, *The Incredibly Strange Creatures Who Stopped Living and Became Mixed-Up Zombies!!?* (Steckler, 1964)	131
Figure 6.1A–D	Torgo (John Reynolds), shown from different angles in *Manos: The Hands of Fate* (Warren, 1966)	144
Figure 6.2A–E	Bad editing obliterates the natural logic of the landscape, *The Beast of Yucca Flats* (Francis, 1961)	149
Figure 6.3A, B	Suggesting shared space through editing, *Plan 9 From Outer Space* (Wood, Jr, 1959)	153
Figure 6.4	The swamp creature reveals itself, *Curse of the Swamp Creature* (Buchanan, 1968)	159
Figure 7.1	Portrait of Jesus, *Ben & Arthur* (Mraovich, 2002)	166

ACKNOWLEDGEMENTS

This book began as a doctoral thesis, and so my first thanks go to my supervisors, Ian Garwood and Dimitris Eleftheriotis, as well as all the staff in Film and Television Studies at the University of Glasgow for their advice, support and encouragement. My thanks to Gillian Leslie, Senior Commissioning Editor at Edinburgh University Press, for her patience. My thanks also to my family and friends, and my husband, Colin. I am also grateful to everyone who has provided feedback, suggestions and bad movie recommendations since this project began.

1. INTRODUCTION: BAD FILMS AND BADFILMS

> 'Greetings, my friend. We are all interested in the future, for that is where you and I are going to spend the rest of our lives. And remember my friend, future events such as these will affect you in the future. You are interested in the unknown, the mysterious, the unexplainable. That is why you are here'.
>
> Criswell, *Plan 9 From Outer Space*

Watching bad movies is often a strange, unsettling, disorienting experience. Bad movies are weird, preposterous, absurd: they are, to use Dyck and Johnson's term, 'bizarre' (2017: 283). In *The Creeping Terror* (Nelson 1964), for example, giant, strangely sexualised carpet-monster aliens devour hapless teenagers by moving very slowly towards them and allowing the screaming youngsters to clamber into their 'mouths'. In *Jail Bait* (Wood 1954), a doctor performs 'very, very complicated' full facial reconstruction surgery on a lowlife gangster, using the sofa in his living room as his operating table. *The Mighty Gorga* (Hewitt 1969), a cheap and blatant rip-off of *King Kong* (Cooper and Schoedsack 1933), features a giant, occasionally cross-eyed, gorilla (allegedly played by the director in a particularly unconvincing costume) fighting an immobile T-Rex puppet. The same dinosaur also features in *One Million AC/DC* (de Priest 1969), a softcore prehistoric hippy sexploitation movie, where it chomps down on a barbie doll. *Night Train to Mundo Fine*, also released as *Red Zone Cuba* (Francis 1966), suggests that the Bay of Pigs invasion was carried out by a handful of criminals duped into joining the military, although

Figure 1.1 A T-Rex claims its victim in *One Million AC/DC* (de Priest, 1969); the same dinosaur also features in *The Mighty Gorga* (Hewitt, 1969).

the story is so nonsensical and poorly constructed that it is difficult to really ever figure out what is actually happening.

However, it is not just the shoddy special effects and ridiculous plots that make films like these so bad – or so weird. Like the others discussed throughout this book, these films are bad because they are *incompetent*: nothing about them seems to work in the way we might expect. Characters are undeveloped, dialogue is trite and unnatural, acting ranges from flat to histrionic, continuity errors are frequent, plots are incomprehensible, and attempts at spectacle fail – spectacularly. The deviations from expected, established standards of cinematic representation seldom seem to be intentional: these films are inappropriate, inconsistent, incoherent and baffling. Yet, precisely *because* of their blatant awfulness, they are not just weird but *intriguing*. Bad movies like these can be so confusing and so bizarre that they encourage us to investigate further: how did these films get made? How were they ever deemed acceptable for release? Surely it is not possible that the filmmakers responsible for them thought they were making *good* movies? It was these questions, among others, that first motivated my investigation into bad cinema. Like so many other cult film scholars, my fandom motivated my academic studies, which in turn led me to ask new questions: why should we study bad movies? What can be learned through a serious, scholarly investigation of cinematic badness, of complete and utter failure, of 'trash'? This book, then, aims to provide some possible responses to these questions.

As a category, 'bad cinema' comprises a rather loose collection of movies described as bad for a range of different reasons. Badness manifests in various, sometimes overlapping ways. Bad movies can be box-office flops and mainstream bombs, shameless vanity projects and cynical money-making exercises. They can be cheap, shoddy pictures made by people lacking the skills and/or motivation to create anything better. Films may be morally suspect, critically disreputable or 'in bad taste', or belong to 'illegitimate' genres like pornography (see Perkins and Verevis 2014; Cartmell et al. 1997; Hunter 2013; Sexton and Mathijs 2011: 98–95). Badness can be determined through a purely subjective judgement, whereby a film is declared to be bad because the viewer simply did not like or enjoy it. Badness is also a characteristic of other categories of cinema, particularly cult. Although cult films are frequently thematically or aesthetically innovative, they can also be bad – even simultaneously (Mathijs and Mendik 2008: 2). With cult films traditionally positioned in opposition to the 'mainstream', badness can be transgressive, challenging standards and conventions of taste, style and quality. Furthermore, the diversity of bad movies, as well as the challenges posed by such diversity, is reflected in cult cinema more broadly; both are loosely defined categories that comprise a wide variety of (overlapping) films often united more by similarities in reception than any specifically textual characteristics.

This book focuses on a particular kind of bad movie: the badfilm. Badfilms are primarily characterised by incompetence, which is typically exacerbated by material poverty and particularly restrictive production conditions. The term can be traced back to the critics writing in the cult fanzine *Zontar: The Magazine from Venus*, who used it as a way of differentiating the 'truly great' bad movies from schlocky, intentionally parodic 'trash' films (quoted in Buchanan 1996: 91). Thus, badfilms are often valued, appreciated and celebrated for their ineptitude by cult audiences who 'cherish the "worst" films and the distinctive pleasures made possible by their transcendent "badness"' (Hunter 2014: 484). As a category, badfilm is largely constructed in reception, although a film's inclusion is primarily justified through a focus on textual characteristics and perceived stylistic deviations. The badness of badfilms is predicated on the assumed evidence of incompetence and failed intentions, which cannot be consciously reproduced: as soon as one intends to make a badfilm, it stops being one. Badfilms, then, are understood to be 'simultaneously *striving for and failing to deploy* artistic conventions' (MacDowell and McCulloch 2019: 644; emphasis in original). In contrast to, for example, avant-garde films that deliberately eschew the 'rules' of cinema established in the classical Hollywood system, the unconventional style of badfilms is interpreted as the result of a 'systematic failure . . . to *obey* dominant codes of cinematic representation' (Sconce 1995: 385; emphasis in original). Badfilm, then, is a subcategory of bad cinema marked by incompetence and failure, whereby viewers can recognise – or make claims to recognise – the failed intention to achieve certain standards of cinematic form, content, construction, and representation.

Badfilms and Failure

To date, academic work on badfilms has been firmly rooted in cult studies. As scholarship has expanded and a discourse surrounding badfilms specifically has emerged, it is worth also considering its relevance to what could be termed 'failure studies'. In a special issue dedicated to exploring failures, flops and false starts, the editors of the journal *The Velvet Light Trap* note that the media industry has 'long been fascinated with failure', even citing 'worst director of all time' Edward D. Wood, Jr, as a notable example of a 'hapless' filmmaker who has been the subject of great fascination (2009: 1). Failure can, however, mean different things in different contexts, and determining failure depends on a recognised yardstick of success. Artistic or creative failures can include 'failures of imagination, failures of taste, moral, ideological, or ethical failures, failures of execution, failures due to inexperience or ignorance, failures due to lack of inspiration or talent, failures of nerve, failures of overreaching' (Berg 2009: 101). Many of these are routinely evident in badfilms, either individually or in combination. Berg also identifies reception failures: box-office failures, recognition failures and the failure of critics (2009: 101). Curiously, the cultification of badfilms suggests that, in terms of reception at least, they now enjoy a strange kind of success – albeit not in ways originally anticipated. Ironically, the niche success of these films as cultified objects is precisely because of their demonstrable artistic and creative failures.

The study of failure can be approached in diverse ways, and the value of studying failure itself is reflected in a range of diverse contributions, from studies of failed aesthetics (Mittell 2009), over failures within an industrial context (Sobock 2009; Hunter 2019), to the function of failure in gaming (Juul 2013). Within a media context, failure studies can draw on a broad range of forms, criticism, industries and practices to explore 'not just the question of understanding the generative mechanisms behind specific failures but also the more central inquiry: How is failure itself defined in these diverse contexts?' (Editors [author unknown] 2009: 1). The badness of badfilms is predicated on failed intentions – typically, as discussed in the next chapter, relating to the failure to achieve the intended artistic outcome. Yet, as I demonstrate throughout this book, failure reveals itself in haphazard, ramshackle and inconsistent ways in badfilms, thereby presenting challenges for interpretation. At the same time, it is often precisely because of badfilms' demonstrable failure and incompetence that they are so unusual and so intriguing. Whereas cult studies have tended to identify the 'value' of badfilms in their reception and use by cult audiences, there is, I suggest, intrinsic value in the badness itself. Badfilms can capture our imaginations, but they can also 'expand [. . .] our understanding of the virtues and limitations of moving images and the industries that surround them' (Editors [author unknown] 2009: 1). Jeffrey Sconce, for example, recognises the pedagogical value of badfilms in their ability to 'compel *even the most complacent viewer* into adopting a reading position marked by that rare combination of incredulous amazement and critical detachment' (2003: 21; emphasis added). Often, the incompetence, inconsistency, incoherence and weirdness of badfilms limits the potential for narrative engagement and immersion but, in the process, can provide new and unexpected opportunities to concentrate on diegetic and non-diegetic elements that are typically concealed from us in 'good' films.

There are, however, risks attached to studying failure. Whereas encountering successful works is a 'humbling experience', the opposite can be true when analysing failure (Berg 2009: 101). As discussed more in Chapter 2, for example, badfilm appreciation can be problematic when it is based on *schadenfreude* or positions of superiority. With filmmakers having presumably invested time and money in a creative endeavour, being celebrated for incompetence is not necessarily a comfortable position to occupy, particularly if – when – that celebration comes in the form of laughing *at* failure. After all, no one intends to make a failure, but they may well have tried their best. Berg suggests that, even if 'it didn't come together [. . .] there is something sacred about the trying' (2009: 101). This echoes advice that Ed Wood offers to aspiring filmmakers and screenwriters in the closing chapter of his fascinating 'How to succeed in Hollywood' guide, *Hollywood Rat Race*: 'It's terrible to me to hear someone say about someone else's work, "ah, that stinks". Yet the critic probably couldn't ink his way out of a paper bag. You put it on paper. Good, bad or indifferent. *At least you had the guts to put it there*' (1998: 131; emphasis added). Thus, for failure studies to become a viable critical approach, 'a great deal of humility is required' (Berg 2009: 101). With this in mind, this book proposes a means of examining failure that acknowledges the potential experiential pleasures and the impact of cultification but recognises the badness as intrinsically valuable and interesting in and of itself. In other words, I suggest that badfilms have value that includes, but also extends beyond, their potential instrumental value as objects of fun. By returning focus to the texts themselves, it is possible to locate value in the failure itself.

The Badfilm Canon

Badfilms are, typically, celebrated in cult circles for their naivety, their sincerity, their endearing ineptitude and their overwhelming, unavoidable failure. Their badness is, however, 'not a mere summary of critical disapproval but denotes a complete abrogation of the minimal standards of filmmaking' (Hunter 2014: 487). The badness of badfilms, therefore, is not 'ontologically separable' (Hunter 2014: 487) and, as discussed in more detail below, the category itself represents an effort to move away from the subjectivity of taste towards an understanding of 'objective badness' (Hoberman 1980), established through the identification of failed intentions. This form of badness is by no means restricted to any particular type of cinema – in theory, any film could demonstrably and overwhelmingly fail to achieve its intended aims and therefore be a badfilm. However, only a relatively small proportion of badfilms have gained notable cult status and become canonised as the 'worst films of all time'.

Like cult cinema more broadly, the badfilm canon is significantly oriented towards US-American films. This is not to imply that *only* US-American films can be considered to have failed in some way but, nevertheless, it is 'notable how US-centric' the canon is (Smith 2019: 705; see also Sconce 1995: 372). There are several possible reasons for this, including the existence of certain modes of production associated with American low-budget, independent cinema, as discussed in more detail below, and particular forms of critical reception adopted by fans. Jamie Sexton and Ernest Mathijs, for example, suggest that the dominance of American films at the 'top of the canon of badness' is 'an indication perhaps of that culture's perceived obsession with rankings of cultural achievements' (2011: 38). They point to the tendency among badfilm fans to adopt alternative awards formats and compile lists of the 'worst' films, 'partly in order to ridicule them, and partly to demonstrate the entertainment value of sheer badness, and to celebrate this badness as a mode of reception' (2011: 38), with the result that certain films have achieved and sustained cult receptions precisely because of their demonstrable incompetence.

Identifying badness-as-incompetence relies on viewers being able to confidently ascertain a schism between the intended aim and the actual result and, as such, it is unsurprising that the badfilm canon is replete with US-American films. The films now celebrated as the 'worst of all time' are typically understood to be striving to adhere to the conventions of narrative and continuity established in Hollywood. Badfilms are generally identified as such through their failure to conform to the 'rules' of American narrative cinema specifically; the Medveds allude to this when they argue that it would be 'unfair to apply Hollywood standards' to films made in different cultural and national contexts (1978: 10). Here, it is worth noting that there are some examples of non-American films to be found dotted throughout fan-authored badfilm lists, but none have achieved the same level of widespread recognition as their American counterparts. Furthermore, it is significant that 'even within this grouping of non-Western titles, there is still an emphasis upon reworking established American films and genres' (Smith 2019: 706). For example, roughly one fifth of the entries in Rob Hill's 'ultimate modern guide' to contemporary badfilms made after 1970 are non-American productions that primarily comprise East Asian low-budget action, horror and exploitation films. Like the American films they feature alongside, they are also largely, if implicitly, interpreted and evaluated within a framework that centres the 'rules' established within classical Hollywood cinema as a baseline for technical competence. As discussed further in Chapter 2, claims about a film's 'objective badness' require some understanding of its categorical context. The dominance of US-American films within the badfilm canon suggests a tacit acceptance of this among fans, as well as an understanding that these films offer productive opportunities to recognise the incompetent efforts to reproduce particular standards through a comparative framework, due to their relative visibility within a wider body of widely accepted 'good' films.

Accepting that the cultification of badfilms is a 'largely Western, Anglo-American phenomenon' (Dwyer 2014: 46), it is also notable that the canon features a significant number of low-budget, American genre pictures from the 1950s and 1960s, with these two decades identified in fan-authored and academic literature as particularly lucrative times for badfilm production and subsequent cult appreciation. Almost half of all the films discussed in the Medved brothers' influential book, *The Fifty Worst Films of All Time* (1978), are from the 1950s and 1960s, while their subsequent books also feature a large proportion of films from these decades. In the introduction to *The Psychotronic Encyclopedia of Film* (1983), Michael Weldon explicitly identifies films made between the 'mass acceptance' of television in the 1950s and the creation of the Motion Picture Association of America's film rating system in 1968 as being of particular interest due to a combination of personal and socio-historical factors (1983: xiii). Similarly, Michael Sauter suggests that the 'post-atomic, commie-paranoid, teenage-rebellious, sexually revolutionary fifties and sixties' represent the 'zenith' of 'honest-to-goodness Grade Z atrocities' (1999: 268). The canon, therefore, 'built its archive from mid-century horror, science-fiction, teen-pics and assorted oddities' (Sconce 2019: 667) and features a range of movies that often straddle the line between 'mainstream' genre pictures and exploitation (see Schaefer 1999: 331). More so than at any other time, the cinematic landscape in America during the 1950s and 1960s made it possible for films to be wholly incompetent but still occupy a position within the wider economic and industrial structure of cinema. As Sconce and others have suggested, these decades represent the 'golden age' of badness (Sconce 2019; Hunter 2014: 485). As such, this book does not particularly deviate from this canon: the films discussed in the chapters that follow are US-American productions from the 1950s and 1960s and are all canonical badfilms, to varying degrees. These films, I suggest, have set the standards by which contemporary badfilms are evaluated and, therefore, offer a productive means of investigating a badness-as-failure that can also be applied to post-1970s bad movies.

A range of factors have contributed to US-American low-budget films made in the 1950s and 1960s gaining particular importance within the badfilm canon. Some of these have been outlined by Sconce, who suggests that canonical badness 'dates from a very specific mode of production, exhibition and (re-)circulation' (2019: 666). The two decades represent a period of significant change for the film industry in America, which helped to create the 'optimal' conditions for badfilm production (see Davis 2012). The collapse of the studio system, for example, heralded the 'beginning of an entirely new age for independent filmmaking' (Davis 2012: 27) and enabled filmmakers like Ed Wood, Vic Savage, Coleman Francis and Phil Tucker to carve out a place for themselves on the fringes of Hollywood. There, they worked under particularly restrictive, impoverished and ramshackle conditions that made it more likely that their films would be 'doomed to various forms of implosion and failure' (Sconce 2019: 667) and, significantly, that these failures would remain in the film on release. Independence, then, can present advantages and disadvantages. On the one hand, filmmakers have 'increased choice and control', while on the other there is 'decreased collaboration and oversight' (Dombrowski 2009: 82). The demonstrable badness of these canonised badfilms can thus be understood – positively or negatively – as a potential consequence of an individual's 'unfettered creativity' (Juno and Vale 1986: 5), unhampered by studio interference.

The vague association with the 'legitimate' industry also contributes to the films' subsequent canonisation and reception. As Sconce notes, badfilms like *Bride of the Monster* (Wood 1955), *The Beast of Yucca Flats* (Francis 1961) and *Mesa of Lost Women* (Ormond and Tevos 1953) 'index an entire circuit of naïveté and failure, a now distant order of production and reception that adjudicated these titles to be saleable as *professional* filmmaking; that is, each was a project that someone at some time presumably took seriously enough to finance, execute, release and watch' (2019: 672; emphasis in original). The 'professional' status of these films on an industrial level brings their demonstrably *unprofessional* production into sharp relief, and this clash may help to account for some of the potential pleasures of badfilms. However, I suggest that the presumption of seriousness that Sconce alludes to is also crucial to badfilm appreciation. As discussed in the next chapter, the badfilms most likely to elicit positive responses and elevated status within the canon are those that expose the failed intention to be serious and to be *taken seriously*.

It is significant, also, that the majority of canonised badfilms from the 1950s and 1960s – and beyond, with *The Room* (Wiseau 2003) and, to a lesser extent, *Ben & Arthur* (Mraovich 2002) being notable exceptions – are rooted in horror, science fiction and exploitation. Because they are 'already only loosely moored to realism', these genres have 'perhaps the greatest potential to become entirely and comically unhinged or "so bad they're good"' (Hunter 2014: 485). Horror films, for example, can be transformed into accidental or unintended comedies through incompetence, as discussed further in Chapter 2. This is, however, not the only explanation for the dominance of certain types of cinema in the badfilm canon. Horror, science fiction and exploitation are already closely associated with cult (as well as certain forms of cinematic badness) and come with particular expectations of spectacle, excess and the fantastic. Considering their restrictive working conditions, it can appear as though filmmakers like Ray Dennis Steckler, Al Adamson and Bill Rebane were setting themselves up for failure by repeatedly promising spectacle and attempting to tell stories far beyond their means or ability. The demonstrable failure to achieve the minimum expectations of the genres in any satisfactory or effective way – through elements such as underwhelming special effects, bad science and a reliance on recycled footage – merely emphasises the films' inadequacies. To some extent, then, badfilms can be considered 'failed fantasies' (Sconce 2019: 667); their incompetence obliterates our ability to suspend our disbelief and dismantles the illusory potential of cinema.

This is not to say, however, that *only* science-fiction, horror and exploitation films can expose the kind of failure associated with canonical badness. As I have mentioned already, failure does not reside exclusively in any single genre or category of cinema. Nevertheless, it is notable – and, arguably, unsurprising – that certain kinds of films are prevalent within the badfilm canon. As indicated above and throughout this book, films like *Plan 9 From Outer Space* (Wood 1959), *They Saved Hitler's Brain* (Bradley 1968) or *Monster A-go Go* (Rebane and Lewis [uncredited] 1965) certainly reveal failure on a regular basis, but extraneous factors have also contributed to their canonisation. The cultivation of this 'golden age' of cinematic badness began, in large part, because of the repackaging and repurposing of titles for late-night television in America throughout the late 1960s and 1970s (see Sconce 2019: 667–68), which gave now-adult viewers an opportunity to revisit the films of their adolescence, now from a position of temporal distance (see Smith 2019: 708) and critical detachment. The majority of canonised badfilms address 'juvenile tastes focused on excess and the fantastic' (Sconce 2019: 667), but it is also significant that so many of the fans and critics who have been instrumental in establishing the badfilm canon are Baby Boomers, writing as adults in the 1970s and 1980s about films from their youth. Badfilm appreciation – even in a contemporary context – is steeped in nostalgia (Sexton and Mathijs 2008: 89), with early badfilm literature in particular suggesting a combination of critical superiority and genuine affection for the 'creature features' of the 1950s and 1960s.

The badfilm canon, like other film canons, is a product of those who constructed it, and represents the countercultural tastes of a community that is, historically at least, male, white, Western, middle-class and college-educated (see Sconce 1995: 375). We can also see male tastes dominating canons beyond badfilm: cult cinema itself has been traditionally positioned as masculine, and this gendering has worked to exclude women from the fandom (Hollows 2003: 37–38). One consequence of this, arguably, is the absence of badfilms from less obviously male-oriented genres within the canon. As previously mentioned,

The Room indicates that badness is not restricted to any type of cinema and that the cultification of failure is not wholly dependent on a film's broader categorical context within horror or science-fiction. Nevertheless, as a romantic melodrama, *The Room* remains an outlier in the badfilm canon. Furthermore, male friendships and issues of masculinity are at the heart of Wiseau's film, while queer male relationships are at the centre of *Ben & Arthur*; both films, therefore, only minimally disrupt the 'masculinity of cult' that Hollows identified. At this point, I should acknowledge that my own knowledge of, and appreciation for, badfilms was influenced by the various fan-authored texts (Weldon 1983; Medved and Medved 1980; Juno and Vale 1986) that have helped to establish the canon of the 'worst' movies. This book, then, aims to expand understandings of the canon by drawing on a range of badfilms – some with more established reputations than others – and focusing on recurring, shared characteristics of failure that can be identified across the collection, rather than attempting to establish a hierarchy of the 'worst' (or the 'best').

Although canonical badness can appear to disrupt established taste cultures, badfilm appreciation often represents a 'species of bourgeois aesthetics not a challenge to it' (Jancovich 2002: 312–13). Hunter even suggests that the 'so bad it's good' response to certain badfilms, discussed more below, is 'dismayingly normative' (2014: 491). Film canons are, as Janet Staiger notes (1985), based on a politics of exclusion and inclusion: certain films are repeatedly included, while others are omitted and effectively excised from history. This is particularly pertinent in relation to badfilms because the films themselves generally made little impression when originally released, making access to the texts or to any exegetic material less likely; these are films that were 'treated with indifference or contempt' (Weldon 1973: xii) at the time of release, often precisely because of their intrinsic badness and cultural insignificance. The reputations of certain films and filmmakers as the canonised 'worst' has encouraged their availability across a range of platforms (VHS, DVD, Blu-Ray and via informal circuits of online distribution; see Barefoot 2017: 1–2), but, of course, this is something of a self-fulfilling prophecy: the films are the 'worst' and therefore become culturally significant, leading to more accessibility; and because they are comparatively more available and visible than others, they are more likely to become canonised as the 'worst'. Ed Wood's contemporary importance, for example, is 'not a product of his significance within the 1950s, but of the specific strategies of interpretation on which contemporary "cult" audiences have brought to the period' (Jancovich 1996: 304). Although Richard Birchard argues that Wood is less an 'original [. . . than] one of many toiling in rather fruitless fields' (1995: 450; see also Davis 2012: 200), his posthumous cultural significance as the 'worst' filmmaker of all time and director of the 'worst' film of all time has ensured his position within the badfilm canon. It is also notable that *Plan 9* has been described as the '*Citizen Kane* of bad movies' (for example, Sconce 1995: 388), evoking a hierarchy of badness that is explicitly aligned with, and contrasted against, the established canon of 'goodness'.

As with every canon, there is no real consensus on the 'worst' film but, across fan-authored and academic literature on badfilms, certain films and filmmakers are repeatedly referenced. In addition, particular characteristics are consistently identified as evidence of failure: technical incompetence, incoherent plots, unconvincing acting, bizarre dialogue, impoverished and inept spectacle, bad sound (for example, MacDowell and McCulloch 2019: 643; Sconce 2019; Adams 2010; Medved and Medved 1980, 1986; Hill 2017). Modes of production in America in the 1950s and 1960s created conditions that were conducive to failure, while technological developments since then – digital cameras and editing software, advances in sound technology that have made shooting MOS (without sound) less prevalent and so on – should mean that even low-budget productions today are less likely to fail to achieve 'acceptable' minimum standards of cinematic representation. Sconce suggests that, from a technical perspective at least, the 'proliferation of basic film knowledge [...] and idiot-proof technology makes the unwitting *Verfremdungseffekt* (alienation or estrangement effect) of the canonically bad increasingly unlikely' (2019: 669). However, as I discuss in the final chapter of this book, contemporary badfilms continue to be evaluated using the same criteria as the early entries to the badfilm canon, albeit in some respects expanded or updated to reflect both technological developments and critical standards – failed spectacle is a key characteristic of contemporary badfilms, for example, with badness now identified not in the relatively obsolete tendency to use recycled footage (see Chapter 4) but in the no less shoddy or unconvincing addition of cheap computer-generated imagery (CGI). Furthermore, the critical approaches to technical failure – how fans and academics engage with, write about and value badfilms – share commonalities from the early days of badfilm appreciation in the 1970s to the present day. This suggests that, although tastes undoubtedly change and although there necessarily is a historical-cultural dimension to badfilm identification and appreciation, there still exist similarities in how people identify, analyse and potentially value cinematic incompetence.

Critical Approaches: A Brief History

The relatively recent academic interest in badfilm has led to several articles and chapters elsewhere that usefully summarise the history of badfilm appreciation and the critical debates at play (Bartlett 2019a; Hunter 2014; Barefoot 2017; Sconce 2019). While it is necessary to outline these again here, the following discussion serves as a brief overview that aims to expand on what is already available, rather than repeat it.

If the 'golden age' of cinematic badness is understood to have taken place in America during the 1950s and 1960s, then the 'golden age' of bad movie appreciation can be identified as the 1970s and 1980s, when several key texts were published that helped to establish the canon of badfilms as it is recognised today. There is some evidence of forms of bad movie appreciation prior to this. In the 1930s, for example, the Surrealists believed the 'worst' movies could reveal 'sublime' moments of truthfulness. One of the earliest examples of attempted canonisation can be found in a 1966 issue of the cult fanzine *Famous Monsters of Filmland*, in which a young Joe Dante compiled his selection of fifty worst horror films. As is fairly typical of badfilm literature, including certain forms of contemporary criticism, the list offers little analysis, preferring instead to provide brief synopses. Featuring primarily low-budget, American horror/sci-fi pictures from the 1950s and early 1960s, the list serves as a precursor to books such as *The Fifty Worst Films of All Time*, *The Golden Turkey Awards* and *The Psychotronic Encyclopedia of Film*. Dante includes two of Ed Wood's films – *Bride of the Monster* and *Plan 9* – in his selection, which suggests that the filmmaker was developing a reputation for incompetence as early as the mid-1960s. Dante's description of *Plan 9*, for example, indicates that it had already been marked as a bad movie: 'I'd heard a lot about *Plan 9 From Outer Space* [. . .] and saw it to see if it was as bad as they said. It was even worse!' (1966: 76). Given that Wood's films are entirely omitted from the Medveds' first book and that *Plan 9*'s dubious notoriety as the 'worst film of all time' was due to a readers' poll in *The Golden Turkey Awards* rather than an honour bestowed by the authors themselves, it is not too much of a stretch to suggest that Wood's multiple appearances on Dante's list may well have helped to establish his subsequent reputation.

Although not specifically focused on cinema, Susan Sontag's 'Notes on "Camp"', published in 1964, helped to identify and characterise certain forms of appreciation for failure and artifice that have proved relevant to the cultification of badfilms; Sexton and Mathijs provide a useful summary of her work and its influence on early bad movie scholarship (2011: 86–89). While Sontag's work has been criticised for 'attempting to disarticulate the camp sensibility from its origins in queer experience' (Sconce 2019: 670), her observations regarding distinctions between 'deliberate' and 'naïve' camp remain particularly pertinent to the discussion here. She notes, for example, that deliberate camp, which 'knows itself to be camp [. . .] is usually less satisfying' than unintentional camp (2009 [1964]: 282) and proposes that naïve camp reveals a 'sensibility of failed seriousness' (2009 [1964]: 287). As I demonstrate in Chapter 2, the perceived aspirations to seriousness are central to badfilm identification and subsequent cult appreciation.

Pauline Kael's article, 'Trash, art and the movies', published in 1969, also provides an early examination of the potential pleasures of bad movies. She implicitly aligns badness with a lack of artistry and suggests that the increased focus on art in film means that 'we may be in danger of forgetting that most of the movies we enjoy are not works of art' (1994 [1969]: 89). She asserts, for example, that it is entirely possible to enjoy a film while being aware of its technical inadequacies and uses American Independent Pictures' *Wild in the Streets* (Shear 1968) as an example of a film that is enjoyable despite the 'unskilled' directing, 'banal' music and general lack of attention to detail (1994 [1969]: 89–91). Kael's claims, however, do not extend as far as those writing about bad movie appreciation later: she rejects art not because it is good, but because it is pretentious, and celebrates trash not for its badness, but for the unexpected moments of goodness that can be located within it. Thus, rather than suggest bad films have value *because of* their badness, Kael proposes that they can be enjoyed *despite* their demonstrable failings.

Cult appreciation for bad movies, as it is recognised today, has been notably influenced by Harry and Michael Medved's books, particularly *The Golden Turkey Awards*. The 'awards' format adopted by the authors is typical of fan-authored literature and allows for a broad selection of films to be included, often on a seemingly arbitrary basis. Like cult cinema generally (see Mathijs and Mendik 2008: 1–11), understandings of what constitutes a bad movie are relatively vague. This is evident throughout both fan-authored and academic literature on cinematic badness. While some authors provide lists of examples (for example, Sconce 1995) or different categories of badness (Medved and Medved 1980, 1986; Sauter 1995; Wilson 2005), badfilms also feature in early books on trash, psychotronic and cult encyclopaedias and reference guides (Peary 1981; Weldon 1983; Juno and Vale 1986). Their inclusion in these books indicate that, within the potentially vast and incoherent realm of bad cinema, films that expose a combination of technical incompetence and material poverty provide particular potential for cultification and enjoyment, in addition to offering an opportunity for fans to demonstrate their countercultural, oppositional tastes (see Sconce 1995; Jancovich 2002; Juno and Vale 1986). By challenging standards and conventions of taste, style and quality, badness can be transgressive, and cult fans can celebrate 'neglected' or otherwise ignored films that 'test the limits of contemporary (middle-class) cultural acceptability' (Juno and Vale 1986: 4). For Juno and Vale, for example, low-budget, independent films like *The Wizard of Gore* (Lewis 1970) are 'worthwhile' because they are unconstrained by studio interference and therefore represent 'eccentric – *even extreme* – presentations by individuals freely expressing their imaginations' (1986: 5; emphasis in original). Moreover, they present a challenge to notions of 'good' taste and have the potential to disrupt the authority of 'dictators of public opinion' (1986: 4) who represent the cultural elite.

Badfilm fandom became more visible and commodified throughout the 1980s and 1990s, particularly through the cult television programme *Mystery*

Science Theater 3000 (1988–99) in the United States and, to a lesser extent, *The Incredibly Strange Film Show* (1988–89) in the UK, which took its name from Juno and Vale's book *Incredibly Strange Films*, which in turn was inspired by the notorious badfilm *The Incredibly Strange Creatures Who Stopped Living and Became Mixed-up Zombies!!?* (Steckler 1964). As I have noted elsewhere (Bartlett 2019a), *MST3K* not only provided audiences with an opportunity to experience films about which they might have only read before, but also presented them in a format that created the illusion of a shared viewing environment and directed viewers towards a specific reading of the films that prioritised the identification, and subsequent mockery, of badness. This appreciation is described as 'cinemasochism', whereby fans find 'pleasure in cinema others have deemed too painful to endure' (Carter 2011: 102). Like paracinematic approaches (Sconce 1995) and Sontag's concept of camp, cinemasochism is an ironic reading strategy that champions artifice and exaggeration, and celebrates cinematic badness, particularly when it appears to be naïve or unintentional. Whereas earlier bad movie literature tended to either identify badfilms as a source of humour and mockery, per the Medveds, or to locate value in their subversive potential (Juno and Vale 1986), here we see a more explicit acknowledgement of the potential pleasures of badness itself.

Examining early bad movie literature indicates the various ways in which badness is identified and subsequently appreciated. As Jancovich points out, the authors' fandom regularly impacts their writing, with the tone shifting between 'virtual contempt for the films discussed, through a patronising affection for their pathetic failings, to a virtual awe-filled admiration for true works of art', while the 'sheer eclecticism of the films [. . .] means they are not read in one coherent way, but through a number of different and contradictory strategies that are constantly slipping into one another' (2002: 314). The difficulties in definition and categorisation, as well as the issues of subjectivity that permeate selection inevitably affect how this broad selection of films is written about. What is clear, however, is that much of the appreciation is the result of the enjoyment that can be gleaned from witnessing demonstrable failure. This enjoyment can take different forms: laughing at perceived ineptitude; celebration of the bizarre and unconventional qualities of bad movies; or identification of badness as evidence of eccentric auteurs' perceived resourcefulness, creativity and determination. Thus, badfilms have been celebrated and cultified both because of and despite their badness.

In academia, scholarship on badfilms is firmly positioned within cult studies and has often focused more on the reception and audiences of badfilms rather than the films themselves (for example, Sconce 1995; Vassilieva and Verevis 2010; McCulloch 2011; Sarkhosh and Menninghaus 2016). Although Sconce identifies badfilm as one example of paracinema, an 'elastic textual category' that includes a broad range of trash cinema not restricted to incompetence

(1995: 372), in many ways a badfilm is a paracinematic film and *vice versa*, as implied in Sconce's decision to use two notorious badfilmmakers' works (those of Ed Wood and Larry Buchanan) as case-studies. It is more useful to consider paracinema as a particular interpretive framework and reading strategy adopted by cult fans, as a way of positioning themselves in opposition to 'mainstream' tastes, rather than a coherent category of film texts. Since the mid-2010s, however, scholars have begun to scrutinise bad cinema in more detail (for example, MacDowell and Zborowski 2013; Perkins and Verevis 2014; Hunter 2014; Barefoot 2017; Hill 2015; Telotte 2015; and the publication of a special issue of *Continuum* on 'So Bad it's Good', 2019). Increasingly, badfilm is being acknowledged as a significant subcategory and a useful descriptor of a particular kind of cinematic badness – badness-as-incompetence. This existing scholarship, then, represents an effort to unpack some of the intricacies of badfilms and the forms and methods of appreciation for them.

Contemporary badfilm scholarship draws on and expands ideas that emerged in the 1980s, particularly those proposed by J. Hoberman. His article 'Bad Movies' represents an early attempt to identify films that 'transcend taste and might be termed *objectively bad*' (1980: 8; emphasis in original). An objectively bad movie, he argues, diverts the viewer's attention away from its plot to its construction, with the visible artifice of the filmmaking process creating a heightened sense of realism. Crucially, this dismantling of the diegesis is understood to be unintentional, caused by failed attempts to reproduce 'institutional modes of representation' (1980: 8), which are typically understood to be classical Hollywood cinema. The objectively bad movie, then, enables us to recognise both the intention to adhere to established standards of screen naturalism and the complete and utter failure to do so effectively. Hoberman thus proposes that the 'best' bad movies are made under restrictive conditions, are often rooted in exploitation and contain auteurist signatures that enable the viewer to identify – or claim to identify – the filmmaker's sincere determination to complete their film against all odds. Hoberman's arguments are somewhat weakened by a rather ambivalent approach to intention (1980: 12) – which is, I suggest, central to understanding badfilms (see Chapter 2) – but his article neatly establishes the criteria by which many badfilms can be understood. Notably, his remarks about the 'best' bad movies particularly suggest that it is possible to identify both the modes of production likely to contribute to 'objectively bad' movies and the specific modes of reception that can emerge as a result.

Although the 'worst films of all time' represent a particularly visible form of cult cinema, analysis of the films themselves has been largely left to fans. This is, perhaps, because the films are so obviously incompetent that their failure has been taken for granted within the academy and not considered to require further investigation. It could, however, also indicate that scholarship has traditionally considered the 'value' of badfilms – if value is to be identified at all – to lie in the recuperative ways in which they are appropriated and used by cult audiences rather than in any intrinsic qualities of the films themselves. Nevertheless, although fans can be, and often are, capable of employing a range of sophisticated and insightful reading strategies, even contemporary fan-authored literature tends to comprise either synopsis-based reviews of individual films deemed bad for a variety of reasons (for example, Sauter 2005; Wilson 2005; Hill 2017; Rausch and Riley 2015; see also websites such as *Jabootu's Bad Movie Dimension*), or lengthy analyses of the output of specific filmmakers (Craig 2007; 2009) rather than considering the broader implications of badfilm as a category. Furthermore, although fans regularly demonstrate substantial knowledge about individual films and filmmakers, not all the information used to support their analysis is necessarily reliable. Often, it seems that a good story is prioritised over accuracy. For example, William Routt has identified several erroneous or misleading claims about Wood and his films and acknowledges the irony that 'criticism that depends so strongly on the identification of gaffes should itself be so riddled with them' (2001: 3). It is only relatively recently that a body of literature focused specifically on badfilms has emerged within the academy, opening up avenues to consider in more detail how incompetence and failure is not only recognised and appreciated, but also how it functions within the film text.

So Bad It's Good

To date, the most interesting and useful academic work on badfilms has focused on movies that have gained a reputation for being 'so bad they're good'. This descriptor indicates a correlation between artistic failure and experiential pleasure, with 'goodness' referring to the latter rather than any reinterpretation of the former: '"good" is what it [the film] does to you' (Hunter 2014: 498). The phrase effectively demonstrates the tensions so often at play in simultaneously recognising, valuing and enjoying badness. Taken literally, 'so bad it's good' is problematic and paradoxical, but 'good' in this context is 'almost exclusively used to refer to how humorous something is, as opposed to any other laudable artistic qualities' (McCulloch 2011: 195). MacDowell and Zborowski propose 'so bad it's pleasurable' as a more accurate description, arguing that this 'does justice to the fact that no claim is being advanced for a text's intrinsic value [. . .] but rather its potential instrumental value as an object of fascination or fun' (2013: 17). Dyck and Johnson, meanwhile, suggest that 'good-bad art' – their term for 'so bad it's good' – is artistically bad but aesthetically good, with the former having the potential to produce an 'aesthetically positive effect of *bizarreness*' (2017: 281; emphasis in original). Watching badfilms, especially those described as 'so bad they're good', can be a good experience – they can be entertaining, enjoyable and unintentionally comedic. Yet, this is not an inevitable or universal response, despite what might be implied by the term itself. Thus, the focus on 'so bad they're good' risks complicating arguments that explicitly aim to move critical focus *away* from taste-based judgments of badness towards a more 'objective' approach to cinematic failure.

Evidently, however, some forms of cinematic badness do seem to be more likely to elicit positive responses than others. The challenge is to consider what textual characteristics might result in a film being considered 'so bad it's good/pleasurable'. This is explored in more detail in Chapter 6, in relation to bad editing, but there are some broader implications in 'so bad it's good' that can be addressed here. Focusing on the 'so', MacDowell and Zborowski argue that it can be 'strange, entertaining, and perversely thrilling simply to experience such an overwhelming quantity of failed intentions' (2013: 18). This suggests that there is evidence of *so much* badness – the greater the evidence of badness, the greater the potential for enjoyment. A pleasurable badfilm is also typically one where the badness is *so obvious*. Badfilms expose incompetence and failure in a multitude of ways, with individual elements failing to convince and failing to support one another. Bad performances are made more obvious through bad scripts and bad sound; already unconvincing recycled footage is unsupported by bad editing; incoherent narratives are made more incoherent by implausible mise-en-scène. This indicates that it is possible to identify *so many different kinds* of badness also. The badfilms most likely to be championed as 'so bad they're good', therefore, are those in which badness is excessive, obvious and varied. In contrast, films that are 'just bad' are often characterised by a leaden pace and lack of excess, which can be interpreted as an absence of effort or ambition (see Sontag 2009 [1964]: 283), further hindering their potential to be transformed into objects of fun.

As the term 'so bad it's good' suggests, excessive failure can have a transformative effect on how we respond to the film. Carter notes, for example, that in 'extreme' cases like *Manos: The Hands of Fate* (Warren 1966), 'not only does the horror film become a comedy, the unwatchable becomes enjoyable' (2011: 103). J. P. Telotte, meanwhile, proposes 'watchable [. . .] terrible' as a way of understanding this experience, whereby films like *Robot Monster* (Tucker 1953) are watchable precisely *because* they are so inherently bad (Telotte 2015). As discussed more in the next chapter, this relates to intentionality also: Hunter suggests that the comedy of badfilms 'derives from the gap between intention and achievement, along with a sense of pathos at the filmmaker's delusion' (2014: 490). On the one hand, designating badfilms as 'so bad they're good' risks making problematic assumptions about the universality of the experience as an inherently good one. On the other hand, the terminology acknowledges that badness itself is at the core of appreciation, whereby 'every extreme feature is *simultaneously bad and thereby good*' (Barker 2013: 221; emphasis in original). Furthermore, there is an implicit acceptance of demonstrable failure. We can say, therefore, that in certain cases badfilms are objectively bad to such an extent that they become subjectively good experiences.

Nevertheless, I suggest that it is possible to distinguish between *identifying* badness and *appreciating* it. Just as one 'need by no means attach the value of "good" to conventions in order to make a judgement of "bad" when they appear to be striven for and missed' (MacDowell and Zborowski 2013: 16), we should not assume that recognition of failed intentions and incompetence will necessarily result in enjoyment of those failures. When I have screened badfilms in cult cinema and other film courses, for example, students have overwhelmingly agreed that the movies are inept and bad, but not all have enjoyed the experience of watching them.

An examination of badfilm literature reveals the myriad ways in which fans engage with, interpret and value badfilms. It also reveals the variety of responses to individual movies, suggesting that, although there are certain films that have been canonised as bad films – even the 'worst of all time' – they are not appreciated or valued in consistent ways. Sconce delineates between the 'paracinematic pleasure' that a film like *Glen or Glenda* (Wood 1953) can invoke and Larry Buchanan's AIP collaborations that 'are a test of even the most dedicated paracinematic viewer's patience' (1995: 389–90). For *Zontar* magazine's contributors, however, Buchanan's movies epitomise badfilm, although they are rarely described in such positive terms as 'so bad they're good'. For example, Brian Curran reports being unable to finish watching *Zontar: The Thing from Venus* (Buchanan 1966) when he first viewed it (quoted in Buchanan 1996: 93) and describes the movie as 'a cinema of alienation' (1996: 94). Similarly, Freddie Mertz argues that the looped 'jungle drum' soundtrack in *Curse of the Swamp Creature* (Buchanan 1966) turns from an 'irritant into the very essence of pain, becoming a concrete metaphor for the film's uncanny stretching of time into a tortuous infinity'. He describes the experience of watching the movie as one of 'mind-numbing, time-stopping, cinematic boredom that would make Stan Brakhage green with envy' (quoted in Buchanan 1996: 98). Identifying the 'value' of badfilms only in their potential to be 'pleasurable' or enjoyable in some way thus fails to account for the cultification of films like Buchanan's. Furthermore, assuming that all badfilms will evoke pleasurable responses risks misrepresenting the full experience of even the movies with a 'so bad it's good' reputation, which can contain as many 'boring' bad moments as entertaining or humorous ones.

Whether a film is described as 'so bad it's good', 'so bad it's pleasurable' or 'watchable [. . .] terrible', the underlying assumption is that it *is* pleasurable, entertaining, enjoyable, watchable. This can complicate how we understand badfilms as 'objectively bad' because having the ability to recognise failure – being able to identify the gap between the desired effect and the actual result – does not necessarily mean that one will inevitably enjoy that failure. Rather, the inherent incoherence and consistent inconsistency that characterises badfilm style means that the films are often ambiguous enough to allow for a variety of possible interpretations, irrespective of possible enjoyment. While many of the films discussed in this book have some reputation for being 'so bad they're good', they are included less because of their potential instrumental value as 'good' experiences rather than because their excessive failure provides a wealth of opportunity for analysing badness. The overwhelming incompetence in *Maniac* (Esper 1934) leads Sconce (2003) to argue for the pedagogical value of badfilm, for example. Thus, 'so bad they're good' films can be particularly productive for investigations into how failure functions within the text, because they represent some of the most extreme, excessive and obvious examples of incompetence. In the following chapters, I aim to demonstrate that badfilms have value beyond their potential as a source of entertainment or unanticipated comedy; there is intrinsic value to badfilms, I suggest, because they provide a chance to examine how failure works.

Some portions of this chapter also appear in Bartlett (2019) '"It happens by accident": Failed intentions, incompetence, and sincerity in badfilm', in Jamie Sexton and Ernest Mathijs (eds), The Routledge Companion to Cult Cinema, Oxon; New York: Routledge, 40–49

2. INVESTIGATING INTENTIONS IN BADFILMS

This chapter examines intentionality as a central factor in our identification, understanding and potential appreciation of badfilm. Badfilms are characterised by ineptitude, typically exacerbated by material poverty and restrictive production conditions, with badness relating primarily to incompetence. Assumptions about intention can be found throughout academic and fan-authored writing, suggesting that the visibility of failed intentions is so obvious, so apparent, that they can be taken for granted and do not require any further consideration. Referring to Ed Wood's films, for example, Alison Graham claims it is the '*appearance* of Wood's intentions that so engages cult audiences – the perceived distance [. . .] between his desire to create compelling narratives and his inability to do so' (1991: 109; emphasis in original). Early cult scholarship indicates the underlying acceptance of visible intentions in cult appreciation generally. Jonathan L. Crane proposes the 'allure' of many cult movies lies in the 'unintentional charms that knowing audiences find in the hapless enterprise of earnest but technically challenged film makers' (2000: 90), while Elena Gorfinkel considers the cult film in terms of a 'logic of excess, in which the intentionality of authorship and narrative requirement comes into conflict with the strategies of execution and the primarily budgetary limitations placed upon them' (2000: 158). Of course, not all cult films are bad movies, and certainly not all are indicative of the incompetence that such remarks imply. Comments such as these, however, directly align cult with characteristics associated with badfilm, indicating the significance of badness within the broader category of cult and highlighting how the visibility of intention is central to the cultification of certain films.

Why Intentions Matter

Every time a film or filmmaker is accused of having 'failed' in some way, assumptions are being made about the motivations behind the text. Indeed, if we 'cannot assume that a film intended to achieve certain aims, then we cannot deem it "bad" for failing in those aims' (MacDowell and Zborowski 2013: 5). The look, feel and construction of badfilms are typically understood to be the unintended consequence of filmmaking incompetence. It is intention, for example, that distinguishes between the unconventional style of counter-cinema and the seemingly accidental style of paracinema, despite possible similarities in effect. As Sconce argues, counter-cinema is a 'strategic intervention [. . .] in which the film artist self-consciously employs stylistic innovations to differentiate his or her (usually his) films from the cultural mainstream' (1995: 384). Paracinematic films, in contrast, are understood to 'deviate from Hollywood classicism not necessarily by artistic intentionality, but by the effects of material poverty and technical ineptitude' (1995: 385). As I demonstrate below, acceptance of intention also enables us to distinguish between badfilms and 'bad' films, the latter consciously reproducing 'bad' film style, usually to invoke a deliberately comic effect.

Although badfilm appreciation is predicated on a celebration of incompetence, the apparent visibility of failed intentions has been largely taken for granted. As MacDowell and Zborowski note, intentionality is rarely central to debates even when it is acknowledged and tends to be accepted rather than interrogated (2013: 4). Although there has in recent years been a relative boom in badfilm scholarship, which has led to more focused consideration of the complexities and significance of intention (MacDowell and Zborowski 2013; Dyck and Johnson 2017; Bartlett 2019a; Bartlett 2019b; MacDowell and McCulloch 2019), intention is still discussed in haphazard ways in other academic works. Despite suggesting that Wood's intentions 'are lost to us now', for example, Rodney Hill makes implicit assertions about those same intentions by claiming films like *Glen or Glenda* are 'conscious constructs' that 'deliberately' (that is, intentionally) challenge cinematic conventions (2015: 179–80). Hill's comments indicate some of the ways in which intentionality is inconsistently attributed and used to support wider claims regarding badfilm style and subsequent reception. Intentionality is a complex, slippery concept. Even accepting that the original intent may well be 'lost' to us, badfilms nevertheless seem to suggest a demonstrable gap between intended effect and actual outcome, with failure further revealed in the decidedly inconsistent ways in which that gap is revealed. This gives us an opportunity to discern, with some confidence, that however the films were originally conceived, they were *not intended to be like this*.

Before proceeding further, however, some clarification is necessary. I do not wish to claim that badfilms can, or should, be restricted to any single form of interpretation or reading. Indeed, the ambiguity, inconsistency and weirdness of badfilms enable a wide range of possible responses, and this is part of their appeal. Alternative readings, such as interpretations that seem to go against the grain of the filmmaker's intentions, are welcome and can be individually evaluated on the basis of their effectiveness, persuasiveness and so on. Nevertheless, even interpretations that challenge claims of failure in badfilms (for example, Craig 2009) typically do so by acknowledging the films', or filmmakers', reputation. In other words, all badfilm analysis operates, by definition, within a framework that acknowledges their badness. Thus, issues of intention underpin all badfilm reception, and to declare intentionality irrelevant would require denying the realities of how badfilms are identified, appreciated and valued. Whether explicitly or implicitly acknowledged, whether confirmed or challenged through analysis, intentionality is central to how we categorise, understand and write about badfilms. Given this, it is important to fully consider its implications. This chapter builds on original and existing research to suggest some ways in which we might proceed in such a task.

Whose Intention Is It Anyway?

Reflecting on the complex concept of intention invites consideration of both how intentionality is identified and who, or what, is the subject of intention. As previously noted, there is a tendency in cult studies to focus on reception, which has often led to discussions that emphasise the 'reader's intentions over the author's or film's' (MacDowell and Zborowski 2013: 4; see Carter 2001; Sarkhosh and Menninghaus 2016; McCulloch 2011). Considering badfilm fans specifically, it can appear that the 'phenomenon of audiences consciously enjoying films for their seeming failings demonstrates their ability to appreciate texts in "unintended" ways' (MacDowell and Zborowski 2013: 4) by, for example, enjoying a horror film as a comedy. As I have discussed elsewhere, however, closer examination of badfilm reception suggests that viewers can and often do read badfilms in both intended and unintended ways (Bartlett 2019b). For instance, we can appreciate the films to which Ed Wood contributed as writer and/or director for their intertextual potential, which seems to be both consciously intended in some respects and entirely unintended in others. Badfilms are characterised by inconsistency, with internal contradictions potentially allowing a combination of intended and unintended readings. It is possible to accept certain moments in the films as largely 'successful' and in line with the intended aims, while also responding in unintended ways to other moments that are 'unsuccessful' and fail.

Although the focus on the reader/viewer's intentions is welcome, it does not address the central issue at play in badfilm appreciation, namely that of artistic intention. Incompetence is generally attributed to the filmmaker – typically, although not exclusively, the director (Bartlett 2019a). Auteurist approaches often underpin cult appreciation and badfilm appreciation specifically; badfilm fans often have a 'special interest in authorial intent' (Dyck and Johnson 2017: 292). Juno and Vale, for example, argue that badness can be the consequence of a 'single person's individual vision and quirky originality' and provides evidence of the creative, improvised solutions to issues that arise primarily because of budgetary restrictions (1986: 5). However, although the various roles undertaken by filmmakers like Ed Wood – including writing, directing, editing, producing and acting – can support claims of authorship, the inherent badness of the movies themselves seems to offer a challenge to one of the most fundamental precepts of auteur theory: technical competence (Sarris 2000 [1962]: 132). Yet, it is in part precisely because of Wood's technical incompetence that he, like others, are now celebrated as 'misunderstood' or 'accidental' auteurs (Hill 2015: 173), rather than, or as well as, the 'worst' filmmakers of all time.

Several issues can arise when attributing intentionality to bad 'auteurs.' William Routt is critical of the way in which auteurism has been applied to Wood, for example (see also Birchard 1995). He challenges the assumption that the 'gap between intention and act is apparent only in what is bad about Wood's movies' (2001: 8) and suggests that biographical details about the filmmaker's life – notably his cross-dressing and alcoholism – are used in a 'kind of bonehead auteurist fashion where the badness of the life is taken as evidence for the badness of the work' (2001: 2). Furthermore, as I have argued elsewhere (Bartlett 2019b), Wood's haphazard approach to filmmaking and writing means that auteurist signatures, if they are to be located at all, often emerge accidentally – despite his intentions, not necessarily because of them. As a result, finding a single analytical approach to Wood's films as a body of work unified through his authorship is difficult; to do so often requires drawing on a range of textual, intertextual and extratextual evidence and adopting a relatively ambivalent, and often inconsistent, approach to intentionality.

Putting more general criticisms of auteurism aside, other issues can also arise when we attribute failed intentions to the filmmaker as author. This can constitute a form of *schadenfreude* (Dyck and Johnson 2017: 290) – finding enjoyment in the failures of others. Distancing their approach from this 'morally problematic one', Dyck and Johnson propose that appreciation for, and enjoyment of, good-bad art lies in the 'bizarreness produced by failed intentions, not because of self-aggrandizing pleasure taken in those failures' (2017: 290). Yet, as Hunter points out, laughing at failure, 'even loving recuperative laughter, is a species of cruelty and cannot avoid an edge of contempt' (2019: 687). Similarly, I am not sure that Dyck and Johnson's remarks entirely reflect the realities of badfilm appreciation. Fans often demonstrate a genuine affection for badfilms and their creators, but it is hard to deny that mockery of and derision towards both also permeates badfilm reception. We can find comments throughout fan-authored badfilm literature (for example, Hill 2017: 9) that suggest *schadenfreude* motivates at least some of the celebration of these cinematic failures. The Medveds, for instance, explicitly acknowledge this when they argue that witnessing the mistakes of people held in high regard and in positions of privilege or power is 'deeply satisfying' (1980: 11). While this apparently politically motivated desire to challenge power structures and cultural hierarchies could somewhat justify their mockery of the 'big-budget flops' initially included in their 'worst film' canon, it does not account for the authors' appreciation for the low-budget, independent features that are celebrated for their incompetence. Working on the fringes of Hollywood with limited industrial support, filmmakers such as Phil Tucker, Vic Savage and Coleman Francis can only be considered to have enjoyed minimal positions of privilege or power, so laughing at their failure can seem particularly cruel.

Shifting focus away from the author/filmmaker offers an opportunity to avoid these potentially uncomfortable or unhelpful approaches. MacDowell and Zborowski argue that it is often difficult, and not necessarily preferable, to look to the filmmaker as the source of intention. They note that . . .

> . . . even to interrogate a living author about a text's genesis is merely to invite into being yet another text – one which, if offered in full earnest, could still capture only (a) what an author *remembers* intending, (b) what s/he intended *consciously*, and (c) what s/he is capable of *articulating* about his or her conscious intentions (2013: 6; emphasis in original).

When asked about the incoherence of *Blood of Ghastly Horror* (Adamson 1971) – the final incarnation of a narrative that had been chopped, changed, altered and added to over six years – producer Sam Sherman claimed that he and director Al Adamson 'weren't designing a film like that to make any sense' (quoted in Konow 1998: 115). In doing so, he challenges the film's assumed failure to conform to conventional narrative and editing standards, leading to the question: if the intention truly was for *Blood of Ghastly Horror* to not make sense – or, at least, that some other motivation/intention was prioritised over making sense – can the resulting incoherence be considered evidence of failure?

Regardless of Sherman's claims, however, *Blood of Ghastly Horror* evidently *is* a badfilm. The incompetent and ineffective compilation of unrelated footage, its incoherent narrative, unconvincing acting, bad lighting and shoddy cinematography reveal the kinds of overwhelming and obvious failure that typify badfilm: the badness is 'so completely and unintentionally achieved that denying it would require overhauling all existing criteria' (Hunter 2019: 679).

Here, we can consider Umberto Eco's proposal that between the 'unattainable intention of the author and the arguable intention of the reader there is the transparent intention of the text' (1992: 78). Susan Sontag argues that we do not even need to know the artist/author's intentions because 'the work tells all' (2009 [1964]: 282). The notion that intentionality reveals itself through the text reflects the tendency of badfilm fans to prioritise the perceived visibility of failure within the film, even if it contradicts the filmmaker's stated intentions. No matter how many times Tommy Wiseau now claims *The Room* was intended to be a black comedy, it is still primarily enjoyed as an *unintentional* comedy. Indeed, it is only by assuming badfilms are not intended to be parodies or comedies that the audience is able to laugh at them in the way they so regularly do (MacDowell and Zborowski, quoted in McCulloch 2011: 106). This suggests that the filmmaker's claims are likely to be disregarded as evidence of intention – that is, unless they support the text's visible (failed) intentions.

Developing these ideas further, MacDowell and Zborowski build on David Morley's concept of a 'preferred reading' – an interpretation of the text that the text itself encourages – and Eco's comments regarding the importance of contextualisation (Eco 1992: 62–63). They argue that our assessment of intention is often guided by a text's 'relationship with pre-existing cultural forms and genres, and their attendant conventions'; such a relationship 'will often facilitate identification of, at a minimum, the text's *categorical* intentions' (2013: 8; emphasis in original). For example, if a film presents itself as a horror film, it can be situated among other horror films from the same cultural-historical context, with its success or failure to meet standards and expectations established through comparison. Bill Warren includes several of the films discussed in this book in *Keep Watching the Skies*, an exhaustive compendium of 1950s science-fiction films. Viewed in this categorical context, films like *The Giant Claw* (Sears 1957), *Bride of the Monster* and *Mesa of Lost Women* do indeed emerge as particularly incompetent examples of the genre.

For MacDowell and Zborowski, locating the source of categorical intention within the text itself offers a useful contribution to debates on aesthetic intention because it 'both avoids the "unattainable" flesh-and-blood author's intentions, and qualifies the centrality of the endlessly "arguable" intentions of individual readers, whilst also simultaneously acknowledging readers' active roles in interpretation' (2013: 8). Identifying the 'intention of the text' requires conjecture on the part of the reader/viewer, and our ability (or even willingness) to do this can impact how we draw conclusions regarding the apparent visibility of the text's failed intentions. Hunter provides a useful illustration of this when he suggests that classical exploitation films like *Reefer Madness* (Hirliman 1936) can seem particularly weird and 'out of synch' with conventional narrative cinema when viewed in isolation but, 'if you watch enough of them, they emerge as explicable and conventional products of a specific lost mode of fly-by-night independent production that flourished in the USA from the 1920s–1950s' (Hunter 2019: 679). As I discuss in Chapter 4, *Glen or Glenda*'s categorical context as a classical exploitation film similarly challenges, or at least complicates, assertions of its perceived failure to adhere to the conventions of 'mainstream' narrative cinema. Wood's debut feature poses several challenges to badfilm interpretation and reception, and in any categorical context other than classical exploitation (and, arguably, even within this context) often seems to be an outlier. Nevertheless, at a minimum, the failed intentions of badfilm texts are typically understood in relation to narrative cinema and its attendant forms. In other words, the most basic categorical context in which badfilms are comparatively identified is one aiming to adhere to the standards of cinematic representation and realism established in the classical Hollywood system. Deviations from the conventions of 'mainstream' narrative cinema that were dominant at the time of their production are read as accidental and unintended, as the consequence of ineptitude and incompetence.

Of course, viewed today, the badfilms discussed throughout this book can also be understood to occupy another categorical context, that of badfilm itself. However, given that this is a category predicated on failed intentions, it stands to reason that this can never be the 'intention of the text' as originally designed. As I discuss in more detail below, the failure that characterises badfilm means that it can only ever be unintended: as soon as a film intends to be a failure, it stops being one. Nonetheless, the ability of contemporary badfilm viewers to surmise categorical contexts is complicated – though not necessarily negated – by the existence of new contexts that have emerged through subsequent reception. This will be addressed further in the concluding chapter. For now, it is worth noting that the categorical contexts through which the 'intention of the text' emerge refer to the initial contexts in which the texts themselves were conceived and to which they aim to adhere.

A heightened awareness of intentionality is encouraged by the seemingly obvious failure of badfilms. However, although the 'intention of the text' provides a useful alternative to potentially problematic auteurist-based approaches, more pragmatically it is clear that, just as we assert the technical competence and artistic vision of 'good' auteurs, we regularly attribute intention to the filmmaker when those intentions are deemed to have failed. MacDowell and Zborowski note that one of the possible appeals of badfilm is the 'continual blurring of lines between the extratextual and diegetic drama [that] can allow for an increased sense of closeness between spectator and filmmaker' (2013: 22). Identifying the text itself as the sole source of intention may well be too abstract a concept to be widely adopted, particularly considering how frequently auteurism underpins badfilm criticism. However, to ignore the contributions of those people whose ineffective efforts result in the text's attendant failures seems to also deny part of the appeal of badfilms and does not particularly characterise badfilm fan criticism as it exists today.

While there are certain benefits to attributing intentionality to the text rather than to an author, there is evidence to suggest that the two sources are often used interchangeably. In the same article, Hunter argues that, although contemporary 'exploitation' *films* like *Snakes on a Train* (Mervis 2006) are bad, 'their intention is never, exactly, to be "good"' (2014: 483), and, later, that the viewing experience of watching badfilms goes 'against the grain of the *director's* legible intentions' (2014: 489; emphasis added). As I have argued elsewhere (Bartlett 2019a), this suggests that intentionality may be, and regularly is, variously attributed to either/both film and filmmaker.

The distinction between authorial and textual intent often appears to relate to the amount of extra- and inter-textual information at the viewer's disposal, and the extent of the filmmaker's cultified auteur reputation. This represents a challenge to Eco's approach, which discourages looking beyond the text and instead aligns badfilm fans with Richard Rorty's pragmatic assertion that *any* reading of a text will *inevitably* be influenced by other information at the reader's disposal (1992: 105). Fan interest and labour has produced a relative wealth of information about certain badfilmmakers. Ed Wood has been the subject of several books (Grey 1992; Craig 2009; Rausch and Pratt 2015), documentaries including *Flying Saucers Over Hollywood: The Plan 9 Companion* (Carducci 1992) and *Look Back in Angora* (Newsom 1994), an Oscar-winning biopic (*Ed Wood*, Burton 1994) and numerous websites and articles (the 'Ed Wood Wednesdays' series on *Dead 2 Rights* is particularly recommended). Larry Buchanan published an autobiography, *"It Came from Hunger": Tales of a Cinema Schlockmeister*, which is frequently referenced in Craig's book, *The Films of Larry Buchanan: A Critical Examination* (2007). David Konow's *Schlock-o-Rama: The Films of Al Adamson* (1998) celebrates the fascinating – and tragic – life and career of Adamson who directed badfilms such as *Horror of the Blood Monsters* (1970). Many of their contemporaries have not received such attention, however, meaning that the viewer has less access to extratextual or other contextual information that might contribute to how their films are read. Far less is circulated about Coleman Francis, Hal Warren, Bill Rebane or Vic Savage than about the above-mentioned filmmakers with their established cult reputations, and even less for others such as David L. Hewitt (*The Mighty Gorga*), Barry Mahon (*The Beast That Killed Women 1965*), or even Phil Tucker (*Robot Monster*), although they all have made badfilms. The lack of information about individual filmmakers and production contexts can thus encourage intentionality to be repositioned onto the film texts instead of a specific author.

Pragmatically, we are often confronted with the reality that badfilms are regularly judged on their intrinsic textual characteristics, with an underlying acceptance that these, in some way, expose the intentions of those involved in production. Thus, we need to be mindful of how we engage with intention. One way of doing this is to acknowledge that our ability to do so can vary from text to text and from one specific example of failure to another, and it can be influenced by a range of additional factors. These factors include, but are not limited to, our cultural capital and the availability of, and our access to, extratextual information. For example, if we can ascertain with some confidence the individual responsibilities within the filmmaking process, our approach to intentionality is likely to be different than if such information is ambiguous. At the same time, we must be careful to not adopt the 'bonehead auteurist approach' that Routt identified as prevalent in badfilm literature, in particular through an undoubtedly appealing, although not necessarily justified, understanding of intentionality that attributes all failure to an individual (cultified) artist or author.

Accepting the challenges of attributing intentionality to an individual 'artist' or creator, an alternative approach is to ascertain the visibility of failed intentions within the text, without restricting this claim to any one person or thing. Dyck and Johnson, for example, present a useful and often persuasive argument in defence of appreciation for failed intentions that acknowledges a creator but prioritises the evidence – the film's bizarreness – within the text. To deny the role of individuals seems to deny a crucial element of badfilm identification and reception. Badfilms draw attention away from the diegesis to the effort that went into constructing it; they constantly remind us of the particularly human effort and labour at the heart of cinema, as well as the relatable human tendency to fail (see Hunter 2019: 687). Like Dyck and Johnson, then, I suggest that we can explicitly acknowledge intentionality as crucial in our understanding of badfilm, while still leaving the format of that discussion relatively open. Even if we do not take the abstract approach of the 'text's intentions' wholeheartedly, we can still look to the text as evidence of failed intentions.

The Intention to Do What, Exactly?

Identifying badness in terms of failed intentions suggests that there is a demonstrable disparity between the intended effect and the actual result. We tend to accept that badfilm style is the accidental, unintended consequence of technical incompetence and other formal errors, exacerbated by the restrictive production contexts and material poverty. The question thus arises: what intention(s) are we alleging to have evidently failed? As already noted, badfilms are typically understood to expose the failure to achieve the conventions of classical Hollywood that were the prevalent form of narrative cinematic style in the 1950s and 1960s and continue to dominate today. Badfilms are bad because they fail to adhere to even the most basic standards of technical competence. Dyck and Johnson go further, suggesting that the 'badness of good-bad art is artistic in nature' (2017: 282). While it is possible to be relatively agnostic about what constitutes artistic badness, the authors propose that, at minimum, this refers to the 'product of failed intentions, execution, or poor artistic vision' (2017: 282). Their claims align with comments elsewhere regarding badfilms' formal failure (Sconce 1995; MacDowell and Zborowski 2013; Bartlett 2015, 2019a) and indicates an underlying correlation between competence and art: badfilms seem to demonstrate the failed attempt of art. Certainly, there are some badfilms – or specific moments in badfilms – that seem to be aspiring to high culture: Wood's surreal portion of the dream sequence in *Glen or Glenda*, for example, or Jerry's nightmare in *The Incredibly Strange Creatures Who Stopped Living and Became Mixed-Up Zombies!!?* However, given that badfilms are typically understood to reveal a failure to achieve even the most basic standards of cinematic representation, I suggest that formal competency – a lower standard of achievement than the potentially elitist notions of art – tends to be the benchmark by which success or failure is evaluated. Badfilms can fail to achieve these standards to such an extent that they emerge as accidental art, even if 'art' was not necessarily the original, or primary, intention.

There is a correlation, therefore, between goodness/badness and success/failure: a badfilm has failed to succeed in its intended (artistic) aims. With this in mind, it is useful to consider the distinction between intended and unintended art and, particularly, the possible benefits of making a film that intentionally deviates from conventional narrative cinematic style in seemingly 'bad' ways. This can be done for comic effect – to encourage an 'intentionally ironic' viewing position (Muecke 1970: 8) that, typically, plays on the viewer's knowledge of badfilms or, at least, their knowledge of the existence of badfilms. The ridiculous premise at the core of *Attack of the Killer Tomatoes* (De Bello 1978), the unconvincing performances, stilted dialogue and barren sets of Larry Blamire's films, as well as the trashy aesthetic of *Black Dynamite* (Sanders 2009) can all be understood as deliberately 'bad'. When watching these films, it quickly becomes evident how well judged the 'badness' is. Apparent failures in editing, sound, performance and mise-en-scène are supported by other formal elements, which are carefully placed to maximise their comic potential and often subtly acknowledged within the diegesis. The observer is invited to adopt an ironic viewing position that is promoted by the film itself. Thus, a filmmaker can intentionally flout conventions, drawing attention to the filmmaking process through seemingly incoherent and illogical aesthetic choices, and successfully create an artistically 'bad' film. In this sense, an intentionally 'bad' film can be judged as successful in its aim to produce a humorous effect through the self-conscious replication of incompetence.

Badfilms, in contrast, are characterised by failure identified in the gap

Figure 2.1   The inanimate octopus prop, which was either borrowed or stolen from Republic Studios, *Bride of the Monster* (Wood, Jr, 1955).

between intended and actual effect. Their demonstrable failure limits, or even obliterates entirely, their immersive potential, instead drawing attention to their inept construction. In the process, badfilms challenge our ability to read the film in the way in which it was originally intended: horror becomes comedy; science fiction becomes fantasy; tragedy becomes farce. The insects flying across the screen, attracted by the camera's lights in *Manos: The Hands of Fate*; the unavoidable but unacknowledged visual disparity between the stock footage of a live octopus and an inanimate octopus prop in *Bride of the Monster*; and the thoroughly underwhelming reveal of the titular character in the concluding moments of *Curse of the Swamp Creature* – these all distract our attention *away* from the narrative, unwittingly encouraging us to instead focus on the non-diegetic elements of the film. These moments do not suggest an intentionally ironic position. Instead, they suggest that, if the films are to be interpreted ironically, they are the victims rather than the perpetrators of such an approach.

Our identification and understanding of badness (or 'badness') as intentional or unintentional speaks to a broader relationship between artistic intention and interpretation. We can, therefore, identify different kinds of artistic intention: (1) the intention to be good, the aim of which is recognised by the viewer who judges the film to be a successful representation of the desired effect; (2) the intention to be bad, the aim of which is also recognised and judged to be successfully achieved; (3) the intention to be good, the attempts of which are recognised but judged to have failed; and (4) the intention to be bad, the attempts of which are recognised but judged as good. In these scenarios, 'good' refers specifically to artistic quality with technical competence as a minimal expectation, rather than the experiential pleasures implied in 'so bad it's good' that were discussed in the previous chapter. Notably, whereas the first two categories indicate that the intended effect and actual effect are in alignment, the latter two suggest a schism between the artistic intentions and viewer's response to them. This is not inherently detrimental – it is difficult to think of any reason why a film might suffer because its intentional badness has been read as artistic goodness. The films discussed throughout this book, however, belong to the third category, and this indicates their uniqueness: as soon as one intends to make a badfilm, it stops being one. Precisely because of their unconventional, inconsistent, illogical and unmotivated style being accidental – the consequence of failed intentions – it cannot be consciously reproduced.

However, things are never quite that simple. Comparing two examples demonstrates the different ways in which intentional and unintentional badness can manifest within the text, while also problematising the idea that this constitutes a clear, binary distinction. Consider an early moment in *Plan 9 From Outer Space*: a UFO encounter. The spaceships are regularly cited as evidence of the film's incompetence and cheapness and, over the years, have been variously described as plates, hubcaps and/or toys (for example, Medved and Medved 1980: 205). Although it is now generally accepted that they are models from a popular 1950s children's hobby kit, they continue to be misidentified: Sconce describes them as 'flaming paper plates' (2019: 667). On the one hand, the conflicting descriptions could suggest, somewhat ironically, that despite their obvious fakeness as alien transportation, their 'real' status is elusive. On the other hand, it could be another example of what Routt describes as 'trash criticism', whereby the badness of the trash object is 'so evident that it does not matter how extravagantly or erroneously one writes about it' (Routt 2001: 4). As I mentioned in Chapter 1, there certainly does appear to be a tendency in badfilm criticism to prioritise interpretations and anecdotes that support claims of incompetence, regardless of their accuracy.

No exaggeration of failure is necessary in this instance, however. The UFO's debut in *Plan 9* clearly demonstrates the jarring technical and formal ineptitude that characterises badfilms. Jeff and his co-pilot are mid-flight when their commercial plane is suddenly shaken by something passing by, depicted by a sudden flash of light across the cabin and the actors grabbing onto their meagre props while swaying wildly from side to side. For a brief moment, the light exposes the boom mike's shadow on the cabin's back wall. As the men look stage-right, a point-of-view shot reveals a saucer-shaped UFO wobbling slightly against a painted backdrop of the sky. Staring blankly at this apparently incredible sight, the co-pilot flatly remarks: 'Holy mackerel!' Accompanied by a constant 'whooshing' sound that suggests it is both fast-paced and moving steadily, the spaceship wobbles offscreen.

Most obviously, there is a clash between the way in which the spaceships are depicted visually and aurally; this continues throughout the film. The UFOs jump and bounce on strings that are clearly visible on several occasions, rendering their movements inappropriate and irrational. When they move

Figure 2.2A,B Jeff and his co-pilot encounter a UFO. Note the boom mike's shadow and the UFO's visible strings, *Plan 9 From Outer Space* (Wood, Jr, 1959).

across the screen, it is clear they are being dragged. Although their general physical appearance adequately, if minimally, supports their identification as alien spacecraft, their movements expose the incompetent manner in which they are portrayed, revealing them as fake and distractingly unrealistic. This is further compounded by the sound effects that accompany them, as well as by the witnesses' unemotional reactions, which fail to appropriately relay the shock and awe that the dialogue suggests. Notably, Jeff and his onboard crew never acknowledge the illogically jerky movements of the craft that are so visible, so unexpected – and so demonstrably *weird*. Incompetence reveals itself across all aspects of the sequence, with each individual formal element failing to convince and also, importantly, failing to adequately support other aspects of the diegesis. Conversely, the scene is framed and edited in relatively conventional ways, further suggesting a clash between intention and outcome. The editing, as I discuss further in Chapter 6, is largely faithful to classical continuity; at the very least, it indicates a general understanding of those standards and the effort to reproduce them. Thus, we are presented with a scene that, despite its demonstrable incoherence, is apparently intended to be read as entirely serious. There is no evidence in this scene, or elsewhere in the film, to suggest an intentionally ironic temperament – rather, it appears we are meant to interpret the alien invasion as shocking, impressive and effectively presented.

In contrast, we can look at *Night of the Ghouls* (Wood 1959), which was made within a few years of *Plan 9* but not released until 1984, six years after Wood's death, due to his failure to pay the processing lab's fees. *Ghouls* has received far less critical attention than Wood's other 1950s productions but, as I have discussed elsewhere (Bartlett 2019b), it is one of his more interesting films because it suggests Wood was consciously (albeit ineptly) creating intertextual connections between his films and even, at times, playing with narrative conventions (see also Routt 2001). The film follows a police investigation into the mysterious and seemingly supernatural events occurring in the 'old house on Willows Lake', which is explicitly (mis)identified as the same place where Dr Vornoff had previously conducted his doomed experiments in *Bride of the Monster*. What was formerly described as Willows House on Lake Marsh is now occupied by Dr Acula (Kenne Duncan), a psychic medium.

The scene in question sees Lieutenant Bradford (Duke Moore) observing one of Acula's séances. The room's walls are draped with curtains, and the floor appears to be covered with assorted carpet remnants. Acula sits at the head of a large dining table; three people are seated with him, each facing a skeleton, one of which is wearing a wig. The shot suddenly changes to show a trumpet 'floating' against a crumpled curtain. Despite no obvious visual markers to suggest a shared space, it subsequently seems that we are meant to understand this shot as representing the characters' point-of-view. Like the spaceships in *Plan 9*, the trumpet jumps and bounces on strings that are, here at least, not obviously visible. We are shown the reactions of the people sitting at the table. One, an old man, looks confused. None of them appear impressed or startled at the sight of a trumpet seemingly floating on its own volition, nor do they react to the plaintive, tuneless wail that accompanies it. Yet, their expressions suggest a reaction different from the blank ambivalence of Jeff and his airline crew in *Plan 9*. As the old woman looks beyond the frame in disbelief, what is clearly a person draped in a sheet sidesteps from one side of the curtained space to the other, accompanied by a comical sound effect. What appears to be a cup and saucer – a moment of intentional irony, perhaps? – also bounce around. These shots are intercut with reaction shots from the séance's participants, now showing expressions suggesting confusion, bewilderment and disbelief. Bradford wryly smirks and shakes his head. The only character treating this patently absurd, surreal situation with any seriousness appears to be Acula himself.

Superficially, the portrayal of apparently supernatural events here is at least as bad as the UFOs in *Plan 9*. The erratic movements of the 'floating' objects in *Ghouls* never adequately suggest that the items are truly possessed by some unidentified force, while the appearance of what is so indisputably a person wearing a sheet to impersonate a ghost makes the scene utterly preposterous. These wholly un-spectacular special effects also seem to expose the impoverished conditions in which the film was produced. Although textual evidence suggests that we are not meant to question the appropriateness of *Plan 9*'s barren cockpit, spaceship and graveyard sets, can we say the same about this unconvincing portrayal of psychic phenomena in *Ghouls*? In contrast to *Plan 9*, the visual absurdity is supported – even acknowledged – by other diegetic elements. The sounds accompanying the objects and the 'ghost' add a comic edge to the scene, while the characters' reactions imply that they too share at

Figure 2.3A,B 'Supernatural' activity, *Night of the Ghouls* (Wood, Jr, 1959).

least some of our disbelief. Indeed, Acula is subsequently exposed as a con artist, confirming that these 'supernatural' events are exactly what they appear to be: obviously staged and demonstrably fake. This indicates that at least some of the 'badness' of *Ghouls* is intentional.

These contrasting examples illustrate one of the central, though underexplored, aspects of intention as it pertains to badfilms: the intention to be serious and, significantly, to be *taken seriously*. There is no obvious evidence of an ironic disposition in *Plan 9* and no textual or extratextual evidence to suggest that it intends to be received as an object of humour or comedy. *Ghouls*, in contrast, seems to indicate a certain amount of self-awareness and, at times, a conscious attempt at comedy and self-parody. This difference is reminiscent of that between naïve and deliberate camp, as outlined by Susan Sontag. For her, 'pure' examples of camp are more 'satisfying' than deliberate efforts, not only because they are unintentional, but because they reveal a 'seriousness that fails' (2009 [1964]: 283). *Ghouls* reveals itself to be at least partly 'in on the joke' and *not* taking itself entirely seriously. Certain moments of apparent failure are later revealed to be deliberate: our recognition of the 'supernatural' evidence as patently fake and incompetently depicted actually aligns with the intended interpretation of the scene. In this sense, *Ghouls* could be understood to be '*intentionally ironic* rather than *sincerely bad*' (Dyck and Johnson 2017: 291–92; emphasis in original). There are, however, plenty of other moments in which *Ghouls* fails 'sincerely'. It is cheaply made, features several inept attempts at intertextuality and parody, haphazardly incorporates obviously unrelated, recycled footage without acknowledgement and presents an incoherent narrative. Thus, we can say that *Ghouls* is both intentionally ironic *and* sincerely bad, marking yet another way in which badfilms reveal themselves to be thoroughly inconsistent both aesthetically and artistically.

The intention to be taken seriously extends beyond the contents of a film to the film itself. Badfilms seem to lack the self-awareness of more consciously ironic bad movies; instead, they invite us to receive them seriously as 'good' films, sincerely made in good faith both as competent artworks and commercial products. This aspiration to seriousness and sincerity is significant in how badfilms are identified and subsequently received. Joel Hodgson, one of the creators of *Mystery Science Theater 3000*, argues that 'if people are winking at the camera like they're saying "we know we're in a bad movie so we're being silly" it didn't work [. . .] You had to feel like the movie was genuinely trying to move the audience' (quoted in Begy and Fierro 2011: 196). Similarly, Rob Hill argues that there is 'nothing worse than an *intentionally* bad movie, no matter how cleverly calibrated it might be [. . .] It's vital that there was a sincere attempt to do the best work possible' (2017: 16; emphasis in original). An emphasis on the 'heart, sincerity and earnestness' of the filmmakers responsible for badfilms (Pehl 2011: 253; see also Davis 2012: 13; MacDowell and Zborowski 2013: 15; Hill 2017: 16) is indicative of the broader tendency within badfilm reception to attribute intentionality, when possible, to an individual, as discussed earlier. Perhaps as a way of avoiding the moral dilemma of *schadenfreude*, the emphasis on the sincere intention to be taken seriously enables fans to use evidence of failure to promote the effort behind it. Bill Warren, for example, advocates for Phil Tucker's inclusion in the 'ranks of fascinatingly bad directors', arguing that the filmmaker's 'sincerity, his desire to make a worthwhile film, is obvious in every frame [. . . and] he's just as earnest as [Ed] Wood, and just as inept' (2010: 704). Recognition of the (failed) intention for the film to be taken seriously, by a filmmaker also apparently aiming to be taken seriously as the creator of the work, allows for an appreciation of both the aesthetic incompetence and the sincere effort that has produced such inept results.

As *Night of the Ghouls* indicates, however, intentionality in badfilm is rarely fixed or consistent. Not all badfilms have been interpreted as having such sincere pretensions to art. Gary Hentzi, for example, argues that the 'studied goofiness' of certain psychotronic (and bad) films such as *Incredibly Strange Creatures* suggests a 'certain level of awareness on the part of the directors, who have accepted the unlikelihood of their making a good film and so are aiming for a campy one instead' (Hentzi 1993: 24). We should nevertheless be careful to not impose a wholesale alignment of narrative trashiness with aesthetic badness. To do so runs the risk of assuming a filmmaker could not possibly make a film titled, for example, *Santa Claus Conquers the Martians* (Webster 1964) and intend for it to be, at a minimum, competently constructed. Generally, badfilms seem to invite us to take them seriously as 'good' films, irrespective of how objectively 'silly', 'trashy' or absurd their narratives are; in other words, their presentation typically does not suggest that we are meant to construe them *as failures*. Consider, for instance, the obvious disparity in *Robot Monster* between Ro-Man's patently ludicrous appearance – a man in a gorilla suit wearing a diving helmet with added antennae – and his characterisation as a highly advanced, intelligent alien being who has already destroyed (almost) all of humanity. This clash is never acknowledged: there is no knowing glance to suggest that we should not take him, or the threat he poses to the human protagonists, seriously. His ruthlessness is emphasised in a particularly disturbing scene in which he murders a young child. As in *Plan 9*, where no acknowledgement is made regarding the spaceship's absurd presentation, none of *Robot Monster*'s characters ever remark on Ro-Man's preposterous appearance. They take him seriously, and the film invites us to do the same.

Nevertheless, Hentzi's comments serve as a useful reminder of the slipperiness of intentionality. A film can be narratively trashy and incompetently made, but these forms of badness are not synonymous: ineptitude constitutes just one form of badness. Plenty of low budget sci-fi and horror movies from the 1950s and 1960s contain 'silly', generic stories and ridiculous monsters, but are competently and effectively made and therefore do not meet the criteria to be considered badfilms. What Hentzi's remarks indicate is that the intention behind a film can change in response to production conditions or other factors, and that self-awareness can help to mitigate against some of the possible assertions of failure or incompetence. It is certainly a more comfortable position to be 'in on the joke' than to be the joke itself. Of course, a film could also fail in its efforts to be campy or self-aware, while conscious campiness might not adequately distract from other evident failures. However, sincerity and seriousness remain central to badfilm identification and appreciation: unsurprisingly, the most widely celebrated badfilms are those that appear to fail in the most 'honest' and 'sincere' ways. Dyck and Johnson propose that good-bad artworks 'don't just have to fail, they have to fail in the right ways' (2017: 290). They identify this 'special ingredient' as bizarreness. While not disputing this, I propose that, primarily, the 'right way' to fail is to do so *sincerely*.

To date, the limited scholarship on intentions in badfilm has tended to focus on artistic intention. However, even the intention to produce competent work can be superseded by other, more prosaic intentions – namely, to make a film within the timeframe and conditions imposed on production. For example, Larry Buchanan signed a contract with AIP for three films, which were 'so successful' that he went on to write, produce, direct, edit and market nine features for the company between 1965 and 1970, in addition to another five he made without AIP's backing (Buchanan 1996: 78). In this instance, it seems likely that he, like other low-budget filmmakers at the time, was hired primarily for his 'speed and efficiency' (Davis 2012: 8) rather than any notable artistic talents.

Buchanan's AIP films – a mix of original concepts and remakes commissioned for television – are so notoriously bad that one, *Zontar: The Thing from Venus*, inspired the name of the fanzine that coined the term badfilm.

Buchanan's movies were subject to particularly restrictive conditions and constraints: they each had to be eighty minutes long, in colour and made for no more than $30,000 (for comparison, *Bride of the Monster* is sixty-nine minutes, filmed in black and white, and cost around $70,000). We can reasonably propose, then, that Buchanan was at least partly motivated by a need to meet these criteria. His own comments support this. He recalls, for example, that because the effects budget for *Mars Needs Women* (Buchanan 1967) was 'zero, zip, nada' he used a 'Frisbee as a spaceship' (Buchanan 1996: 101), knowing that he 'had no choice but to deliver the banality, crude structure, rough editing and in many instances bad acting to *satisfy my contract*' (1996: 102; emphasis added). His comments suggest that not only was Buchanan aware of the challenges of producing a competent film – let alone an artistically impressive one – but that competence was not necessarily his or AIP's priority. In this scenario, then, we can propose that the intention here was a more functional one: to complete the work to a minimal standard according to the specifications, irrespective of quality. Arguably, he succeeded in this aim. Likewise, when Hal Warren made *Manos: The Hands of Fate*, the intention was – according to anecdotal evidence – to win a wager between him and screenwriter Stirling Silliphant. Warren bet that anyone, even he, could make a movie. Ultimately, he succeeded: he made a movie. There did not appear to be any conditions or expectations of quality attached to the wager.

The haphazard and inconsistent style that characterises badfilms often suggests an ambivalence towards the film as a finished product. It is telling that Sconce asserts that Ed Wood was 'unable (*or unwilling*) to master the basics of continuity, screen direction or the construction of cinematic space' (1995: 387; emphasis added). The cultification of badfilmmakers as accidental auteurs, as well as the assumption that badness reveals itself through failed artistry, does not fully reflect what often appears to be a disregard towards quality. Badfilms are often shoddy, cheap movies; their formal badness is not just indicative of incompetence but also of carelessness. The technical failure in badfilms seems to suggest a lack of effort, whereby attempts to provide continuity, to tell a coherent story, or to present visual spectacle seem to be minimal at best. Badness, in this sense, reveals itself in the carelessness, the absence of effort and the apparent conceit that the bare minimum will suffice. Can we really claim that the set design of the spaceship's interior in *Plan 9* is the result of a wholehearted attempt to construct an impressively alien setting? The spartan aesthetic evident throughout the film seems more often to suggest minimal effort: a case of 'that'll do'. The numerous mistakes, contradictions and repetitions in and across Wood's films (see Bartlett 2019b) are not particularly suggestive of effort or care. Rather, textual evidence supports anecdotal claims about his chaotic, erratic approach to writing (various in Grey 1992: 139–41) and indicates a lack of research and self-editing. The swamp creature so widely ridiculed in Buchanan's movie (for example, Curran, quoted in Buchanan 1996: 96–98) does not just appear in one film; the costume features in two of Buchanan's other films (*Creature of Destruction* 1967; *It's Alive* 1969). No obvious effort has been made to *improve* the costume, just to alter it slightly so that it may be re-presented as new. As these examples indicate, the badness, shoddiness and internal inconsistency in badfilms can often suggest ambivalence. The mistakes and errors remain – no apparent effort has been made to remove them, or even to minimise their negative effect on narrative or aesthetic coherence and continuity. This apparent aim of minimal functionality can complicate our understanding of failed artistic intentions, while also implying a certain resourcefulness and even a cavalier attitude that assumes – correctly, some might argue – that the bare minimum will indeed suffice.

We should also acknowledge another possible intention: the aspiration to make a commercially viable and profitable movie. Pauline Kael suggests that this aspiration can take precedence over other aims in any movie, arguing that 'whatever the original intention of the writers and director, it is usually supplanted, as the production gets under way, by the intention to make money – and the industry judges the film by how well it fulfils that intention' (1994 [1969]: 92). For the people attempting to carve out some semblance of a career on the fringes of Hollywood, it is likely that they were always motivated, in part at least, by the possibility of a paycheck. We should, therefore, be careful not to dismiss the financial intentions behind film production – or the possibility that these can be successfully achieved in badfilms. There is a difference between critical and commercial success; one does not guarantee or negate the other. Kael's comments regarding the industry's – rather than the critic's – evaluation of films in terms of their financial returns aligns success with profit. Using this criterion, several badfilms can be considered successes. *Robot Monster*, for example, was shot on an estimated budget of only $16,000 (or $35,000, or $50,000, depending on who is asked; see Warren 2010: 703), but grossed $1,000,000 in the United States alone (Davis 2012: 10–11). Indeed, several people responsible for the badfilms discussed throughout this book enjoyed relatively productive and stable film careers lasting several decades. Badfilmmakers such as Buchanan, Adamson, Steckler, Rebane and even Wood succeeded in carving out a place for themselves in the industry. However, a film's financial success did not always serve to benefit its creator. Despite *Robot Monster*'s substantial returns, its director allegedly struggled to get further work and (unsuccessfully) attempted suicide (Warren 2010: 703). Ed Wood died homeless and destitute, having already pawned most of his possessions. For them, personal failure followed commercial success, with their incompetence dually revealed through their struggles to master either the creative or business aspects of their chosen career.

Having been largely taken for granted in fan-authored and academic bad movie criticism, the recent focus on intentions in badfilm is certainly welcome. As MacDowell and Zborowski note, aesthetic approaches to badfilm require us to address a fundamental question: 'on what basis can we presume to infer artistic intention, given that we [. . .] clearly and necessarily *do* so regularly?' (2013: 5; emphasis in original). However, as I have shown here, artistic intention represents only one aspect of intention that contributes to the style of badfilms and how we respond to them. It is likely, for example, that interpreting badness in terms of failed artistic intentions will elicit a more sympathetic and positive response than focusing on the often successful, but arguably less creative and admirable, intention to make money. Yet, precisely because of badfilms' haphazard, inconsistent qualities – what Dyck and Johnson might describe as their 'bizarreness' – intentionality reveals itself in different ways and in different contexts. The badness of badfilms exposes intentionality through failure in ways that 'good' films do not by, for example, drawing attention to production contexts and formal processes of cinematic construction, but it does so in ways that are often open to a range of possible interpretations and responses. Thus, we must be mindful of how we approach intention – who or what we attribute intention to, and what we understand intentionality to relate to – and how this can impact how we respond to the films themselves, including how we potentially value, appreciate and enjoy them.

Intention, Taste and the Problems with 'So Bad It's Good'

Although certain films may be described as 'so bad they're good', they are not necessarily received that way universally. For example, Dyck and Johnson use *The Room* to examine failed intentions in what they describe as 'good-bad art'. Referring to the sex scenes in particular, they propose that these are unintentionally ironic due to the failed, entirely unerotic attempts to be sexy through the use of common tropes such as roses, candles and soft music. This, they argue, is 'certainly funny' (2017: 283), with the emphasis 'certainly' suggesting an absolute. However, although the contradiction may be entertaining initially, the scenes carry on interminably. It is an awkward, increasingly uncomfortable and voyeuristic viewing experience, one that seems more likely to invite a kind of involuntary, nervous laughter rather than sustained enjoyment. Later, the authors distinguish between 'good-bad' (so bad it's good) and 'bad-bad' (what I term 'just' bad) art. As Dyck and Johnson acknowledge, not every failure warrants appreciation; it is their example of 'bad-bad' art that is so unusual. They propose that 'many films are simply too bad for us to enjoy; they are too boring, for example. Many [uncited sources] find that this is true of *Plan 9 From Outer Space*, which is just boring' (2017: 290). For these authors, *Plan 9* – arguably the most canonised 'so bad it's good' movie there is – is not good-bad art, but bad-bad art. It is hard to not read this as evidence of subjectivity infiltrating what is otherwise an astute and relevant investigation of intentionality. I suggest that this demonstrates the inherent problem of attributing the 'only' value of badfilms to appreciation in terms of enjoyment.

More useful, then, are Dyck and Johnson's comments regarding the 'bizarreness' of failed intentions. In many ways, their discussion of intentionality aligns with my own. They suggest that badfilms are unique precisely because of their failure, which cannot be reproduced consciously without slipping into more conscious parody or deliberate camp. Their identification of 'bizarreness' as an inherent quality of badfilms correlates with my focus on the films' incoherence and inconsistency. Bizarreness, to use their term, can encourage a certain kind of active viewer engagement (see also Sconce 2003). In one sense, Sontag's claim that the 'work tells all' appears to be correct: the badness of the work reveals itself through the text, and badfilms seem to expose their failed intentions in particularly obvious ways. At the same time, however, badfilms do not 'tell all'. Their weirdness, inconsistency and seemingly unmotivated incoherence often invite more questions than they provide answers, and we are left 'genuinely curious and bewildered, wondering: *How could someone think this is a good idea?*' (Dyck and Johnson 2017: 283; emphasis in original). As Adams asserts, badfilms can be 'thought provoking, if only because you were made to wonder *how* they'd ever been made' (2010: 4; emphasis in original). Their excessively obvious, unavoidable, seemingly unintended failure draws attention to the non-diegetic elements of the film (Hoberman 1980; Sconce 1995, 2003) and encourages us to investigate further – to try to understand the failure, to rationalise what we are experiencing. We can, however, dispute the apparent inevitability of laughter as a response to bizarre badness; curiosity and bewilderment do not necessarily equate enjoyment.

Enjoyment of badfilms, then, is necessarily subjective. Although the recent academic attention to failed intentions in 'so bad they're good' movies (or 'good-bad art') begins to address this as a crucial, but previously underexplored aspect of badfilm appreciation, the focus on failed intentions in relation to potential pleasure can complicate otherwise astute and insightful arguments. It can appear, for example, that the authors are justifying certain tastes through a model that only seems to be objective and evidence-based. In other words, the prioritisation of 'so bad they're good' movies in discussions of failed intentions seems to suggest that there can be no 'intrinsic' value of badfilms – that 'value' can be located only in their instrumental value as objects of fun. This is, however, not the case. As I demonstrate in the remaining chapters of this book, badfilms offer vast scope for analysis beyond their reception contexts. It is precisely *because* of the visibility of failed intentions that the films' inconsistent, incoherent, bizarre qualities cannot be reproduced. Badness, then, has intrinsic value because it is accidental and unintentional, producing an aesthetic that is distinct and different from 'conscious' style.

3. THE DISRUPTIVE EFFECTS OF BAD VOICES

Introduction

As viewers, we often take it for granted that cinematic sound and image will work together in a coherent manner, and that they will not only co-exist, but also support each another. Typically, the aim of narrative cinema is to create an immersive diegesis that is easily understood and accepted by its audience: we are presented with a film world that is highly constructed, but which actively works to conceal this construction and to deflect attention away from it. For viewers accustomed to narrative sound cinema, there is often a tacit assumption of coherence, cohesion and synchronisation. We *expect* sound and image to be unified, and certain conventions to be adhered to. There is a complicity in watching movies, and film form works to encourage this complicity by 'exploit[ing] the illusory characteristics of the medium to present a world that on some level is taken to be reality by its audience' (Donnelly 2014: 7). Although an inherent separation exists between sound and image due to cinema's mechanical, technical and industrial structures, evidence of that separation is minimised and the illusion of a coherent reality is maintained, when the two complement and work to support each other.

When successfully employed, cinematic conventions typically work to conceal the processes that go into constructing the diegesis, encouraging narrative immersion and emotional engagement instead. Conversely, when sound and image fail to cohere, this can have a significant impact on how we understand, engage with and respond to the film's world, particularly when this lack of cohesion appears to be unintended. Kevin Donnelly suggests that cinema 'makes the audience wide-eyed, unable to see and hear beyond the thin veil of the illusion of the mechanism that grips them in a state of such awe' (2014: 7). Badfilms regularly disrupt and dismantle the relationship between sound and image that we so often take for granted in 'good' films. They challenge our complicity and draw attention away from the diegesis to its construction. Being able to see beyond the veil, therefore, offers viewers an opportunity to engage with cinematic form in dynamic, different, although not always intended, ways.

This form of active viewer engagement is inherent to cult audiences. Like film aesthetes, paracinematic and badfilm fans are considered to be 'extremely conscious of cinema's characteristic narrative forms and stylistic strategies' (Sconce 1995: 387) and can appear to be predisposed to have a desire to look beyond the diegesis. However, I suggest that this claim needs some qualification. Certainly, badfilm fans are particularly attentive to cinematic form and often demonstrate their ability and tendency to employ sophisticated reading strategies that draw on a range of textual and exegetic material. Nevertheless, badfilms regularly invite – and even unintentionally encourage – this mode of engagement, by drawing attention to the 'truth' that cinematic conventions so often aim to conceal: the diegesis is a construction, the 'reality' unfolding before us is a composite of disparate parts, and the film world is merely an illusion. Badfilms thus unwittingly encourage a more detached, critical position. The inherent inconsistency and strangeness of such evident failure also, I suggest, makes it more likely that we will try to look beyond the frame to the processes of production, even if only in an attempt to make sense of the seemingly unmotivated and unintended deviations in cinematic style.

This chapter examines post-production sound techniques, specifically voice-over narration and post-synchronisation, in badfilm. Film sound plays an important role in communicating information in an 'aesthetically and stylistically appropriate manner' (Pauletto 2012: 129) and voice-over and post-synchronisation have both been recognised for their functional, practical and corrective potential. When incompetently and inappropriately used, however, they can have particularly disorienting and distancing effects. These post-production devices are regularly exploited in badfilms, but in such shoddy, inconsistent and ineffective ways that they serve to expose the attempts to 'stitch together' the sound- and image-tracks. The blatant discrepancies between sound/voice and image/body draw attention to the constructed nature of the film world. Rather than successfully concealing or correcting other errors, badly integrated post-production sound draws attention to them and even exacerbates them further. Badfilms thus demonstrate the disconcerting, disturbing effects of sound that fails to support, and is itself unsupported by, the image it accompanies.

As well as providing an opportunity to interrogate the unintended consequences of inept cinematic construction, examining the voice in badfilms also provides an opportunity to consider the broader relationships between cinematic sound and image. The film image has long been prioritised over sound: although the historical and ontological hierarchies that underpin this belief have been dismissed as 'fallacies' (Altman 1980a: 14), and more attention is now being paid to the complexities of cinematic sound, certain assumptions still carry some weight. There remains a tendency, for example, to assume that 'when words and images absolutely contradict each other, the images always seem to be the truth-tellers' (Kozloff 1988: 144). Film sound is both 'constructed and highly manipulated' (Pauletto 2012: 129) and perceived to *be* manipulative (Dykhoff 2012: 174); it can have a powerful, significant impact on how we respond to the film world but is usually designed to be unobtrusive and invisible. Its 'manipulation' – a term with negative connotations – is concealed through the ability of sound to work in collaboration with the image to render the illusion of a coherent film world. The success – or failure – of this illusion often depends on the process itself remaining hidden (Donnelly 2014: 3), with discrepancies between sound and image, either through asynchrony or some other clash, believed to 'undermine the film experience' (2014: 4). Examining post-production sound in badfilm, therefore, addresses an aspect of cinematic construction that has often been ignored or downplayed and allows for consideration of formal devices that are usually meant to go unnoticed.

Critical Approaches to Voice-Over Narration

Several of the most notorious badfilms of the 1950s and 1960s feature voice-over narration. This device was popular in low-budget films of the time, ostensibly assumed to be included not for artistic or creative reasons, but because it gave filmmakers an opportunity to 'straighten out their discontinuity' (Kozloff 1988: 37) in post-production. When effectively and appropriately utilised, voice-over narration has the potential to mitigate against continuity problems. Conversely, when ineptly applied, it exacerbates those problems by drawing attention to them and adding new layers of incoherence to stories already beset with discontinuity. As I demonstrate below, voice-over in badfilms regularly fails in its attempts to impress upon the viewer the seriousness and importance of the story being told, while blatant contradictions between the narration and the image typically work to undermine the former, exposing it as unreliable. Thus, poorly conceived voice-over narration can also unintentionally invite us to consider broader issues of control and authority that extend beyond the text.

Voice-over narration refers to 'oral statements, conveying any portion of a narrative, spoken by an unseen speaker situated in a space and time other than that simultaneously being presented by the images on the screen' (Kozloff 1988: 5). There are two main types: first-person and third-person. The former, spoken by a character within the diegesis but recounted from a time and/or space non-concurrent to the main narrative, is commonplace in American fiction film and can create a more 'subjective' perspective, as well as enable the viewer to forge a more intimate relationship with the character relaying this narration. Third-person voice-over, in contrast, often works to maintain distance and suggest the objective authority of the speaker over the image: it is constructed as 'fundamentally unrepresentable in human form, connoting a position of absolute mastery and knowledge outside the spatial and temporal boundaries of the social world the film depicts' (Wolfe 1997: 149). This is the form taken by most voice-over narration in American badfilms of the 1950s and 1960s. As a narrative device, the qualities of third-person voice-over, particularly its 'supposedly authoritarian yet often presumptuous' style of address (Nichols 1983: 17), have long been negatively perceived as 'elitist, oppressive, and offensive' (Kozloff 1984: 41) by filmmakers, scholars and critics. Even at the peak of its popularity in the 1940s, this 'voice of God' narration was associated with 'lower' forms of entertainment – television, genre pictures and low-budget productions. By the time the films discussed in this book were made, therefore, third-person voice-over had already fallen out of favour and was subject to criticism and derision, even when employed effectively.

Although the most common form of narration in badfilms is third-person, at times voice-over is used in ambiguous ways and can blur with other forms of sound, such as voice-off. However, it is not always clear how intentional this ambiguity is. Hack radio psychic Criswell's roles in two of Wood's loosely related films, *Plan 9 From Outer Space* and *Night of the Ghouls*, demonstrates this well (see Bartlett 2019b; Routt 2001). Voice-over is also a significant feature in *Glen or Glenda*, where various narrators feature, each used in unconventional, complicated and frequently confusing ways. Dr Alton's first-person narration is used as a framing device, but the tone he adopts is more akin to third-person, omniscient narration, while sequences within the stories he is apparently recounting are overlaid with multiple voice-overs, possibly intended to be interior monologues, emanating from unidentified characters. Occasionally these are accompanied by images of fragmented bodies – an ear, an eye – but it is never clear whether the voice is meant to be understood as belonging to those bodies. The appearance of a god-like character called The Scientist (Bela Lugosi) complicates matters further. Although he remains largely outside *Glen or Glenda*'s main narrative, The Scientist seems to control it to such an extent that he has been described as narrator (Medved and Medved 1980: 178), despite his voice only ever being heard in conjunction with his onscreen image. The haphazard, inconsistent ways in which voice-over are employed draw attention to the ambiguous relationships between voice and body, but also suggest an inherent incoherence in narrative form. Thus, it is unclear who, if anyone, has authority over the image or can be considered a reliable, effective source of information.

Just as Altman identifies certain 'fallacies' associated with sound in cinema, Kozloff recognises the existence of prejudices within the academy and among filmmakers towards voice-over narration in general. Some of these relate to the broader historical tendency to prioritise the film image over sound, as mentioned earlier. There is an underlying assumption, for example, that 'since real filmmakers know that film is essentially a visual medium, it is the unimaginative and incompetent who turn to voice-over' (Kozloff 1988: 21–22). Certainly, voice-over has practical benefits that may well appeal to low-budget and novice filmmakers working under restrictive conditions. It can be utilised to conceal or correct mistakes or narrative discontinuity, for example, and can also provide a cheap way of providing information that would be costly and/or difficult to relay through visual means. This functional use, however, can appear to work counter the guiding principle of 'show, don't tell' in cinema. When voice-over serves to replace, rather than work with, the image, it can suggest apathy and/or inability; it is seen as a last resort, a poor substitute for more 'appropriate' and preferable forms of visual representation. The criticisms do not end there, however. Voice-over has also been considered particularly manipulative and tainted by a subjectivity that curtails the interpretive and polysemous potential of a film text. Alternatively, it has been rejected as an unnecessary and 'redundant' technique that does little more than reiterate and confirm the contents of the image, although such criticisms do not account for the ways in which voice-over can, and often does, provide 'disjunction, independence, interrogation, and even negation of the image' (Browne 1980: 234). As I demonstrate below, voice-over can work in seemingly redundant ways but nonetheless expose disjunction through failure to appropriately support the image. By failing to even accurately describe the image, voice-over can expose itself as not only unnecessary but detrimental to the film.

Although scholars such as Kozloff have successfully countered many of these criticisms of voice-over narration, the tendency to dismiss its inclusion in low-budget, genre pictures as a cost-cutting, functional and (implicitly) lazy device remains. Like recycled footage, to be discussed in the next chapter, it appears that not all forms of voice-over narration have been deemed equally worthy of closer investigation and possible re-evaluation. The casual assumption of voice-over as a functional, money-saving tool for 'incompetent' filmmakers suggests a homogenous approach whereby it is used in the same way, to the same effect, across low-budget narrative cinema. This is certainly not the case. Superficially, we might expect the third-person voice-over narration in *The Beast of Yucca Flats* and *The Creeping Terror* to work in similar ways: both are low-budget, science-fiction/horror movies that were filmed without sound

(MOS) and include narration, in part, to compensate for this lack of diegetic sound. Yet, the style of voice-over varies significantly between the two films, with significantly different outcomes. The narration in *Yucca Flats* is notable for its brevity and characterised by staccato, disjointed and fragmented sentences that are uttered by the director himself. These either offer unmotivated, irrelevant pseudo-philosophical comments ('Flag on the moon, how did it get there?') or repeat non-specific remarks ('Man and wife, unaware of scientific progress') that have little obvious benefit to the viewer in terms of either narrative development or emotional engagement. In contrast, *The Creeping Terror*'s narrator adopts an authoritarian and often literary approach, regularly speaking over characters as they are shown talking onscreen to provide insights into their emotional and mental state.

Incompetence can be identified in a variety of seemingly unmotivated and inconsistent deviations in film style; failure reveals itself in a multitude of ways. Advocating for a more positive approach to voice-over narration, Kozloff proposes that 'what matters is not whether the narration was a forethought or an afterthought but *how well it is thought out*' (1988: 22; emphasis added). In this sense, voice-over narration can be understood as either appropriate or inappropriate; it can work positively to enhance the filmic experience, or it can negatively impact our understanding and engagement, irrespective of when the decision was made to include it. Whereas *Yucca Flats*' narration appears to be an example of 'forethought' style, there have been suggestions, discussed in more detail later in this chapter, that the voice-over in *The Creeping Terror* was included as an afterthought to conceal a problem that arose during production. Nevertheless, although used in very different ways, the voice-over in neither film could be considered 'well thought out' or even minimally successful. By failing to achieve even its most functional potential to correct problems and compensate for or minimise the effects of other deficiencies, the voice-over in badfilms regularly exposes itself as inappropriate.

Beyond the academy, voice-over narration is regularly cited as evidence of badfilms' incompetence, although this does not guarantee any more consideration or analysis than is found in scholarship. For example, Bill Warren recounts a passage of third-person voice-over to support his claim that *Mesa of Lost Women* is a 'leading contender for the worst film of all time' (2010: 571), but his critical review does not extend to considering how the inflated language and authoritarian tone affects the film's subsequent ability to meet expectations, although this would certainly work to support his argument. The tendency to include direct quotations – not limited to voice-over – as evidence of failure is common in fan-authored criticism (for example, Juno and Vale 1986: 206–11) and points to the significance of 'atrocious scripts' (Sconce 2019: 670) as a potential source of entertainment and enjoyment in badfilms. When voice-over is referenced, quotes often appear to be selected based on their inherent oddness, their bombastic nature and the likelihood of the film's narrative or aesthetics to fail to meet the narrator's claims. Citing specific examples without narrative context – as I have done above, arguably, in relation to *Yucca Flats* – can also emphasise the films' badness and suggests ways in which individual elements of the film can be, and often are, disentangled from one another. In this way, dialogue provides evidence of badfilms' incompetence and weirdness, and effectively 'speak for themselves'; no context is required.

Impossible Expectations, Unintentional Irony and Narrative Redundancy

Badfilms featuring voice-over narration regularly expose a disparity between sound and image, which can result in both the narrator's and the filmmaker's authority being thrown into doubt. When appropriately acknowledged within the text, this tension can be understood as evidence of the narrator's ironic temperament, which can be intentional or unintentional. Eric Smoodin distinguishes between the two by proposing that intentional irony differs from unintentional irony in that the 'narrator chooses to be ironic, and does not himself [sic] speak with an unintentional irony that only the spectator or reader, and not the narrator, can appreciate' (1983: 26). In the case of the former, the voice-over narrator takes advantage of a clash between literary and cinematic devices to offer a deeper understanding of what is being presented, avoiding the allegedly redundant exercise of describing the image over which it speaks. In the latter situation, irony is inferred by the viewer, particularly through knowledge of the full filmic text or extratextual information about the film's production. Intentionality, therefore, does not extend beyond the voice-over itself; irony is assumed to be beneficial to the viewer's understanding of the film because it does not call into the question the authority or competency of the filmmaker/image-maker.

Intentionally ironic first-person narrators can display authority over the narrative through an obvious self-awareness that is emphasised by their position as a diegetic character. In Russ Meyer's low-budget sex-comedy *Eve and the Handyman* (1961), for example, Eve observes her subject cleaning out a washing machine in a laundromat. As he sticks his entire head in the barrel, she says, via first-person voice-over, that this gave the handyman 'time to use his head for planning and plotting. Obviously, he was self-disciplined to think deeply, so that nothing would ever pass him by'. However, his moment of reflection means that he fails to notice that the woman at the machine next to his has completely disrobed, placed all her clothes into the washer and walked away naked. This deliberate, obvious, immediate contradiction between the voice-over's description of events and the accompanying image appropriately infuses the scene with humour, adding a light-heartedness to the narrative that is in keeping with the rest of the film. The voice-over narration also helps to conceal the film's low-budget production, particularly its lack of synchronised sound. It is consistently ironic throughout the film; it supports and is supported by other formal elements, including the musical score. As this ironic temperament can also be found in other Meyer productions, such as *The Immoral Mr Teas* (1959), it is easy to accept this as both a deliberate stylistic device and one that appropriately and successfully achieves its intended result.

In other situations, inferring the ironic temperament of a third-person narrator can lead to their assumed authority being disputed, particularly if irony appears to be unintentional. Because of their heterodiegetic position, third-person narrators are often perceived to be superior to the onscreen characters and 'unconstrained by our questioning their right or power to know so much' (Kozloff 1988: 74). When the narrator does not appear to be aware of his or her (usually his) own ironic position, it can create doubts as to their authority over the narrative. This is further complicated by the implication of a closer relationship between narrator and image-maker due to the former remaining off-screen, creating a situation whereby the 'voice ultimately becomes for us the voice of the image-maker' (Kozloff 1988: 74). In badfilms like *Yucca Flats*, such a reading is justified since the filmmaker and narrator are one and the same. Positively, the third-person voice-over draws our attention beyond the frame and, potentially, could help us forge a closer relationship with the image-maker. Negatively, however, the perceived correlation between voice-over narrator and filmmaker – whether accurate or not – can result in suspicions about the voice-over's authority extending to the image-maker, particularly when the image-maker already demonstrates little authority over their film through evident incompetence elsewhere.

When contradictions between image and sound emerge, generally the former is perceived to be more 'truthful' than the latter, and irony – intentional or otherwise – can be inferred in this disjunction. As Kozloff notes (1988: 119), the lack of simultaneous visual corroboration of a spoken statement must be considered within its wider context. In badfilms, this requires acknowledging the impact of extratextual information and the film's established reputation, as well as the (in)consistency of the narrator's individual statements in the context of its function in the entire narrative, and the success or failure of other elements of film form in relation to one another. For example, in *The Creeping Terror*, the third-person voice-over narrator's claim that Martin (played by director Arthur Nelson White under the pseudonym Vic Savage) and his companions 'looked at the rocket with utter amazement' is undermined by the image over which it speaks. There is no evidence of 'amazement' on any of the three characters' faces. Instead, they stare blankly beyond the frame, and the voice-over thus exposes itself as an unreliable source of information. This

Figure 3.1 Martin and his companions 'look at the rocket with utter amazement', *The Creeping Terror* (Nelson, 1964).

could be interpreted as a moment of unintentional irony, but not entirely as Smoodin describes. Neither the narrator nor the image-maker appear to be unaware of his statement's ironic potential. There is no obvious advantage in exposing the actors' failure to portray appropriate emotional responses adequately, and no clear benefit to establishing the narrator's unreliability at this moment, given their seemingly omniscient position and predominantly authoritative tone throughout the film. Rather, it appears that the obvious discrepancy between sound and image is meant to go unnoticed. This suggests that, if irony is inferred by the viewer, it works to undermine both narrator and image-maker through recognition of their failed intentions.

The discourse surrounding the ironic potential of voice-over narration indicates a tendency to assume that any such reading is appropriate, beneficial and intended by the filmmaker. Kozloff even suggests that our confidence in the image-maker is so strong that 'whenever a discrepancy arises [. . .] we seek for – and if necessary, invent – a rationale' for it (1988: 115). An unreliable voice-over narrator, therefore, is usually assumed to be the 'victim of the image-maker's irony' (1988: 112). As the following analysis of *Monster A-go Go* demonstrates, however, ironic readings are not necessarily intended, nor are they inevitably beneficial to interpretations of the film text. Poorly conceived voice-over narration can emphasise the filmmaker's incompetence and lack of control or authority, thereby becoming a marker of failed intentions. Although irony may be inferred as an interpretive strategy to provide a 'rationale' for the all-too obvious discrepancies between image and narration, badfilms rarely provide textual support to suggest that this approach is intended by either narrator or image-maker.

'What You Are About to See May Not Even Be Possible': *Monster A-go Go* and the Unreliable 'Voice of God' Narrator

In addition to exposing itself – and, by extension, the image-maker – as unreliable, inept voice-over narration regularly fails to conceal or mitigate against other formal incompetence. When voice-over draws attention to unconvincing acting, underwhelming spectacle or moments of discontinuity, for example, it fails to achieve even its most basic, corrective function. Although the third-person voice-over narration in *Monster A-go Go* was allegedly added at a late stage in an attempt to rectify problems that had emerged during production, much of the film's reputation as a badfilm rests on its narrative incoherence. The voice-over regularly exacerbates this, while also exposing itself as unreliable, frequently redundant and lacking authority. The narration is not dissimilar to other 'voice of God' narrators found in low-budget science-fiction films a decade earlier: *The Astounding She-Monster* (Ashcroft 1957), *The Giant Claw* and *Mesa of Lost Women* all feature similarly bombastic third-person narrators. Each assert, with minimal success, the seriousness, importance and shocking nature of what will be shown, apparently in an effort to fill the viewer with trepidation and awe. Given the films' tiny budgets, generic narratives and often amateur or inexperienced crews, the unintended yet seemingly inevitable consequence of such grandiose narration is that expectations are raised to impossible levels and the various failures are emphasised rather than minimised.

Monster A-go Go, a 'mutant monster on the loose' movie originally titled *Terror at Halfday*, was Bill Rebane's directorial debut. Its production was beset with problems, largely due to union disputes that ate into its already tight budget. According to Rebane (2010), principal photography was staggered throughout 1961, with around six months separating each of the three week-long shoots. Several cast members who had featured prominently in the original script had to drop out due to other commitments, with the result that entirely new characters are introduced midway through the film but mostly fulfil the same roles as their predecessors. Rebane managed to complete around 80 to 90 per cent of the film, which ended up in the hands of independent producer Herschell Gordon Lewis, who had briefly worked on the project as production manager and cinematographer under the pseudonym Sheldon Seymour. Allegedly, Lewis added a couple of scenes and the voice-over narration before releasing the film in 1965. If accurate, this suggests that the voice-over was a later, intrusive feature added, possibly without the original writer-director's knowledge or permission, and that it was included out of necessity rather than being integral to the film as it was initially imagined. Uncertainty lingers over the details surrounding production: only a handful of actors have been identified, for example. Some fan-authored literature (Begg

2010; Petersen 2010) attributes large portions of the narrative to Lewis, rather than to Rebane, while others (for example, Tucker 2015) provide accounts that contradict Rebane's version of events. Looking to the film text itself for evidence is a largely fruitless exercise because it is so inherently incoherent that it seems to neither adequately confirm nor refute the various claims. That the haphazard production partly contributed to the film's incoherence is not disputed, but there seems to be no clear consensus on who is responsible for its various failures.

At least everyone seems to accept that, at some point, *Monster A-go Go*'s original writer-director lost – or ceded – control over his project. Even Rebane himself admits that the film has 'a lot of weaknesses', due in part to his own inexperience and inability to see the project through to completion (Rebane 2010). In the absence of a consistent image-maker guiding production, the voice-over could thus potentially fulfil an important function as a heterodiegetic authority figure. The narrator is presented in such a way as to suggest omniscience and precognition, indicating control over the image and story. Voice-over features in the opening scene, for example, framing the film's narrative. The redundant tendency to foretell events marks the narrator as largely irrelevant, however, and any sense of authority or reliability is quickly undermined through the obvious but unacknowledged discrepancies between the voice-over's descriptions and the visual evidence. These discrepancies could be read ironically, but to do so requires us to accept the narrator as unreliable and fallible. As demonstrated below, this approach works counter the presentation of the narrator as authoritative and omniscient, suggesting that any such reading is unintended and ultimately renders the narrator as an oblivious victim of the viewer's ironic disposition.

The voice-over narration in *Monster A-go Go* provides a lot of information at some points and remains silent for long stretches elsewhere. It offers a substantial amount of exposition in the opening scene – too much, perhaps, to adequately emphasise the relevant points. After being told that communications with a recently launched space capsule on a mission to 'observe new objects circling the Earth' have been lost, we are informed that a 'search team, headed by Colonel Steve Connors, began an intensive search of the entire area' and only subsequently learn that a 'strange object had fallen to Earth'. Over repetitive images of a helicopter hovering above a field and two men in a car, the voice-over continues to report on events in a literary, authoritative style, asking rhetorical questions ('*Was* it the space capsule?'), providing details that are, at this point, meaningless (references to the 'the Space Agency Astrophysical Laboratories') and pre-empting events. The few brief remarks uttered by the onscreen characters immediately contradict the narrator's comments. For instance, while speaking over a transistor radio, one of the characters identifies himself as Captain – not Colonel – Connors.

This seems too minor a discrepancy to be intentional. Rather, it appears to be a basic continuity error, but has the effect of suggesting that the narrator is fallible, despite presenting as omniscient.

The overabundance of information provided by the voice-over narrator in the opening minutes makes it difficult to establish what is relevant – the mysterious satellites orbiting Earth are never referred to again – while other details are ineffectively relayed. As Connors arrives at the helicopter's location, the voice-over confirms that 'without question, this *was* the capsule that had put Douglas into orbit, and without question, Douglas was gone without a trace'. Although the narrator's authoritative tone never wavers, its statement is rendered ludicrous by the accompanying image of the missing capsule, which is revealed to be a tiny, pepper-pot-shaped object that any average-sized person would struggle to fit into. Furthermore, although Douglas, the supposed 'monster' of the title, is an important character, he is inadequately introduced as a vague afterthought. Characters discuss Frank's whereabouts in a subsequent scene; only retrospectively can we infer that Frank and Douglas are one and the same, a man called Frank Douglas. Rather than provide clarity, the voice-over's comments are confusing, making an already convoluted story even more complicated, for no obvious reason. Instead of concealing or correcting errors, it draws attention to and contributes to them, indicating the failure to achieve even its most perfunctory purpose.

Inferring irony often depends on recognising a simultaneous clash between image and sound; as time passes, it becomes increasingly difficult to accept the voice-over's comments as intentionally ironic, because the contradiction between its claims and the 'truth' of the image is not immediately evident. Near the capsule, the men discover a body on the ground. As the camera focuses on their faces, the narrator asserts that the 'helicopter pilot, who discovered the capsule, was dead – horribly mangled in a way no one had ever seen before'.

Figure 3.2 The space capsule, *Monster A-go Go* (Rebane, 1964).

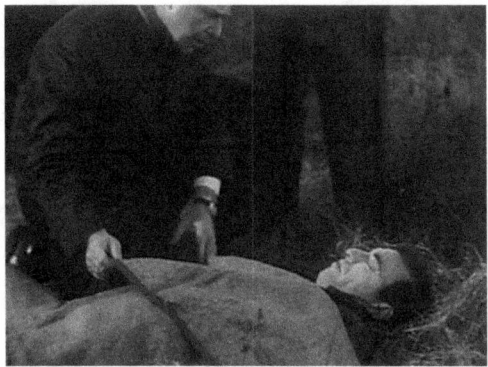

Figure 3.3   The 'horribly mangled' corpse, *Monster A-go Go* (Rebane, 1964).

Almost five minutes (and several scenes) later, the notably unblemished corpse is eventually revealed. Charitably, we might suggest that this is an example of an ironic narrator choosing to overinflate their commentary to engender 'humorous disparities' (Kozloff 1988: 111), but because this exaggeration can only be identified retrospectively, it seems less evidence of ironic inflation than unironic overstatement. Here, the voice-over draws unhelpful attention to *Monster A-go Go*'s inadequate special effects and lack of impressive spectacle. Having been denied the image for such an extended period, the 'big reveal' is particularly anticlimactic because it fails so completely to meet the expectations created by the voice-over.

The voice-over narration in *Monster A-go Go* seems intended to impress the seriousness of the story on the viewer and, practically, to provide exposition, contextual information and explanatory statements. Although attributing inclusion of the voice-over to either Rebane (possible) or Lewis (more probable) depends primarily on accepting anecdotal information as accurate, we can nevertheless look to the text itself to assess its effectiveness and appropriateness. The relationships between the narration and both image and narrative are inconsistent, rarely helpful or complementary. The narrator fails to either adequately present itself as an authority figure or to assist in relaying plot details or character motivations in any coherent manner. The voice-over is often absent when its inclusion would be most beneficial – when almost every major character inexplicably disappears and is replaced by others who perform almost identical narrative functions, for example – but imposes itself onto scenes that do not require narration. It appears that neither the two directors nor the voice-over narrator are in control of this thoroughly incoherent story.

At times, the voice-over entirely disrupts any sense of narrative, spatial or temporal continuity by seemingly imposing itself unnecessarily onto the story. Around midway through the film, after a character remarks that no attacks or monster sightings have occurred for eight weeks, we are shown Dr Conrad Logan, brother of the now-deceased Dr Logan, in a laboratory filling a syringe, while the narrator offers a convoluted combination of misinformation and foreshadowing. The voice-over claims this new Dr Logan has secretly captured Douglas and is giving him an antidote that appears to be working but has 'unpredictable side effects'. On this specific occasion, however, he is late – 'too late'. An eerie tracking shot, focused on Logan's feet as he walks along a long corridor, suggests that Logan is going to administer the antidote. But when he returns to his laboratory, it has been vandalised. The voice-over confirms the damage to be the monster's handiwork, compromising the narrative's temporal structure by insinuating that Douglas is being treated by Logan, while at the same time he has escaped and is destroying the lab. There is a potential benefit to the narrator exposing Logan's secret: it provides the viewer access to information of which the characters are not aware and could help to create suspense or tension. However, the scientist reveals the same information via diegetic dialogue in the subsequent scene. This suggests that the voice-over was not included solely as a substitute for missing scenes; its purpose is ambiguous here, but the effects are detrimental, revealing narrative redundancy, reducing suspense and negatively affecting the film's pacing.

Monster A-go Go's final scene exemplifies the film's narrative incoherence and the voice-over's ineffectiveness as a corrective device. Much of the final twenty minutes comprises footage, apparently shot MOS, featuring the Chicago Fire and Rescue Department as they assist in the search for Douglas, who is now highly radioactive and roaming the tunnels beneath the city. The different quality of the footage, the relatively generic action it depicts and the addition of the voice-over's comments to provide narrative context has led to some erroneous descriptions of the sequence as stock footage (for example, Tucker 2015: 153), despite some familiar characters appearing in the shots and Rebane having confirmed in 2010 that this was original footage. Thus, the origins of the most visually and technically impressive sequence of the movie are called into question, in part because of the voice-over's failure to provide adequate support. Any knowledge of the film's chequered history is likely to encourage such a reading: since we know that *Monster A-go Go* was completed by someone other than the original director, we cannot be certain what has been added or altered, what meanings have been lost or gained, and to whom to attribute responsibility (or blame).

As always, we must be careful to not rely too heavily on extratextual information, such as filmmaker anecdotes recalled years after production has ceased, particularly when claims are not fully supported by the text itself. *Monster A-go Go* features a wholly nonsensical 'twist' ending: the voice-over informs us that 'suddenly . . . there was no giant, no monster, no thing called Douglas to be followed', and the 'puzzled men of courage' now find themselves alone in the tunnels. Logan passes his superior a telegram that is framed in extreme close-up, allowing us to easily read that Douglas has been rescued, alive and well, in the North Atlantic. This information is redundantly repeated by the voice-over. The twist is illogical and incoherent. Why, for example, did everyone mistake this creature for Douglas? Why did the antidote appear to be working if the monster was not actually human? Is this an alien and, if so, why did it impersonate an astronaut? Instead of providing answers to these or any other number of questions that the telegram raises, the voice-over emphasises the discontinuity by posing its own series of rhetorical questions – such as 'has the cosmic switch been pulled?' – while providing no insight whatsoever. Initially, Rebane's comments seem to shed some light on the mystery: he claims that he had intended Douglas to receive his antidote and be cured, providing the film with a contained, complete narrative arc (Rebane 2010) and, implicitly, attributes this seemingly 'new' ending to Lewis. While it may suit Rebane to absolve himself of responsibility, the film itself offers contradictory evidence: why would he have shot footage showing the contents of the telegram, if the radioactive monster was Douglas all along? Alternatively, if this scene was added by Lewis – which seems unlikely, given its aesthetic consistency with the preceding footage that Rebane has confirmed as his – this suggests that Lewis may have contributed more to the film than Rebane admits. Either way, any attempt to make sense of *Monster A-go Go* proves futile, and the more extra-textual information we are provided, the more incoherent the film becomes.

Monster A-go Go demonstrates the impact of voice-over narration when it fails to fulfil even its most basic function: to aid narrative coherence and give the impression of a controlling figure at the helm. Rather than correct problems and minimise discontinuity, badly utilised voice-over exacerbates and emphasises them, while adding a new layer of incoherence. Attempts to impress upon the viewer the remarkable and extraordinary visual and narrative content have the opposite effect by creating impossible expectations to which the film cannot live up. Despite being presented as omniscient and authoritative, *Monster A-go Go*'s narrator seems 'pompous' (Tucker 2015: 153) and unreliable. This is typical in badfilm. While discrepancies between a narrator's claims and the accompanying visuals can, in certain instances, be rationalised through irony, there is rarely any indication that this is the intended interpretation. Irony also cannot account for moments when the voice-over exposes itself as unnecessary and irrelevant. Through inept integration and poorly conceived contributions, the 'voice of God' narrators common to badfilm are regularly exposed as fallible, untrustworthy and lacking authority. In this way, they can invite us to look beyond the frame, to try to locate evidence of a guiding voice elsewhere. Voice-over in badfilm can, therefore, work counter its more typical use: although designed to give the illusion of control, bad narration instead draws our attention to the *absence* of authority and control that seems to so often characterise badfilms, by suggesting that no one – neither the narrator nor the image-maker/filmmaker – is truly in charge.

Disembodied Voices and the 'Uncanny' Effects of Bad Post-Synchronisation

Thus far, this chapter has concentrated primarily on the *content* of sound – the words spoken via voice-over – in relation to badfilms' narrative (in)coherence. However, it is important to also consider the *construction* of sound itself. Michel Chion argues that the voice in cinema has traditionally been ignored in the academy because 'we usually retain only the significations it [speech] bears, forgetting the medium of the voice itself' (Chion 1999: 1). The remainder of this chapter aims to address this gap by focusing specifically on the technical process of incorporating sound and image, voice and body, through analysis of post-synchronisation techniques in badfilm. As I demonstrate, badly integrated sound detaches voice from body, unwittingly drawing attention to the cinematic construction of a relationship that tends to be hidden in 'good' films.

Several of the badfilms discussed in this book were filmed MOS (without sound) with dialogue and, occasionally, voice-over narration added in post-production. There are economic benefits to this approach: generally, it is cheaper to film without sound. This decision, however, presents different challenges for low-budget, often inexperienced filmmakers. In particular, post-synchronisation of dialogue – a 'technical procedure by which a voice [. . .] is 'glued' to a visible speaking figure in the image' (Shochat and Stam 1985: 48), commonly referred to as dubbing – requires precision and expertise to ensure an appropriate audio-visual match. Post-synchronisation aims to 'restitch' the cut between voice and body in cinema (Chion 1999: 125). Typically, the desired effect of dubbing is synchrony, whereby 'synch points' such as moments of dialogue serve to anchor the images and sounds together. Donnelly suggests that it is only through direct synchronisation that cinema can produce the 'illusion of a coherent reality' (2014: 9) and 'hold together the film experience' (2014: 12). In contrast, as I demonstrate below, bad synchronisation – unintentional, inappropriate asynchrony – can compromise the immersive potential of a film and draw attention to its artificiality. Asynchrony, then, can shatter the illusion, instead emphasising the reality of a film's disjointed construction and breaking apart the film experience.

Cinema is 'essentially conventional in character' (Donnelly 2014: 11), with these conventions functioning ideologically to maintain the illusion of reality through a careful collaboration between sound and image. Each conceals the work of the other, the aim being that the work itself goes unnoticed. This perhaps explains why most writing on cinema implicitly endorses this 'illusionist perspective' (Donnelly 2014: 12), even in a contemporary context.

As an audience, we 'desire to believe that the heard voices actually emanate from the actors/characters on the screen' (Shochat and Stam 1985: 49); we are predisposed to accept the unity of sound and image, even if we are aware that this is constructed in post-production. Donnelly even suggests that human perception has an inherent tendency 'to "join up" elements of an object into a meaningful, coherent – and seamless – whole' (2014: 23). Synchronisation, therefore, is central to our understanding and acceptance of the diegesis but appears to be so widely taken for granted that it has received no sustained academic attention. Donnelly's book represents an effort to rectify this, and my work here aims to expand this further by considering the effects of asynchrony.

Like voice-over narration, post-synchronisation has been subject to criticism. It tends to be discussed in terms suggesting subterfuge or deception: it has been claimed, for example, that post-synchronisation 'exploits' the viewer's 'naïve faith in cinematic reality' (Shochat and Stam 1985: 50). Chion, meanwhile, argues that dubbing is predicated on audio-visual matching 'in order to fool us' and suggests that the synchronisation of sound and image functions 'not so much to guarantee truth, but to authorise belief' (1999: 127). Ginette Vincendeau's research indicates that dubbing has induced in viewers 'a feeling of being duped' for almost as long as sound cinema has existed (1988: 33), due to its ability to disrupt the spectator's position and their relationship with the characters onscreen. When voice and image are successfully matched together, dubbing works to conceal the true source of film sound: by associating the sound with a visible signifier, the viewer's attention is diverted from the 'technological, mechanical, and thus industrial status of the cinema' (Altman 1980b: 69). Post-synchronisation is, by its nature, duplicitous but, by drawing attention *away* from the true source of sound, it also assists in presenting sound/voice and image/body in a coherent, unified and unobtrusive manner.

Successful synch points alone are not enough to cohere voice and body, however. Whether a character has a real or implied physical presence, the voice 'needs to be appropriate for the bodies producing it, for their actions and emotions, and for the spaces they inhabit' (Pauletto 2012: 131). Shochat and Stam refer to this as 'character synchrony', whereby the timbre, volume, tempo, tone and style of speech of the speaker is matched to the physical gestures and facial expressions of the actor onscreen (1985: 49). The speaker and actor do not need to be the same person, but the voice must be accepted as 'belonging' to the body if this synchrony is successful. Certain conventions, established through repetition, can encourage this acceptance, but we are often already willing to 'play along [. . .] even if we know the film is dubbed, provided that the rules of a sort of contract of belief are respected' (Chion 1999: 129). In this way, the success or failure of post-synchronisation is, in part at least, dependent on our complicity as viewers and our willingness to, for example, overlook slight deviations or discrepancies.

Challenges arise, however, when the voice does not seem appropriate to the body with which it is aligned. Conventions of age and gender are important: if the visible body is that of an old man, for example, we expect the accompanying voice to also be that of an old man. Discrepancies are likely to engender confusion. While this can be deliberately utilised for humorous effect, in badfilms it is more often an accidental consequence of an inappropriate and unbelievable matching of voice and body – of failed character synchrony, or character asynchrony. In *Manos: The Hands of Fate* (Warren 1966), young Debbie's dubbed voice is disconcerting because it can be quite easily identified as an adult woman imitating a child, rather than the authentic voice of a six-year-old girl; Jackey Raye Neyman-Jones, who played Debbie, recalls 'bursting into tears' when she first heard the voice now emanating from her mouth onscreen (Neyman-Jones 2012c). Character asynchrony can also extend beyond phonetic synchronisation between lip movement and dialogue, as can be seen in the clash between the voice and performance of alien-robot-gorilla Ro-Man in *Robot Monster*. Although the character's face is concealed beneath a helmet, which should minimise the visibility of badly constructed synch points, other disparities between Ro-Man's movements and accompanying dialogue are evident. Actor George Barrow's overly emphatic physical gestures 'rarely relate well' to John Brown's accompanying dialogue (Warren 2010: 703). The Medveds cite a moment in the film, for example, in which Ro-Man 'claps his hands and points a furry finger to his chest while the voice on the soundtrack declares "You will all be destroyed!"' as evidence that the 'entire dubbing process [. . .] failed miserably' (1978: 196). In this instance, Ro-Man is rendered incoherent, not because of specific moments of phonetic asynchrony, but because of paralinguistic elements such as how dialogue is delivered. Brown's voice, added in post-production, seems intended to imbue the character with gravitas and authority, but this is incompatible with the creature's absurd physical presence. Character asynchrony can, therefore, extend beyond phonetic synchronisation between lip movement and dialogue – the most basic technical requirement of successful dubbing. As the Medveds' comments indicate, this asynchrony draws attention to the inept stitching together of voice and body, pointing actively, albeit unintentionally, to the incoherent construction of the character himself.

Due to the influence of American narrative cinema, which has traditionally been 'obsessively concerned with synchronisation that has no detectable "seams"' (Chion 1999: 130), there is an expectation that sound in films adhering to the conventions of classical continuity will be 'unremarkable' (Donnelly 2014: 30) and constructed to maintain the illusion of a coherent, seamless diegesis. Where there are recognisable efforts to conceal potential moments of asynchrony in badfilms, they reveal attempts to conform to the expectations of coherent, synchronised sound film conventions, despite the unconventional aesthetic that can emerge as a result. The frequent cutaways to random, inanimate objects employed by sexploitation filmmaker Doris Wishman, for example, remove the need to match lip movement to dialogue added in post-production. This results in an editing style that can seem not dissimilar to the avant-garde style of the same period but, as discussed further in Chapter 4 in relation to recycling practices, is differentiated by intention. Comparing Wishman with Jean-Luc Godard, Michael Bowen suggests that the former's style comprises a 'unique combination of eruptive mobility and unexpected stasis' (2002: 115), located in her films' cutaway editing style combined with the often hollow-sounding sonic density of voices recorded in a sound booth. What distinguishes Wishman from avant-garde filmmakers is that 'her transgressions were not intentionally ironic' (Bowen 2002: 114). Thus, whereas radical filmmakers such as Godard consciously challenge conventions by deploying 'explicitly disruptive strategies to highlight the factious nature of post-synchronisation' (Shochat and Stam 1985: 51), any similar stylistic deviations in badfilms seem to emerge accidentally, as an unintended consequence of attempts to limit the textual danger of asynchronous sound by either concealing or ignoring the films' MOS production.

In addition to cutaways, badfilms reveal a variety of other techniques exploited to avoid, or at least reduce, the possibility of asynchrony dismantling the 'illusion of sound and visual unity into a miasma of disparate and potentially meaningless elements' (Donnelly 2014: 11). Some of these, such as filming characters in long shot to reduce the need to match lip movements to dialogue or keeping the body from which the voice is supposed to originate offscreen or facing away from the camera, will be explored in the case-studies below. Voices emanating from beyond the frame can have 'uncanny' effects, suggesting that when a sound is 'no longer anchored by a represented body, its potential as a signifier is revealed' (Doane 1980: 40). Although Altman has questioned the need to simultaneously show a speaker as he or she speaks (1980b: 68), this convention – one of many regarding the relationship between sound and image – has been so firmly established that it is now largely taken for granted. Donnelly suggests that the 'overwhelming majority of films exploit the illusory characteristics of the medium to present a world that on some level is taken to be reality by its audience' (2014: 7). In contrast, badfilms are notable because they break this illusion through the incompetent and inconsistent application of post-synchronised sound, adding to the failure of the film while also unwittingly drawing attention to the technical, phonetic and linguistic challenges that the technique entails.

In badfilms, discrepancies between sound/voice and image/body regularly expose the diegesis as a construction. The inconsistent ways in which these discrepancies emerge, combined with an apparent effort to minimise the impact of obvious asynchrony, make it difficult to interpret deviations from classical cinematic style as a deliberate flouting of conventions. Dubbing, when employed in badfilms, often seems to be a cost-cutting device but regularly fails to result in an appropriate synchronisation of sound and image. While Donnelly suggests that an 'awareness of the illusion of cinema ought to lead us to be concerned with perception and artifice' (2014: 7), failed attempts at post-synchronisation dismantle this illusion, inappropriately exposing the construction of the diegesis instead and compromising the film's immersive potential.

FAILED POST-SYNCHRONISATION IN *THE BEAST OF YUCCA FLATS* AND *THE CREEPING TERROR*

Examining asynchrony in badfilms thus offers significant potential for understanding the complex, but often unacknowledged, co-dependent relationship between cinematic sound and image. As noted earlier in this chapter, *The Beast of Yucca Flats* and *The Creeping Terror* were both filmed MOS and dubbed in post-production, and each employs a combination of voice-over narration and dubbing. The ways in which these are used in the films, however, suggest very different approaches to how sound and image are 'stitched' together. Whereas demonstrable efforts are made to limit the disruptive potential of post-synchronisation in the former, the latter makes little or no effort to conceal its moments of asynchrony. Despite these differences, both in their own way unwittingly draw attention to their construction through the unconventional relationship between sound and image that they present.

The first of these films, *Yucca Flats,* was the directorial debut of Coleman Francis. It was made on a budget of around $34,000 (Tube 1961: 6) and shot almost entirely outdoors near Los Angeles. Narratively, it is similar to other science-fiction films of the 1950s and 1960s, loosely playing on contemporary fears of the Cold War and nuclear warfare. Former Swedish wrestler Tor Johnson plays Joseph Javorsky, a 'noted scientist' defecting to America from behind the Iron Curtain, with a briefcase full of secrets. He is transformed into the titular Beast after stumbling onto an active atomic testing ground while attempting to escape from a couple of Kremlin agents, then spends the rest of the film wandering around the desert looking for people to attack while two patrolmen hunt for him. Having mistakenly shot at an innocent man from a small airplane, the police eventually find and kill Javorsky, who dies after kissing a wild hare that accidentally hopped into the final shot.

In addition to its thoroughly disorienting editing (see Chapter 6), the sound in *Yucca Flats* is a key signifier of its incompetence. With its meagre plot, undeveloped characters and minimal, poorly executed action sequences, there is little to divert attention away from the way in which the narrative is relayed through sound. The score, recycled from *The Astounding She-Monster*, dominates the soundscape, likely as a way of avoiding the need to add ambient sounds in post-production. Fan-authored reviews, however, largely focus on the film's dialogue and voice-over narration as evidence of the film's badness and inherent oddness. For example, the Medveds misleadingly describe Johnson's role as a 'mute Russian scientist'; they appear to mistakenly conflate *Yucca Flats*' lack of synchronised sound with the character's lack of spoken dialogue (Medved and Medved 1986: 208). Michael Weldon's claim that the viewer 'might have been appalled (and delighted) watching *The Creeping Terror* because it had no dialogue, just offscreen narration [. . . but *Yucca Flats*] uses the same silent technique and it's even worse!' (1983: 43) draws a direct correlation between the two films, but inaccurately describes them: both, in fact, feature a combination of narration *and* dialogue. Although these reviews point to the challenge of accurately remembering the relationship between sound, narrative and image, the repeated references in fan-authored literature to *Yucca Flats*' unconventional sound indicates it is a widely accepted and particularly obvious example of failure that has notably weird and, potentially, enjoyable effects.

The disjunctions between sound and image in *Yucca Flats* are often unavoidable. Dialogue, whether from the third-person voice-over narrator or the characters onscreen, is sparse. The film's narrative often does not require the characters to speak and frequently isolates them from one another, further reducing the need to include conversations. In the first thirteen minutes – a quarter of the film's runtime – only one line of diegetic speech is heard: as Kremlin agents start shooting at the scientist and his aides, we are shown a close-up of Johnson looking around, while a male voice is heard saying 'Mr Javorsky, get in the car'. This provides an early example of the 'uncanny' effect of voice-off and the unconventional dynamics of sound/image for which *Yucca Flats* has been both criticised and celebrated. Although one of the most prominent 'rules' of classical narrative cinema assumes that 'an individual who speaks will in all probability be the object of the camera's, and thus of the audience's, gaze' (Altman 1980b: 68), this is not the case here or elsewhere in the film. The dialogue is not anchored to a body, and the source of sound remains ambiguous: it is never clear who has spoken. Contra to Altman's claim, speech – the contents of the dialogue itself – is prioritised in *Yucca Flats*, not the speaker.

Framing decisions throughout *Yucca Flats* regularly separate voice from body in disorienting, confusing ways, but seem to be motivated by a desire to conceal the film's MOS production and limit the effects of obvious phonetic asynchrony, rather than any conscious attempt to challenge or disrupt the established 'rules' of cinematic construction. Characters are shown in long shot, speakers face away from the camera, and characters are kept out of the frame altogether, with conversations relayed via voice-off, thus avoiding the need to match lip movements to sound added in post-production. By resolutely *not* showing characters as they speak, however, the conventions that enable the viewer to associate a voice with a specific body are broken. Phonetic synchrony in film serves to anchor the image and sound together and makes explicit what otherwise remains ambiguous, thus reducing the 'tension' of unanchored sound (Altman 1980b: 74). The seemingly conscious decision to not include synch points at various points in *Yucca Flats* conceals potential moments of asynchrony but, in the process, unintentionally breaks the 'spell of diegetic effect' (Donnelly 2014: 3) by denying us an explicit source of the sound. The uncanny effect of voice-off in *Yucca Flats* suggests that, even when the source of the sound – the body implicitly accompanying the voice – is visible, tension still exists when the character's face remains hidden. In this situation, we can *infer* a relationship between sound and body, but never *confirm* it.

When conversations do occur in *Yucca Flats*, they tend to be delivered as voice-off. Around midway through the film, for example, we are introduced to the Radcliffe family who are travelling by car when a tyre blows out. Having completed the necessary repairs, Mr Radcliffe and his wife realise that their two young boys have wandered off. With the camera positioned inside the family's car, Mrs Radcliffe walks across the desert towards her husband, who is leaning against the vehicle. The shot is static and claustrophobic in its intimacy, and it encourages a voyeuristic perspective: the car's interior is much darker than the bright, naturally lit landscape, and the characters' chests are awkwardly framed by the vehicle's window. The couple only begin speaking to one another once their faces are obscured from view, suggesting that the unusual framing has been motivated, in part at least, to conceal potential phonetic asynchrony caused by ineffective dubbing. Even this fails, however. The occasional visibility of Mr Radcliffe's chin is just enough to suggest that the words being heard do not correspond to his facial movements, accidentally revealing asynchrony despite apparent attempts to avoid it. The relationship between voice and body remains ambiguous due to these discrepancies and the absence of an appropriate visual anchor – specifically, moving lips accurately corresponding to the speech. Further exacerbating the ambiguity, the scene lacks foley or ambient sounds and is unnaturally silent in contrast to the clarity and hollowness of the voices. We see desert plants move in the breeze but hear nothing; Mrs Radcliffe makes no aural impression as she walks to the car; Mr Radcliffe lights and smokes a cigarette without making a sound. The visible, diegetic space is thus unsupported by appropriate aural markers. The dialogue is neither anchored effectively to the bodies onscreen nor adequately rooted in the landscape; instead, the characters' voices seem to emanate from some unearthly space beyond the frame.

The conventions of narrative cinema suggest that the sound- and image-track should work together to help 'hide the work of the other' (Altman 1980b:

Figure 3.4 Mr and Mrs Radcliffe discuss their sons' whereabouts, *The Beast of Yucca Flats* (Francis, 1961).

70) and to create an authentic, immersive diegetic world through appropriate synchronisation. In *Yucca Flats*, however, sound and image are regularly kept separate from one another: when the image shows people speaking, the soundtrack rarely provides supporting dialogue, while audible speech is not supported by visuals anchoring the voice to a body. This division appears to be less a conscious, artistic rejection of conventions and more a necessity borne out of a desire to minimise the potentially disturbing, damaging effects of obvious asynchrony: Francis' subsequent films, shot with sound, do not repeat this aesthetic, for example. However, the ambiguous ways in which sound, particularly voice, is associated with onscreen bodies in *Yucca Flats* is inherently disturbing and draws attention to the failed co-dependence of sound- and image-tracks, a co-dependence that is usually invisible and taken for granted. It is only when such conventions are dismantled that they become obvious. As Donnelly and others have suggested, we are predisposed to making connections: we are naturally inclined to find ways that enable us to accept the diegesis as a coherent whole, which also supports Altman's claim that 'as long as each [sound and image] reinforces the other's lie then we will not hesitate to believe them both' (1980b: 70). Through this complementary system, the 'work' of filmmaking – the process of constructing a coherent whole from disparate parts – is concealed. As *Yucca Flats* demonstrates, however, when sound and image are kept separate, the work comes to the fore, and the illusion of a coherent diegesis is obliterated by the obvious tension that exists between the various, unsupported elements used to create it.

Failure is evident in *Yucca Flats* through the inept and ineffective attempts to conceal the film's MOS production and remove the textual danger of obvious asynchrony. A seemingly unintended consequence of these efforts is that they complicate our ability to accept, and be appropriately immersed in, the diegesis; trying to align sound with image requires work on the part of the viewer and thus serves as a distraction from the events presented to us. The lack of synchronised sound is evident throughout, contributing to and exacerbating the spatial, temporal and narrative incoherence – among other failings – that characterises Francis' inept debut. However, asynchrony can be just as unsettling when it reveals itself in other ways. It is not immediately obvious, for example, that *The Creeping Terror*, a science-fiction film about two aliens (the 'terrors' of the title) landing on Earth and terrorising a small American town, is also shot without sound; its characters tend to be framed in reasonably conventional ways that seem to adhere to the principle that '*I speak, therefore I am seen*' (Altman 1980b: 68; emphasis in original). There is no obvious attempt to make the work of post-synchronisation easier or to minimise the potential textual danger of badly dubbed dialogue by, for example, concealing moving lips, as does *Yucca Flats*. Thus, it appears that those responsible for *The Creeping Terror*'s production were either unaware of, or ambivalent about, the potentially disruptive effects of asynchronous sound (or, perhaps, that they were confident in their ability to appropriately synch sound to image in post-production). Yet, as the film progresses, the strange, unconventional relationship between sound and image becomes increasingly obvious, while the lack of diegetic sound is confirmed with every additional moment of jarring asynchrony.

Occasionally, at least, *The Creeping Terror*'s characters are afforded the dual privilege of being both shown and heard speaking. The opening scene shows newlyweds Martin (Vic Savage) and Brett (Shannon O'Neill) returning home from their honeymoon by car. The camera is mounted on the dashboard, and their faces are clearly visible in medium shot, making it likely that phonetic asynchrony would be difficult to ignore. If there is only a slight delay or the film is only marginally out of synch, we can 'mentally "overlook" the discrepancy by "compensating" and concentrating less on the conduct of dialogue and lips on-screen' (Donnelly 2014: 3). In this scene, there is little to distract our attention from characters' expressions and their moving lips but, despite the odd rhythm and tempo of the speech (suggesting that the dialogue was added in post-production with the aim of matching the visible movements onscreen) and the synch points being rather shoddily constructed, they are more or less adequate. Despite the brief moments of asynchrony, at this point it is possible to 'repress' our awareness of the discrepancies (Shochat and Stam 1985: 49) and, if we are feeling charitable, to perhaps accept the relationship between voice and body as it seemingly intends to be understood.

However, although we might be willing to accept the voices as belonging to the bodies onscreen through acceptable phonetic synchrony, they lack the sonic density required to firmly root the voices in the diegetic space. It becomes increasingly difficult to ignore the hollowness of the voices and the lack of appropriate, accompanying ambient sound, which continues throughout *The Creeping Terror*. The volume of the voices remains constant, regardless of where the characters are positioned within the frame, while foley is inconsistently utilised: we hear a car moving along a road, for example, but after it stops and its passenger exits, there is no sound that accompanies the car door being closed. This aural inconsistency grows ever more obvious; as it does, the illusion of the diegesis is first compromised, then obliterated. There is a demonstrable division between sound and image exposed through a combination of unnatural silence, post-synchronisation efforts that achieve varying degrees of success, as well as moments of unavoidable asynchrony.

Whereas the third-person voice-over narration in *Yucca Flats* barely even tries to compensate for the lack of character dialogue, at the other extreme, the device is used excessively in *The Creeping Terror* where the 'voice of God' narrator adopts an authoritative, literary tone and regularly dominates the soundscape. For example, we initially hear Martin and Brett's conversation in the opening scene, but the omniscient narrator quickly takes over and, in the process, compromises our potential affiliation with the characters. Although the visuals indicate that the characters are still speaking to one another, we are no longer privy to the exchange. Instead, the voice-over offers context – who the couple are, their relationship, where they have been and where they are going – but provides no insight into their conversation. This is typical of how the voice-over works throughout *The Creeping Terror*; it alternates between intruding upon the soundtrack to summarise conversations happening concurrently onscreen and denying the audience any insight into what is being discussed. Although presented as omniscient, the narrator's authority is regularly called into question through obvious disparities between the narrator's claims and the accompanying image or, occasionally, diegetic character dialogue. This constitutes another form of asynchrony, whereby the narration corresponds neither to the bodies onscreen nor to the words they are speaking. In contrast to attempts in *Yucca Flats* to conceal post-synchronisation, *The Creeping Terror* regularly does not even *try* to provide synch points. Tantalisingly, we are repeatedly shown conversations that we cannot hear, the effect being akin to watching a sound film on mute. As a result, however, we gain only partial access to the diegesis, and the 'whole story', as it were, remains just beyond our reach.

Conversely, when character dialogue is heard in *The Creeping Terror*, it is often asynchronous, suggesting a failure to adequately provide phonetic synchrony through appropriate audio-visual matching. When the army arrives to investigate the crashed spaceship, for example, there is a clear discrepancy between voice and body. The small troupe is initially framed in long-shot and extreme long-shot. This, combined with generally poor image quality, means that it is not possible to see the men's faces as they speak, thereby reducing the potential identification of phonetic asynchrony. Yet, the origins of the voices heard on the soundtrack are uncertain because they are not sufficiently anchored to specific bodies. At one point, a male voice is heard saying: 'Sergeant, take one man and check it [the spaceship] out'. During this sentence, the camera's view changes from long to medium shot, allowing the characters' faces to be clearly visible. There is a clash, however, between sound and image: the response heard – 'Yes, sir!' – does not correspond to the facial gestures of the man shown speaking. As well as obliterating the illusion of the diegesis as a unified whole, this asynchrony compromises narrative coherence, by inadvertently implying that the man physically motioning another forward is also the person receiving the orders.

As I have already noted, we do not need to explicitly see the source of sound – such as a character's moving lips – to identify asynchrony between sound and image. During the largest action set-piece in *Yucca Flats*, for example, Mr Radcliffe is repeatedly shot at after being mistaken for the Beast, but the use of what appears to be two stock 'gunfire' sounds fails to establish any appropriate sense of proximity, compromising the scene's ability to create tension or imply peril. In *The Creeping Terror*, meanwhile, one of the aliens' first victims is heard screaming long after the majority of her body has apparently been consumed by the creature. The screams are muffled and indistinct even before the woman is eaten; the volume and density of the sound remains constant before, during and after she clambers into the alien's 'mouth'. The screams also appear to be one repeated sound on a loop, exposing the artifice of the sequence. It is difficult to care about the tragedy of this poor woman's death when it is presented in such a blatantly unnatural, inauthentic and unconvincing manner. In this moment, the distancing, distracting effect of poorly integrated sound also draws attention to *The Creeping Terror*'s other failures, including, notably, the incompetent design of an alien that requires its victims to insert themselves into its body in order to be devoured. In both films, the repeated use of the same sounds dismantles the logic of the diegesis, exposes the scenes as constructed and negatively affects the films' emotional and immersive potential.

One of the oddest aspects of *The Creeping Terror*'s asynchrony is that it is evident, in part, because the film appears to have been shot without any obvious attempt to adapt its visual style for post-synchronisation. In this way, it is aesthetically quite different from other badfilms that were shot without sound. Whereas the unconventional and frequently distracting, disorienting and awkward framing and editing in films like *Yucca Flats*, *Manos: The Hands of Fate* and Doris Wishman's sexploitation movies – to give just a few examples – can be largely attributed to their efforts to limit the possibility of phonetic asynchrony, *The Creeping Terror*'s visuals regularly emulate those of conventional sound cinema. Conversations are shown in typical shot-reverse-shot, for instance, but the dialogue is either replaced by loosely related voice-over narration or misrepresented through dubbed speech. Indeed, the haphazard disregard for synchronisation suggests that, were one able to read lips, *The Creeping Terror* would be an altogether different experience. It is the absence of even *attempted* post-synchronisation that is often most obvious, revealing a slapdash disregard for conventions that normally work to create the illusion of a coherent, authentic diegesis.

This apparent ambivalence towards synchrony, and the excessive use of voice-over narration, draws attention to the film's constructed nature, but the motivations behind these strange decisions are not easily established through textual evidence alone. It is not clear, for example, why some scenes in *The Creeping Terror* are dubbed, while others are overlaid with lengthy, literary narration. As is so often the case in badfilms, the ambiguous presentation of the diegesis can encourage a heightened awareness of processes beyond the frame, while attempts to understand and make sense of what we are experiencing require more information than the film itself can provide. In the case of *The Creeping Terror*, extratextual information can seem to provide a possible explanation for its unconventional presentation of sound and image. As with many of its contemporaries, details about the film's origins and production context are limited, but certain legends surround it and have become part of its mythology. The most infamous claim is that it was originally intended to be a conventional sound film, until its writer-director-star accidentally dropped the sound-reel into Lake Tahoe (Medved and Medved 1980: 18). As the story goes, he then had no choice but to add the voice-over and dubbed dialogue in post-production.

In some respects, the aesthetics of *The Creeping Terror* appear to support this legend. There is no particular evidence of attempts to mitigate against the possible 'textual danger' (Donnelly 2014: 8) of obvious asynchrony. Rather, the film indicates a certain level of textual *ambiguity* because of an inconsistent mix of synchrony and asynchrony. However, although the 'dropped into Lake Tahoe' story provides a humorous explanation for the diegetic inconsistency evident throughout the film – while also suggesting a comic combination of ineptitude and misfortune that can then support sympathetic cult auteurist approaches – it is probably inaccurate and, at the very least, has been disputed. In their subsequent book, *Son of Golden Turkey Awards*, the Medveds again discuss the film, but this time claim that it was deliberately shot MOS. The excessive use of voice-over narration in certain scenes is explained by actor William Thourlby, who recalls that the plan to 'mouth our lines, and then [. . .] come back later and dub in the words' (quoted in Medved and Medved 1986: 198) was forced to change after the director lost the script and several of the cast were unavailable for this post-production work. Although this explanation seems more likely, the original legend can still be found repeated in more recent fan-authored literature (for example, Wilson 2005: 211; the film's IMDb page also still includes it as unchallenged trivia). Thus, extratextual information provides two possible explanations for the film's unconventional presentation of sound and image; both could be supported by textual evidence, and both suggest – in different ways – the filmmaker's incompetence. Conversely, it is precisely the film's inherently ambiguous and inconsistent approach to (a)synchrony that enables both versions of events to be possible, just as it is equally possible that neither are.

As these examples indicate, the failure of sound and image to support each other has direct impact on a film's narrative coherence and immersive potential. We do not require any particular expertise to recognise, for instance, the blatant asynchrony of poorly dubbed dialogue; nor do we need to understand the intricacies of voice-over to identify when there is an obvious clash between the narrator's claims and the 'truth' revealed through the image. Furthermore, our expectations of cohesion between sound and image, and especially between voice and body, make the clashes and other moments of asynchrony even harder to ignore or overlook. Recognising discrepancies, particularly when they appear to be unintentional and therefore inappropriate, forces us to acknowledge the diegesis as a construction, and an inept one at that. This can help to account for why badfilms so often seem to compel viewers to adopt an unusual reading position marked by 'incredulous amazement and critical detachment', as suggested by Sconce (2003: 21).

Badfilms such as *Yucca Flats*, *Monster A-go Go* and *The Creeping Terror* are characterised by excessive incompetence: *nothing* works in the way in which we expect it to work. Although this chapter has focused on the inept ways in which dialogue and voice are presented, it should be noted that failure is typically revealed through a demonstrable clash between sound and image, whereby each fails individually and they both fail to support one another. As Hoberman notes, the failure to reproduce institutional modes of representation 'deforms the simplest formulae and clichés so absolutely that you barely recognise them' (1980: 14). Crucially, incompetence does not entirely dismantle these modes of representation – we can still recognise the attempts. In other words, we can identify what outcome was intended and what effect was being striven for, but we can also judge it to have demonstrably failed to achieve this aim. Meanwhile, blatant contradictions between sound and image draw our attention away from the diegesis to the film's formal construction. Thus, by failing to create coherent sound and image in any appropriate or effective manner, the technical processes of cinematic construction are unintentionally emphasised. This then enables the viewer to more easily recognise other examples of failure within the film, such as narrative discontinuity, unconvincing acting, bad set design and underwhelming attempts at spectacle.

In this way, then, poorly integrated and ineffective post-synchronisation can activate a heightened awareness of formal devices that we normally take for granted, reminding us that, no matter how 'natural' or 'realistic' the filmic world appears to be, this is always an illusion – and that some illusions are more convincing than others.

4. RECYCLED FOOTAGE, PLAGIARISM AND BAD ART

Badfilms are characterised by a combination of technical incompetence and material poverty, with the latter contributing to, and likely exacerbating, the former. Lacking adequate resources or skill, the filmmakers responsible for the films discussed throughout this book regularly had to find 'creative' solutions to practical problems that hampered production (see Juno and Vale 1986; Sconce 1995), to varying degrees of success. In the previous chapter, I discussed this in relation to post-production sound. This chapter examines another common practice in low-budget production that can suggest a certain amount of 'creativity' and resourcefulness: the incorporation of pre-existing footage into otherwise 'new' films. This footage includes stock footage filmed without a specific purpose, footage poached from previously released movies, documentary footage and newsreels, as well as footage taken from unreleased or uncompleted films and repurposed for new productions. The practice of recycling and re-using existing footage provided filmmakers with the chance to include scenes of visual spectacle and excess that they had neither the means nor the motivation to produce themselves, while also providing new narrative possibilities. When poorly integrated, however, recycled footage draws attention to itself in inappropriate ways, exposing badfilms' impoverished production conditions as much as their inherently incompetent construction.

Examining recycled footage in badfilms reveals diversity in terms of its integration, use and visibility within new narrative and aesthetic contexts, which are deserving of rigorous critical investigation. There has been limited academic interest in recycled footage, however, and the scholarship that does exist almost exclusively focuses its attention on 'found footage' practices associated with a specific form of avant-garde and experimental cinema. This is not to say that 'mainstream' traditions of using recycled footage have not been acknowledged, merely that these are typically assumed to be motivated by expediency and economy rather than artistry (for example, O'Pray 1987; Johnson 1996), and therefore do not merit further investigation. This seems somewhat remiss of the academy, given that several of the avant-garde filmmakers championed for their recycling techniques were 'acutely aware of the widespread use of stock footage in B-movies and serials' (Jarosi 2012: 239) and regularly used footage from low-budget Hollywood genre pictures in their experimental films. As I discuss below, similar images repeat themselves across high and low cultural objects and, at times, recycled footage is appropriated in badfilms in ways not dissimilar to the experimental approaches for which avant-garde filmmakers are celebrated. This chapter, therefore, aims to expand the existing discourse through an examination of recycled footage in badfilm. This approach continues along a path initiated by Guy Barefoot, whose investigation of Hollywood uses of recycled footage serves explicitly to remind us that 'recycling and remixing are not just practices of isolated avant-garde artists' (2011: 164) but were regularly also integrated into the commercial structure of low-budget American cinema. Like Barefoot, I suggest we can accept that recycled footage in low-budget, narrative-based cinema was often included as a 'cost-cutting measure' (2011: 154), without this disqualifying it from further investigation.

Recycling practices in cinema are not inherently bad, nor are they solely associated with any particular form of cinema, irrespective of what scholarship's focus might imply. There is a long, rich tradition of recycling footage, stretching back to the earliest days of cinema and spreading across mainstream and avant-garde films. Although recycling itself does not inevitably suggest incompetence or failure, how recycled footage is presented can render it bad in a variety of ways. Central to consideration, I propose, are the appropriateness of its visibility, the forms of appropriation and underlying purpose for inclusion, as well as the extent to which its pre-existing status is acknowledged within the 'new' film. Recycled footage tends to serve different purposes in mainstream and avant-garde cinema, and it is integrated in different ways. Generally, it is intended to go unnoticed in the former, while the latter presents it in ways that draw attention to the images, inviting us to recognise them as recycled. In badfilms, there is rarely any indication that we are meant to notice the footage as anything other than new and original, despite the all too obvious visual discrepancies on display. This suggests that visibility is the unintended consequence of failed attempts to reproduce 'mainstream' standards of cinematic representation, signifying incompetence. As I discuss below, however, the apparently unintentional visibility of badly integrated recycled footage can, on occasion, seem to invite a form of interpretation more obviously associated with the avant-garde.

This chapter, then, acknowledges that the differences between 'high' and 'low' culture are not always easy to define. Both avant-garde and trash cinema are regularly positioned as alternatives to the loosely defined cultural 'mainstream'. Differences can be located in their underlying motivation and intent: whereas the avant-garde is seen to be consciously experimenting with the boundaries of experience, aiming for formal originality and interrogating intellectually significant questions, exploitation cinema is considered to be 'inarticulate and regressive' (Bowen 2002: 110). As counter-cinema, avant-garde style tends to be perceived as a 'strategic intervention' (Sconce 1995: 384), while trash cinema's countercultural status is usually established through reception (see Jancovich et al 2003). Joan Hawkins, meanwhile, suggests that avant-garde and trash cinema can be distinguished from one another through the spectatorial responses they offer, particularly in relation to bodily affect, but she recognises that one cultural use does not necessarily preclude the other (1999: 17). Additionally, different viewing and cultural contexts can directly impact the way in which a viewer might respond to a film (see Mathijs 2005), and reception can change significantly over time, with certain badfilms now even described as a form of 'accidental' avant-garde cinema (Hill 2015).

Found footage cinema, in its many forms, highlights the ambiguous distinctions between 'high' and 'low' culture. Roger Luckhurst suggests that the diverse forms of found-footage science fiction, for example, can 'challenge the spectator to rethink some critical categories in their conjuncture of high and low or avant-garde and popular cultural resources and formal techniques' (2008: 211). The same can be true of badfilms. The often excessive, and seemingly unintended, visibility of recycled footage as a result of inept or careless integration can, at times, challenge aesthetic conventions and narrative expectations in unexpected, intriguing ways. In their own slapdash, inconsistent ways, some badfilms can even be understood as precursors to the more widely discussed, critically acclaimed avant-garde found footage films. Martin Norden argues that avant-garde filmmakers such as Bruce Conner are important because their films 'intentionally destroy the illusion of reality commonly found in mainstream movies' (2002: 77). Badfilms can work in similar ways. Through the failed efforts to present recycled footage as new and original, despite the obvious differences in style, quality and so on, badfilms can also unintentionally call attention to the images '*as* images' (Wees 2002: 4; emphasis in original). Even when they do not invite the same kind of interpretive potential as avant-garde found footage cinema, the inappropriate visibility of recycled images provides an opportunity to consider, as Barefoot does in relation to 'mainstream' recycling practices (2011), broader issues of intertextuality and adaptation. Badfilms, therefore, can seem to blur the line between mainstream and avant-garde practices, sharing similarities with both, but occupying neither category comfortably.

Plagiarism, Self-Plagiarism: Recycled Narratives

Whereas avant-garde found footage cinema invites viewers to recognise recycled images as precisely what they are, badfilms typically seem to aim to conceal their pre-existing footage, whether this comprises brief stock shots or entire sections of another movie that have been repackaged and minimally repurposed. In this sense, many badfilms are guilty of a form of plagiarism, through their 'direct *but unacknowledged* use of segments from another film' (Verevis 2006: 19–20, emphasis in original; see also Hutcheon 2013: 9). Each time a film uses pre-existing material without adequate acknowledgement, it attempts to present someone else's work as new and original. This is particularly evident in badfilms that use recycled footage from other feature films as the basis of a supposedly 'new' movie, with original (new) footage minimally edited into the existing narrative. As discussed in more detail below, this was a common practice in low-budget filmmaking. Of course, labelling recycling practices as plagiarism carries its own implications and negatively suggests a form of deception, intentional or otherwise. In badfilms, textual evidence often indicates a conscious effort to limit recognition of the footage as recycled, irrespective of the aesthetic differences on display. Indeed, the relatively common practice of appropriating footage from previously released films can only be understood as 'successful' if the audience is unaware of the existing production and does not notice the footage as recycled: it is only then that old narratives can be passed off as new. Ineffective execution, however, draws attention to both the attempt and the failure to adequately conceal the appropriation, thereby revealing the badness of this form of recycling. Here, badness is not only located in the decision to plagiarise existing works, but in the incompetent ways in which that plagiarism is attempted.

Unsurprisingly, given their low-budget and largely independent contexts, recycling practices are commonplace in badfilms made on the fringes of Hollywood during the 1950s and 1960s. It is quicker, cheaper and easier to simply repackage an old film than to create a new one, particularly when quality and artistry are not primary concerns. Using existing films as the basis for supposedly 'new' stories, however, raises intriguing issues relating to power and control because the footage already has its own, pre-existing narrative content. The power dynamic between recycled and new footage in these 'new' films is not necessarily what might be expected: new footage is created to support the recycled footage and, usually, works to preserve and reaffirm the latter's previous narrative significance, not to supplant or subvert it. This creates an unusual relationship between new and old footage, whereby it is the latter and not the former that is prioritised and emerges as the dominant force. In their apparently conscious attempt to maintain the original meaning of the pre-existing footage while aiming to conceal its recycled status, those involved in the 'new' production cede artistic control: it is not their creative vision that is prioritised, but that of whoever produced the original work. For their plagiaristic tendencies to go unnoticed, the 'new' filmmaker has little choice but to respond and react to the original work, to allow it to dictate the terms of the 'new' production.

Nevertheless, the attempts to pass off existing work as new and original are often obvious. This form of compilation results in films that are aesthetically and narratively inconsistent and frequently seem 'wrong', somehow: actions are unmotivated, plotlines are abandoned, characters respond to events in odd ways. These problems draw attention to a power struggle within the film text itself. Only the new footage is 'aware' of the existence of the old, so any attempt at interaction between the two can only ever be one-sided. While the new footage can – and often must – adapt to the needs of the old, the recycled footage remains in a kind of stasis, unaware of its new context and unresponsive by default. For example, *The Bride and the Beast* (Weiss 1958) initially sets up one narrative arc before abandoning it and focusing instead on the narrative embedded in the recycled footage that makes up much of the film's last hour. Initially, we are introduced to a newly married woman, Laura (Charlotte Austin); she is attacked by her hunter husband's captive gorilla, learns that she may once have been a gorilla herself and decides to travel to Africa in an attempt to cure her unhealthy obsession with apes. Once the newlyweds arrive in Africa – represented conventionally through stock footage of generically 'exotic' scenes and wild animals – there is a marked shift in narrative focus, necessitated by the decision to use large portions of footage from a decade-old American jungle movie set in India, *Man-Eater of Kumaon* (Haskin 1948), alongside more typical, though no less obviously recycled, documentary footage of real hunting expeditions.

The recycled footage, particularly from Haskin's film, becomes increasingly prominent as *The Bride and the Beast* progresses and appears to be the dominant factor in decisions made regarding plot developments, costumes and character actions. As in similarly structured films such as *Man Beast* (Warren 1956), *Monster from Green Hell* (Crane 1957) and, to a lesser extent, *The Skydivers*, the new characters are required to adapt their actions and appearance to create visual and narrative continuity; generally, the less obvious the matches, the more 'successful' the plagiarism. Evidence of efforts to conceal the seams where the footage has been 'stitched' together strongly suggest that we are not meant to recognise any discrepancies but should instead accept the film as a single, original narrative. Yet, the attempts to combine two completely unrelated narrative strands – the psychological motivation behind Laura's trip to Africa and the series of tiger attacks that form the basis of *Man-Eater*'s story – are tenuous at best. The problems that originally established Laura's need to travel to Africa are entirely abandoned for most of *The Bride and the Beast* and are only 'resolved' in the final few minutes after this new, and poorly justified, tiger threat has been neutralised.

Tensions between old and new footage are evident in other badfilms. For example, *Horror of the Blood Monsters* (Adamson 1970; also released as *Vampire Men of the Lost Planet*) is a science-fiction/horror hybrid, shot in colour and set predominantly on an alien planet that features extended scenes from *Tagani* (Bayer 1965), a black-and-white Filipino film about warfare between two prehistoric tribes. With ready-made scenes of spectacle including vampire-like creatures, crab people and bat people, Adamson recognised *Tagani*'s potential. By chopping it up and editing the most visually 'impressive' scenes into newly shot scenes, he was able to create a seemingly 'new' film at minimum expense. The recycled monochrome footage is disguised by tinting all the scenes on the alien planet with different filters, with the unusual colour changes explained through character dialogue as 'chromatic radiation' and even promoted in *Blood Monsters*' marketing, with theatrical posters declaring that it was shot using 'Spectrum X!' However, although it was ostensibly the spectacle that drew Adamson to *Tagani*, that film's narrative content also remains largely intact. Other than transplanting the tribes onto an alien planet, no real effort is made to recontextualise or alter the story itself. Yet, as discussed below, attempts are made to conceal the recycled footage, which are evident in both the film's aesthetics and its narrative structure.

Blood Monster's first twenty minutes or so, which features a group of astronauts who have been sent to investigate the source of a virus plaguing Earth, is entirely comprised of new footage. Mechanical problems on their spaceship force the astronauts to land on a planet to conduct repairs and, from this point on, the original mission is side-lined so that they can observe a civil war between two 'alien' tribes on the planet. As the film progresses, *Tagani*'s footage and narrative become increasingly visible and dominant, and Adamson's original characters are rendered little more than passive spectators. Recycled footage makes up some thirty minutes of *Blood Monster*'s final hour, with inserted sequences ranging from a few seconds in length to over four and a half minutes, uninterrupted. The relationship between the new and old footage collapses as their narratives diverge and fewer attempts are made to integrate the footage through editing. Reaction shots disappear, emphasising the spatial and temporal distance between Adamson's characters and *Tagani*'s spectacle. Voice-over that featured at the beginning of the film is replaced with dubbing, while flashback sequences that somewhat explained some of the visual discrepancies are replaced by scenes that bear no relation to the astronauts whatsoever, drawing attention to the increasing separation between the two narrative strands. Recycled scenes become longer and more prominent until, by the end of the film, Adamson's characters are not even witness to the spectacle and entirely unaffected by the action presented in these recycled sequences. As *Blood Monsters* reaches its conclusion, neither narrative strand is adequately resolved, and no real attempt is made to unite them.

In the above examples, claims of plagiarism seem justified. *The Bride and the Beast* and *Blood Monsters* present all of their footage as new, with neither explicit nor implicit acknowledgement of the recycled sections. Yet, recognition of the footage as *not* original is often unavoidable due to the marked aesthetic and narrative discrepancies. At the very least, the decision to chop up an existing narrative and insert sections of it into a new story means that incoherence is more likely. The viewer is not granted access to the 'whole' narrative as it was originally intended; inevitably, some of the meaning will be lost. It is little wonder, then, that *Blood Monsters* has been described as a 'bewildering mishmash' (Adams 2010: 159) and a 'paste-up science-fiction atrocity' (Weldon 1983: 332). In both *Blood Monsters* and *The Bride and the Beast*, we can identify the efforts to pass off existing footage as new. This is not just apparent in the attempts to create some visual, spatial and temporal connections between old and new footage. The majority of new footage features at the beginning of both films, encouraging viewers to (falsely) believe that this is an original story, with recycled sequences typically getting longer, less integrated through editing and more abundant as the film progresses; it is only after we have already dedicated some time and attention to the films that their patchwork nature becomes apparent. In addition to the inherent badness of these plagiaristic tendencies, the films' failure is established through recognition of visual discrepancies despite the attempts to conceal them, the unacknowledged appropriation of an existing narrative through its presentation as new, and the uncomfortable realisation that the original elements of the screenplay ultimately serve as little more than a McGuffin exploited to allow an old, recycled story to be (re)told.

Other badfilms seem to exploit footage recycled from pre-existing movies in similar ways, but not all invite the same accusations of plagiarism. In *They Saved Hitler's Brain*, for example, new footage adds to the narrative contained within the original source material, a Nazi mad scientist movie called *The Madmen of Mandoras* (Bradley 1963). Despite its rather ludicrous plot, *Madmen* is photographed and staged well and, in general, is competently made and entertaining. In contrast, the new scenes created for *They Saved Hitler's Brain* are notably amateurish and of a far lower quality. This new footage features exclusively at the beginning of the film. It introduces characters who appear to be the film's main protagonists and features a convoluted storyline that is tangentially related to *Madmen*'s narrative. Some attempts are made to integrate the new and recycled plot threads – conversations between new characters directly refer to events from *Madmen*, while some scenes are cross-cut between new and old footage to give the impression of spatial and temporal unity – but these are poorly executed and thoroughly unconvincing. With the new footage shot several years after *Madmen*'s original release and no obvious effort made to maintain period accuracy, there are clear differences in costume, character appearance and accompanying score, as well as cinematography, editing, dialogue, acting and general filmmaking quality. After twenty-five minutes, everyone central to the story thus far is dead. From this point on, Bradley's original film plays, unaltered, in its entirety.

They Saved Hitler's Brain complicates claims of plagiarism, however, because it is the new footage that is inadequately attributed, not the old. Demonstrating the unusual power dynamic at play, *Madmen*'s opening credits introduce the film, with two differences: a new title card, and the addition of an extra slide unobtrusively declaring 'additional post-production by Paragon Films, Inc. (Hollywood)'. This vague reference to some form of post-production work fails to adequately acknowledge the later contributions of people unrelated to the initial production, and no specifics are provided: we do not know who directed, wrote, edited or even acted in the newly added scenes, and they do not appear to attempt passing off Bradley's work as their own so much as aiming to maintain the illusion of his authorship over the entire film. Looking beyond the text can help to understand why: allegedly, new footage was added to *Madmen* by a group of film students to make the movie a more suitable length for television. This suggests that the aim was not to rework the footage, but simply to make the film longer. Yet, we should be careful not to entirely dismiss *They Saved Hitler's Brain* as merely an extended version of an earlier movie. Its new title implies that it is a new film, as does the narrative content of the first half-hour. At the very least, this implies a degree of attempted subterfuge that, curiously, results in a form of reverse-plagiarism, whereby the anonymous people responsible for the unspecified 'post-production' additions absolve themselves of responsibility and attempt to pass their inept work off as someone else's, without their knowledge or approval.

It is also possible to find examples of self-plagiarism in badfilms. As I have discussed elsewhere (Bartlett 2019b), Ed Wood regularly recycled his own ideas, stories and characters, as well as previously shot footage. Scenes from one of his unfinished films called either *Hellborn* or *Rock and Roll Hell* appear in both *The Sinister Urge* (Wood 1960) and *Night of the Ghouls*, with the latter also featuring portions of a pilot episode ('Final Curtain', 1957) from the filmmaker's doomed television series *Portraits of Terror*. Famously, *Plan 9 From Outer Space* includes original footage of Bela Lugosi that was filmed just before the actor's death, either without any specific purpose or as preliminary shots for a film possibly titled *The Ghoul Goes West*. Wood's proclivity for recycling and repurposing his own footage indicates that he was quite willing to self-plagiarise. He was not alone: Al Adamson and his business partner, Sam Sherman, also regularly repackaged and repurposed footage from their back catalogue in order to create 'new' films. They appear largely ambivalent about quality, with profits being the primary aim (see Sherman quoted in Konow 1998: 118). For example, a 1964 production called either *Echo of Terror* or *Two Tickets to Terror* had footage added to capitalise on the then-popular 'go-go' dance craze, becoming *Psycho A Go Go* in 1965. New scenes featuring John Carradine were added two years later, and more scenes were inserted some years thereafter. In its various incarnations, the film was also released as *Man with the Synthetic Brain* and *Fiend with the Electronic Brain*. Finally, in 1971, it became *Blood of Ghastly Horror*. What was initially a cheap, but reasonably straight-forward heist movie had, by this point, morphed into an utterly incoherent genre hybrid that attempts to unite disparate plot strands including a jewel heist, a serial killer, a mad scientist and zombie slaves.

Recycling, repackaging and (minimally) reworking existing films provided filmmakers who were already working under restrictive conditions an opportunity to cheaply create apparently 'new' movies. While there is a clear economic advantage to this approach, it often comes at the cost of artistic and aesthetic quality, not to mention narrative coherence. Through the failed integration of recycled footage, these 'new' films can be identified as bad not just through their inconsistent and inept construction, but because they can constitute a very obvious form of plagiarism, with all the negative connotations that this implies. Furthermore, the visibility of the pre-existing footage suggests that even the attempt to effectively plagiarise can be considered unsuccessful. At the same time, however, this visibility can open new interpretive possibilities and invite us to question aspects of these films' production that we might otherwise take for granted. For example, Wood's proclivity for recycling his own films offers a chance to identify seemingly unintended moments of intertextuality within and between his various works (Bartlett 2019b). These can, in turn, be used as evidence of an 'authorial signature' and helps to collate a collection of films that 'virtually defy classification' (Hill 2015: 172) into the marginally more coherent category of 'Ed Wood films'. Elsewhere, recycling practices invite other forms of unintended intertextuality, some of which will be explored in more detail below.

Conversely, accusations of plagiarism do not fully account for the vast, widespread and diverse ways in which recycled footage is used and incorporated into other films. It does not appropriately describe films featuring copious amounts of stock footage, for example, because this footage was created for the precise purpose of being sold for use in new productions. The inappropriate visibility of stock footage can certainly have detrimental effects on how a film is interpreted, as discussed below, but its badness is neither inherent nor inevitable. Although its origins tend to not be acknowledged within these new films, the inclusion of stock footage does not constitute plagiarism as it is traditionally understood. Instead, the unsuccessful integration of stock footage, and/or an over-reliance on it, draws attention beyond the frame, reminding us of certain commercial practices associated with *all* forms of cinema. Thus, while recycling practices associated with badfilms can, at times, be understood in relation to plagiarism, at other times they seem to operate in different ways, opening up new possibilities for interpretation and meaning-making. When this occurs, badfilms can collapse – or at least blur – the boundaries between 'high' and 'low' cultural forms. Before proceeding further, then, we can look to a form of recycling that is not derided as plagiarism but acclaimed for its appropriation of pre-existing materials: avant-garde, experimental, 'found footage' practices.

A 'Thousand Possible Whys': Recycled Footage and the Avant-Garde

The concepts of appropriation and recontextualisation are central to many avant-garde and experimental found footage films. Filmmakers such as Bruce Conner and Craig Baldwin rely on their audience's familiarity with the recycled images and cinematic conventions in order to challenge that familiarity through montage, collage, or other means. Newsreels, B-movies, science-fiction, exploitation films and soft-core pornography proved to be valuable sources of footage, in part due to the easily identifiable textual connotations that their generic and often stereotypical images offer (Luckhurst 2008: 195–96). Consequently, several of the most notable found footage films draw inspiration and footage from low-budget genre pictures, with 1950s American films in particular considered to be 'key sources' of found footage material (Danks 2006: 243). In this way, similar images repeat themselves across high and low cultural objects – avant-garde cinema and narrative-based genre pictures – but are presented in very different categorical contexts that encourage markedly different reading strategies.

Scenes of real atomic bomb detonations, for example, can be found in experimental cinema (Wees 1993: 36–41), 'mainstream' movies and badfilms, but tend to be integrated, appropriated and recontextualised in different ways. In *A Movie* (Conner 1958), nuclear bomb footage is part of a collage that works to produce a 'series of visual gags and metaphoric links between sexual desire and military aggressiveness' (Wees 1993: 39). *Dr Strangelove or: How I Learned to Stop Worrying and Love the Bomb* (Kubrick 1964) concludes with a montage of nuclear explosions signifying humanity's destruction through war, ironically accompanied by Vera Lynn singing *We'll Meet Again*. Recognising this footage as real and recycled enables a deeper appreciation for the film's blackly satirical, political message. In badfilms, atomic bomb footage seems to be included primarily for its potential as spectacle and tends to be presented in fairly unambiguous ways. In *The Beast of Yucca Flats*, for example, it has a clear narrative function: to illustrate the cause of 'noted scientist' Joseph Javorsky's transformation into a beast. Elsewhere, atomic bomb footage concludes *Bride of the Monster*, with the explosion apparently caused by a giant octopus and its mad scientist creator Dr Vornoff being struck by lightning while fighting. Allegedly, the inclusion of this footage was a condition imposed upon the film by its financial backers (Rodriguez quoted in Grey 1992: 69–70) who wanted to make a political statement but, if this was the aim, it has been poorly executed. Rather than invite a 'more analytical reading' through self-referentiality, as avant-garde found footage films do (Wees 1993: 11), nuclear bomb footage in badfilms seems predominantly included as cheap spectacle, with its minimal recontextualisation within the narrative suggesting that we are meant to understand it literally, not figuratively.

Whereas experimental found footage films draw attention to their recycled status and use that awareness to encourage a more critical, analytical response, the 'ideal goal' of recycled footage in narrative cinema is that it 'won't be noticed by its audience' (Danks 2006: 246). This is evident in the commonplace use of recycled footage – often stock footage or documentary footage of people, landscapes and animals – as establishing shots. In the opening scene of *Bela Lugosi Meets a Brooklyn Gorilla* (Beaudine 1952), for example, brief recycled shots of various 'jungle' animals are accompanied by authoritative third-person voice-over narration that does nothing more than describe the images onscreen. The images are recontextualised only in so far as they are compiled together. This compilation works to construct an easily identifiable, although by no means accurate, 'exotic' setting: the 'jungle of the middle-class American imagination' (Schaefer 1999: 269). For all its cheapness, the film generally uses recycled images in ways that are typical of a broader tendency within low-budget narrative cinema. Contra to more critically acclaimed avant-garde practices, narrative function is prioritised, and efforts (here, voice-over narration) are made to minimise any non-literal interpretations of the images or recognition of them as recycled images. While the quality of the footage varies and is all entirely dissimilar to the rest of the film's constructed jungle studio set, it is possible to understand the footage not as evidence of the actual jungle in which the majority of *Bela Lugosi Meets a Brooklyn Gorilla* takes place, but as the figurative representation of what the jungle might look like. To paraphrase Paul Arthur (1997), the footage can be read as depicting 'a' jungle rather than 'this' jungle and 'some' animals instead of 'these' animals; subsequently, it can be considered relatively unobtrusive and functionally successful. This example indicates that success or failure, therefore, can be established by evaluating the functionality of the recycled footage, its integration – or lack thereof – within its new context, its visibility and quality in relation to the film's original footage, and its effectiveness in establishing a setting for the action that occurs in the rest of the film.

As I have already noted, badfilms can, on occasion, produce an effect similar to experimental found footage cinema. This is usually because of a failure to achieve the intended 'ideal' goal of invisibility, rather than a deliberately self-aware or self-reflexive approach to how the footage is appropriated. Discussing avant-garde found footage practices, Wees argues that montage, in particular, deliberately exploits the inherent discrepancies between the original and present functions of the image: it 'does not disguise the fact that the shots came from different sources; yet, at the same time, it prompts us to recognise an appropriateness in their juxtaposition' (1993: 12–13). It is only through recognition of the footage as recycled from a pre-existing source that its original meanings can be dismantled, enabling a 'new structural relationship' (Norden 2002: 77) to be constructed. This is possible because all film footage is 'extraordinarily malleable, its meaning and significance provided by context as much as by image 'content''' (Zyrd 2003: 48). The meaning of a single image, shot, or scene is influenced by the images, shots, or scenes surrounding it, and images can be recontextualised through montage, collage and compilation to create new meanings and invite new interpretations. Using familiar imagery and altering its context enables filmmakers to create new chains of meaning. Standish Lawder describes this as 'ironic decontextualisation' whereby . . .

> . . . original context is obliterated. The shot is re-presented in a new context and, invariably, with a different soundtrack. Stripped of its original context, the shot becomes veiled with layers of speculation, subjective evocation and poetic ambiguity. Questions of intentionality and meaning become slippery. The true significance of the *a priori* original image hovers just off-screen; we cannot be certain exactly *why* it was filmed. Yet *what* was filmed remains firmly fixed, only now surrounded by a thousand possible new *whys* (quoted in Zyrd 2003: 51; emphasis in original).

Not all found footage cinema aims to create new meanings out of existing footage, although, arguably, the images are always recontextualised – even if they are unedited and unaltered – through their re-presentation. Found footage films 'draw attention to the body of the film itself, to the film's own image-ness' (Wees 1993: 11) and invite us to reflect on their status as images, first, and the new meanings that reveal themselves through their new contexts, second. The potential of filmic techniques such as montage, collage and voice-over narration to elicit these new meanings has proven of particular interest to filmmakers and scholars alike. The most widely celebrated found footage films, for example, tend to be those that appropriate generic and stock images – usually images that function as icons but lack inherent narrative meaning – and use these to construct new narratives through their compilation and recontextualisation. Editing is crucial, helping to create these new meanings through the combination of previously disassociated shots. In particular, processes of montage can construct associations whereby each shot 'contributes to a reading of the one next to it, so the accumulated readings produce thematic categories or paradigms in which most if not all of the film's images fit, no matter how unrelated their original contexts might have been' (Wees 1993: 15). In this way, recycled images both maintain their own individual meaning – they depict a specific, albeit decontextualised, moment in space and time – *and* they become multivalent, revealing new, metaphorical, satirical, figurative, illustrative and ironic meanings through recontextualisation and their association with other similarly ambiguous images.

The addition of a new soundtrack, particularly voice-over narration, can also assist in re-presenting recycled images in a new context and directing the viewer towards a specific interpretation. This is particularly relevant when stock footage is used: voice-over limits the polysemous potential of these generic images and reduces their inherent ambiguity. Voice-over narration, already discussed in Chapter 3, can provide a 'more subjective point of view' (Wees 1993: 22) and, in the case of avant-garde found footage films, also frequently adopts an ironic tone that encourages a similarly ironic spectatorial position. The soundtrack acts to 'regulate what might seem to be a largely scattered field of images [. . .] or [functions] as a counterpoint that can both resonate with and grate against what we are seeing' (Danks 2006: 248). In particular, voice-over narration helps to draw attention to the images' individual and collective new meanings, and often works to 'expose, satirise, and produce new readings of the banalities, clichés and conventional modes of discourse [. . .] that are endemic to mass media' (Wees 1993: 21). As the following examples demonstrate, however, even when recycled footage is integrated into badfilms through montage and collage in a way similar to avant-garde practices, the added voice-over does not necessarily adopt an ironic position. This suggests that, primarily, the aim is to fully integrate this footage into the new film, disguise its recycled origins and, usually, to encourage the viewer to take the contents of the image at face value.

Challenging the High-Low Distinction: *Glen or Glenda*

One notorious badfilm in particular seems to exemplify the blurring of distinctions between 'high' and 'low' culture discussed by Hawkins and others. In many ways, *Glen or Glenda*, Ed Wood's feature debut, does not appear to be trying to replicate the established conventions of traditional narrative cinema. Conversely, despite its experimental style, particularly in relation to its copious use of stock and documentary footage, it seems to lack the self-awareness and ironic disposition that often characterises avant-garde cinema. Rodney Hill suggests that, although Wood is not an avant-garde filmmaker, *Glen or Glenda*'s style is 'proof' of Wood's '*awareness* of the avant-garde' (Hill 2015: 178; emphasis in original). However, even though Wood's appreciation for Hollywood genre films is well-documented (see Grey 1992; Wood 1998), I have yet to find any extradiegetic evidence to suggest he was aware of early avant-garde filmmakers, let alone that he was attempting to replicate their style in any conscious way. Rather, *Glen or Glenda*'s unconventional approach to cinematic construction, loose narrative structure and pseudo-documentary style can be best understood when contextualised within classical exploitation, an industry that existed 'in the shadow of Hollywood' (Schaefer 1999: 2) between roughly 1919 and 1959.

Classical exploitation, as Schaefer identifies it, is a distinct category of cinema, with films generally conforming to four main features: a 'forbidden' or taboo subject matter; extremely low production values; independent distribution; and comparatively few prints in circulation at any one time (1999: 5–6). Unsurprisingly, there is an overlap between these films and bad movies, with certain classical exploitation films – notably *Maniac* and *Reefer Madness* (Gasnier 1936) – gaining an audience among badfilm fans who celebrate the 'cinematic ineptitude' (Schaefer 1999: 2) on display. However, classical exploitation and badfilms are not synonymous. Schaefer suggests that the former's incompetence was often the result of their production contexts and, by prioritising 'forbidden spectacle' as their organising sensibility (1999: 5), they 'could be "bad" because there was no compelling need for them to be "good"' (1999: 42–43). Thus, whereas the majority of established badfilms fall into recognisable genres favouring narrative coherence and seamless continuity, classical exploitation tended towards different priorities, and their contemporaneous audience was likely to have had different expectations.

Nevertheless, certain stylistic tendencies and production strategies are shared across classical exploitation and badfilm. Notably, due to the restrictive working conditions that typify most low-budget, independent filmmaking, both make significant use of recycled footage. This is often ineptly integrated and clashes uncomfortably with other formal elements. Schaefer suggests that recycled footage in classical exploitation differs to that found elsewhere because it 'could provide the primary instances of spectacle' (1999: 57). As I discuss later in this chapter, however, recycled footage often serves the same purpose in badfilms. Furthermore, although recycled footage in classical exploitation is rarely, if ever, acknowledged as such, it was frequently 'old, poorly lit, and badly shot, and in many instances [. . .] is abrupt and startling, drawing attention to itself' (Schaefer 1999: 57). Such aesthetic discrepancies are evident in badfilms also, but in these it is often the case that the recycled footage is of a *better* quality, with higher production values, than the surrounding, original footage.

Acknowledging *Glen or Glenda*'s classical exploitation context helps to demonstrate the collapsing of boundaries between high and low culture. Just as avant-garde cinema often produces a viewing condition whereby we are 'constantly reminded that we are watching a movie: representation of reality, rather than a window on it' (Norden 2002: 78), classical exploitation films also 'consistently reminded the viewer that he or she was watching a film' (Schaefer 1999: 80) through their discontinuity, prioritisation of spectacle and disregard for, or ambivalence towards, traditional Hollywood conventions. Similarly, badfilms offer heightened realism through their failure to be believable and draw attention to the construction of the image, rather than the image itself. Michael Adams' description of *Glen or Glenda* as a 'weird, wild one-off work of art' (2010: 61) in his book on the 'worst films of all time', for example, typifies the tendency among cult fans to ascribe oddness and artistry in equal measure and demonstrates how these different categories – exploitation, avant-garde, badfilm – collide in Wood's feature debut.

The bulk of *Glen or Glenda*'s narrative centres on two people – Glen/Glenda and Alan/Ann – whose stories are relayed as medical case-studies by Dr Alton to Inspector Warren, so that the latter might better understand what led a transvestite to commit suicide. Although originally intended to capitalise on the publicity surrounding Christine Jorgenson's sex change operation, Wood instead primarily draws inspiration from his own cross-dressing. *Glen or Glenda* offers a rather progressive plea for tolerance of certain non-normative gender identities and thus occupies a notable position within queer cinema history as possibly the 'first American film to portray transvestites and transsexuals as sympathetic human beings' (Benshoff and Griffin 2005: 104). More than any other badfilm, *Glen or Glenda* has been reinterpreted as art (intentional or otherwise) and an example of accidental avant-garde cinema. Despite this, it is consistently contextualised as a badfilm, even if this characterisation is subsequently challenged or even rejected outright (for example, Jenkins 1981; Craig 2009; Hill 2015).

Different understandings of categorical contexts can lead to different responses, as noted in Chapter 2. Within any context other than exploitation, *Glen or Glenda* can seem like an outlier, and even as a classical exploitation film, its biographical inspirations mark it as different. Aesthetically, however, Wood's debut is not dissimilar from other exploitation films of the time. Whereas most badfilm literature tends to emphasise *Glen or Glenda*'s weirdness, unconventionality and uniqueness (for example, Sconce 1995: 388–89), Schaefer appears to find little to distinguish it formally from other classical exploitation. For him, the repeated shots of lightning, traffic on a highway and World War II combat are 'typical' (1999: 57). Yet, *Glen or Glenda* is unusually polysemous: in addition to the narrative strands that never really converge and the earnest, pseudo-documentary style, Wood's reliance on stock footage, edited together through montage and collage with multiple voice-over narrators, creates an aesthetic ambiguity that enables a range of interpretations.

Examining a brief but notorious scene demonstrates how *Glen or Glenda*'s recycled sequences may be alternately read as evidence of ineptitude, or effective metaphor. Glen (Wood, as Daniel Davis) and his fiancée Barbara (Delores Fuller, Wood's then girlfriend) are engaged in conversation, during which Glen admits he has a secret which he fears will cause Barbara to leave him. After reassuring her fiancé that he can tell her anything, Barbara asks him: 'Is it another woman?' Glen physically shrinks away from her, and the image abruptly cuts to stock footage of stampeding buffalo. The Scientist (Bela Lugosi), a kind of god-like figure who presides over the action, is superimposed over the shot, glaring into the camera while shouting: 'Pull the string! Pull the string! A mistake is made. A story must be told'. On the one hand, this appears to be an obvious example of incompetence: an unrelated, misplaced and inappropriate insert that clearly does not belong in a film about transvestism, let alone in a scene intended to convey Glen's emotional anguish (for example, Medved and Medved 1980: 178). On the other hand, the buffalo can be read as a symbolic representation of Glen's torment (Craig 2009: 45). This sequence, therefore, can be alternately read as evidence of Wood's ineptitude and/or his creativity. Craig is not alone in suggesting that the visibility of this recycled footage is less evidence of incompetence than an abstract way of depicting the internalised emotions of Glen in this moment. Tunc and Prescott even locate intention within the scene, suggesting it is 'obvious that the scenes he [Wood] selected are not only strategically placed, but also connected to the complexity of Glen's dilemma' (2003). Here, the psychological symbolism takes precedence over the seamless integration of stock footage; it is the contents of the image and their relationship to the surrounding shots that matters. However, although we should be careful to avoid assuming that Wood's style is evident only in his failure (Routt 2001), he often appears to be motivated by resourcefulness rather than a specific, singular vision. For example, although we see Glen wrestling with his dual identity on several occasions, the buffalo only appear once. It is not clear, therefore, whether Wood would have sought out this particular footage had it not been readily available to him, nor is there evidence of the filmmaker consistently using recycled footage in similarly representational ways elsewhere in his films.

Nevertheless, in this moment at least, an aesthetic and thematic ambiguity is created through the way in which the stock shot is integrated into the scene, thus enabling a variety of possible interpretations. The image itself has no inherent, fixed significance of its own – it is simply a bird's eye view of stampeding buffalo in an unidentifiable location. Wees suggests that found

Figure 4.1A,B Glen and Barbara's conversation is interrupted by stampeding buffalo, *Glen or Glenda* (Wood, Jr, 1953).

footage avant-garde cinema works because 'so strong is the mind's inclination to turn juxtaposed images into something meaningful [...] that every alert viewer will find some way of associating and thematising these images' (1993: 16–17). In other words, when confronted with ambiguity and disjunction, our natural inclination is to find connections, to construct meaning. In *Glen or Glenda*, recycled footage gains meaning and possible significance through its new context, its association with the shots on either side of it and the addition of the Scientist's nonsensical dialogue. In isolation, the buffalo are meaningless but, when recontextualised in this way, they become steeped in potential meaning.

Conversely, when the image is contextualised in unambiguous ways and ascribed explicit narrative significance, we are presented with meaning, rather than invited to discover our own. This helps to explain why, for example, the stock footage octopus in *Bride of the Monster* has not benefited from the interpretive approaches at the heart of *Glen or Glenda*'s re-evaluation. Like the buffalo footage, the octopus footage has no inherent or fixed narrative significance but, unlike the buffalo, its recontextualisation reduces its multivalent potential. The footage is presented as point-of-view, as a literal depiction of a physical creature visible to the characters, in a genre picture with clear roots in narrative cinema. Its presentation suggests that it is intended to be understood as precisely what it appears to be – an octopus – and nothing more. There is no ambiguity created through montage, no recontextualisation through voice-over, just unacknowledged visual discrepancies that draw attention to themselves and expose the scene's compilation of footage from disparate sources. Issues of quality thus become unintentionally foregrounded because there is no particular opportunity to ascribe symbolic or non-literal meaning to this recycled image.

Whereas the stampeding buffalo represent a stock shot inserted into what is otherwise original footage, other sequences in *Glen or Glenda* are entirely comprised of recycled footage, which is recontextualised through montage and the addition of one or more voice-over narrators. Voice-over has the potential to 'turn mass produced public images into components of individual and even autobiographical statements' (Wees 1993: 22–23). *Glen or Glenda*'s loose structure includes stories within stories, shifting perspectives, flashbacks, memories, dreams and odd, tangential conversations, spoken by unseen characters and relayed via voice-over and/or unconfirmed voice-off, with apparently recycled images providing some loosely connected visual accompaniment. One such sequence involves a conversation between Joe and Jack, two characters who are never shown on screen and whose appearances are limited to this single, ninety-second scene. Over recycled images showing cars on a highway during daytime, a panning shot of a factory exterior, machinery inside a steel mill, cars on a highway at night and a flash of lightning, the pair discuss a recent news story about someone undergoing a sex change. The conversation itself has far more relevance to the film's main themes than the images over which it is heard, and the 'twist' conclusion suggesting Joe may have a female alter ego[1] further indicates that the aural is being prioritised over the visual here. Even the way in which the sequence is edited suggests that the images have been organised to complement the dialogue. Alternating shots between a large vat and a molten steel rod coincide with the characters' voices, creating an unusual correlation between sound and image whereby each character is directly associated with one of the stock shots. This strange symmetry appears to be indicative of certain decisions made in the editing process, suggesting a rather rudimentary, but deliberate, method of stitching sound and image together.

Perhaps more than any other scene in *Glen or Glenda*, the sequence outlined above seems to pre-empt the techniques of recontextualisation through montage and voice-over narration that were popularised by avant-garde filmmakers a decade later. Like the buffalo scene, this 'extraordinary' sequence (Craig 2009: 46) has also been ascribed psychoanalytical significance, although Freudian claims regarding the phallocentricity of the steelworks (Tunc and Prescott 2003) and the emotional intent ascribed to the machinery (Craig 2009: 46) are, to me, not always convincing. These interpretations are *possible*, however, because of the polysemous nature of the images, and the ways in which relationships are suggested between the images through voice-over narration and montage.

While psychoanalytical readings that largely bypass issues of construction

---

[1] This moment, along with a handful of other brief scenes, is missing from some currently available versions of the film.

BADFILM

Figure 4.2A–G   Joe and Jack's day, *Glen or Glenda* (Wood, Jr, 1953).

or quality constitute one possible interpretation, the sequence can also be taken at face value. In this reading, the stock shots can be understood to represent a single day in the life of Joe and Jack: they commute to work, discuss current affairs while working a shift in a steel working factory and return home in the evening. This reading draws attention to an uncomfortable clash between the aural and visual: whereas the images are non-specific, presenting an ellipsis through montage and depicting *any* typical working day for the pair, the spoken exchange is specific, relaying a *particular* conversation between them. The scene, therefore, complicates claims about intentionality, which are particularly speculative due to the film's ambiguity and muddled further by Wood's contemporary reputation. For example, it is not clear to what extent *Glen or Glenda*'s unconventional approach to 'storytelling' – in the loosest sense of the word – is deliberate. The recycled footage, for instance, is so frequent and obvious that it seems improbable that anyone could assume it would go unnoticed. The construction of entire scenes from stock footage, meanwhile, suggests at least some time and effort was put into compiling them, which also indicates a certain amount of conscious decision-making. However, we can question how consistent this apparent approach is. Recycled footage comprises approximately twenty percent of the film's content, but many scenes are not subject to the reading strategies outlined above, suggesting a formal inconsistency that could further complicate claims of intentionality.

Closer inspection of *Glen or Glenda* also indicates that at least some of the shots included elsewhere in apparently recycled montage sequences may actually have been created specifically for this film – or, at least, *a* film. The hick farmer ruminating about the 'hosses'; the ears we see in close-up; the 'native' tribespeople dancing in the jungle; even the distractingly inappropriate radiator shot in the opening scene – all of these could be dismissed as stock footage, although they are clearly staged and share a certain degree of aesthetic consistency, suggesting that they are not recycled. Thus, perhaps the stock shots are not as immediately obvious in *Glen or Glenda* as they first appear. Indeed, this hints at a further, presumably unintended consequence of including so much stock footage: the potential misidentification and misattribution of seemingly inappropriate or non-specific original footage as recycled, in an effort to understand its inclusion.

As I discussed in Chapter 2, auteurism underpins much of fan-authored and academic analysis of badfilms. This is particularly true of *Glen or Glenda*. This approach, however, does not adequately account for all the film's recycled inserts. Broadly, auteurist readings fail to acknowledge the possible contributions of 'Bud' Schelling, the film's editor, and instead attribute *Glen or Glenda*'s unconventional style entirely to its writer-director-actor. Additionally, there is evidence to suggest the film was amended by its producer, George Weiss, who is apparently responsible for adding the most substantial and obvious sequence of recycled footage (Grey 1992: 48), possibly without Wood's involvement or knowledge. Lasting just over six minutes, the footage – a series of B&D burlesque scenes attributed to W. Merle Connell – is minimally integrated into the most explicitly experimental portion of *Glen or Glenda*, a surreal dream sequence in which Glen imagines the possible reactions he would receive were he to reveal his true identity to Barbara. Initially, several cutaway shots of Glen and The Scientist show them apparently reacting to these inserted stripteases with confusion, bemusement, fear and excitement. This suggests at least minimal effort to integrate the footage, apparently to justify its inclusion within the wider, original sequence. Yet these reaction shots are soon abandoned, and no further recontextualisation is even attempted. *Glen or Glenda*'s dream sequence provides some of the most persuasive evidence of Wood's experimental approach to cinematic form that, here at least, seems to be intentional, but its effectiveness is compromised by the footage which Weiss subsequently added and which, arguably, constitutes the *least* interesting portion of the film.

This added sequence represents a very different approach to how recycled footage is used and incorporated elsewhere in *Glen or Glenda*, and its very existence complicates claims of auteurism, which necessarily ascribe the film's meaning solely to its director. Tunc and Prescott, for instance, continue their psychoanalytical approach and focus their attention predominantly on Glen's reactions to the recycled images (2003). This suggests that the recycled footage only becomes meaningful for the authors through its recontextualisation; notably, it is Wood's original footage, not the recycled images, that allows them to continue their psychoanalytical analysis. Hill, meanwhile, concedes that there is 'some doubt' about the scene's origins but acknowledges Wood's reputation for using stock footage and suggests that the burlesque scenes 'do "fit" aesthetically with the rest of the sequence' (2015: 177). I am not convinced; in addition to the footage clearly being of a different quality, the scene's minimal camerawork and lack of editing also mark it as different. The soundtrack – a muffled jazz score – and sound editing also jar uncomfortably with the rest of the film. Unlike elsewhere in *Glen or Glenda*, including the above-mentioned sequence with Joe and Jack, there is an obvious disjunction between aural and visual elements, with music tracks stopping and being replaced by new ones mid-scene on multiple occasions.

The challenge, then, is how to best analyse this sequence in relation to the rest of *Glen or Glenda*. Aesthetically, it has not been integrated in the same way as recycled footage elsewhere – editing is minimal, techniques of montage and collage are not employed, the contents of the footage have not been repurposed, and voice-over has not been added to direct the viewer towards any particular interpretation. Although contained within a surreal dream sequence, any attempts to conduct a psychoanalytical reading depends on the surrounding context and Wood's original shots, rather than the recycled images themselves. The footage has no obvious, inherent meaning or narrative significance – it is just a series of unconnected, burlesque-inspired scenes – and is given no particular new relevance through its new context. Yet, it is almost the same length as Alan/Ann's entire story and remains an important part of the film as it exists today, although not, perhaps, as Wood originally intended. Thus, for anyone with knowledge of *Glen or Glenda*'s production context, ascribing authorship entirely and exclusively to Wood is misplaced. Furthermore, the sequence added by Weiss results in the narrative effectively being paused and forced to give way to spectacle, likely contra the filmmaker's original 'vision'; in this moment, *Glen or Glenda*'s status as classical exploitation is confirmed.

Recycled Spectacle

As already noted, recycled footage was regularly used as a cheap source of spectacle. Much of *Glen or Glenda*'s visual spectacle, for example, is located in its recycled shots; in contrast, original images in Wood's feature debut and elsewhere are frequently characterised by 'banality and generality' (Routt 2001: 11). However, badfilms typically adopt a more conventional approach, whereby recycled footage usually functions as a visual representation of a moment or event motivated by, and rooted within, the narrative. Acknowledgement of the images' recycled origins is rare. More often, we can identify attempts to conceal their status as existing material, leading to claims of plagiarism, as discussed at the beginning of the chapter. This charge is particularly relevant when considering the unacknowledged but obvious inclusion of recycled footage as a primary source of spectacle. It is unsurprising, for instance, that, although classical exploitation films already tended to receive poor critical reception, the movies made from recycled material account for 'the most scathing criticism levelled at the form' (Schaefer 1999: 61).

On occasion, of course, it makes aesthetic as well as financial sense to use recycled footage for its spectacular potential: recreating atomic bomb footage, for example, is unlikely to achieve the same effect as the real thing. Similarly, recycled military footage is commonplace in low-budget, independent cinema. Like bomb footage, it may contain its own pre-existing cultural and historical significance, as well as effects and production values that would likely be expensive and difficult to reproduce, but it tends to lack fixed narrative meaning. Footage depicting training exercises and army drills, for instance, can be appropriated and recontextualised while retaining at least some of their original textual connotations. On occasion, its use suggests an ironic disposition. For example, *The Monster of Camp Sunshine* (Leroget 1964) concludes with an explosion of recycled war footage, depicting everything from re-enactments of the American civil war to World War II fighting, to illustrate – in notably self-aware, delirious and intentionally comedic ways – the military's efforts to stop a mutated monster running rampant in a nudist camp.

By rooting the footage within a clear, explicit narrative context, however, military footage in badfilms is usually indicative of attempts to 'conceal the status of pre-existent materials' (Luckhurst 2008: 194). This is evident in Alan/Ann's story in *Glen or Glenda*, which contains military and war footage, edited together as a visual accompaniment to Dr Alton's first-person account of his former patient's life. Similarly, *Plan 9 From Outer Space*'s most notable sequence of recycled footage occurs around twenty minutes into the film and features some generic, stock shots of Los Angeles, alongside recycled footage of the military conducting missile tests and new footage depicting Colonel Edwards (Tom Keene) standing against a blank backdrop and looking heavenwards through binoculars. The military footage is thus recontextualised, albeit minimally: now, the soldiers are shooting at UFOs. Nevertheless, the third-person voice-over narration and the way in which the footage is presented strongly suggest that we are meant to accept the contents of the footage at face value. Despite its new narrative context, the military footage remains just that and is presented without irony, commentary, critique or acknowledgement of its recycled origins.

These recycled images in *Plan 9*, however, do offer easily recognisable, widely available, cheap spectacle and often contain more to 'fascinate the eye of the spectator' (Schaefer 1999: 76) than the surrounding, new footage. This was particularly important in classical exploitation, which often depended on forbidden spectacle as the primary method of attracting its audience. In contrast, films aiming to adhere to more traditional forms of cinematic storytelling are assumed to have other priorities and could relate the same information via character dialogue or voice-over narration. Admittedly, both above-mentioned military scenes could be 'handled in less "spectacular" ways without damaging the narrative coherence of the film' (Schaefer 1999: 77). Although *Plan 9* cannot be understood as classical exploitation, as Schaefer defines it, the ability to provide spectacle was still important to these low-budget, independent genre pictures; like classical exploitation, there was often very little else worth promoting that might attract an audience. Indeed, *Plan 9*'s decision to include recycled spectacle, accompanied by voice-over narration that emphasises the narrative relevance of the images, hints at the liminal position that these films occupy. These are films made on the fringes of Hollywood, neither entirely exploitation nor benefitting from the money, expertise and resources of the studio system. As such, they exploit recycled footage as a cheap source of spectacle that is also imbued with explicit narrative justification, however tenuous.

The prevalence of recycled footage in low-budget cinema demonstrates one way in which pre-existing resources are exploited by filmmakers who may be less concerned with aesthetic consistency than profits, or who do not have the time, money, motivation or ability to produce a similar effect to the same standard themselves. Positively, recycling practices can indicate the creative approaches that resourceful filmmakers employ to complete their picture; conversely, however, these practices can also draw attention to other failings, whether that is an inability to produce original spectacle to any satisfactory standard, or the apparent assumption that, somehow, we will not notice the obvious visual discrepancies caused by such shoddy and ineffective integration. Yet, there is a further tension inherent in many of the genre-oriented badfilms that rely on recycled footage as their primary source of spectacle. Luckhurst suggests that, by bringing together the 'typically avant-garde or underground experimental cinematic practice' of using recycled or found material and a 'typically mass cultural genre', recycled science fiction ought to be a 'contradiction in terms' (2008: 194). Thematically, science fiction is a genre with mainstream appeal, whereas avant-garde cinema eschews conventions and is aimed at a niche audience; aesthetically, science fiction is associated with visual innovation, while recycled footage uses pre-existing materials and is oriented to the past (2008: 194). Although Luckhurst counters this distinction by noting the potential for new forms of temporality through repurposing old material, badfilms – including those obviously rooted in science fiction – already blur the line between high and low culture. Here, the tension arises primarily *because* of the unacknowledged appropriation of recycled spectacle. As the case-study below demonstrates, too often we cannot help but recognise the footage as not only recycled but old; oriented to the past, despite being presented as new. Identifying recycled footage in bad science fiction, then, challenges the genre's assumed innovation and forward-thinking. It exposes the inevitable disjunction between the old, recycled spectacle – which is frequently of a higher quality due to a tendency to reuse 'footage from earlier productions, especially such expensive-to-stage scenes as chases, fights, battles, and natural disasters' (Flynn and McCarthy 1975: 23) – and the inadequate, cheap and unconvincing attempts to provide new spectacle.

Recycled Footage as Spectacle: *Robot Monster*

Contemporaneous reviews of *Robot Monster* suggest that its reputation as one of the worst films of all time developed after its initial release. A contemporaneous review in *Variety* is somewhat complimentary when it reports that the picture 'comes off surprisingly well, considering the extremely limited budget and schedule', although the performances 'barely rise to a professional level' and Tucker's direction is 'off' (Neal 1953: 16). In contrast, today *Robot Monster* is firmly established as a badfilm and has gained significant cult status as a result of its combined seriousness, sincerity and absurdity. Warren, for example, describes it as one of the 'most watchable of all terrible movies'

(2010: 701), while Telotte argues that its cult reception is the result of what he refers to as science-fiction's 'double character' (2015: 161) – a combination of the serious and the strained. Shot over only four days, with no interior sets, on a budget of somewhere between $16,000 and $50,000 (Warren 2010: 703), *Robot Monster* attempts to tell an ambitious, post-apocalyptic story, including the global annihilation of almost all of humanity by an invading alien race of robot monsters. It does this, in large part, by using recycled footage.

Like other badfilms, there are plenty of amusing anecdotes and myths surrounding *Robot Monster* that, irrespective of their accuracy, have been used to both support claims of badness or failure and to endear the film to cult fans. Notably, there appears to be some confusion regarding *Robot Monster*'s use of recycled footage. *Monthly Film Bulletin*'s contemporaneous review claims that it includes a 'sequence of prehistoric monsters previously seen in *King Kong*' (Anonymous author 1954: 180), even though no footage from that film appears in any currently available versions. The Medveds, meanwhile, state that recycled footage of dinosaurs lasts 'about fifteen minutes' (1978: 195), although the scene in question lasts just under two minutes, and they also describe 'bison running downhill, woolly mammoths stampeding, and even a volcano erupting' (1978: 195), but none of these elements feature in currently available versions of the film. Rather, it seems that the authors have conflated *Robot Monster* with *One Million B.C.* (Roach and Roach Jr 1940), the film in which much of the recycled spectacle originally featured.

By relying almost exclusively on recycled footage for *Robot Monster*'s spectacle, the filmmakers have an opportunity to visually relay a story that otherwise would be far beyond their means or ability. As Telotte notes, its similarity to other alien invasion narratives, particularly *Invaders from Mars* (Menzies 1953), compounds a sense of 'meta-textual presence' that invites informed (cult) viewers to 'reposition themselves as knowing players in that revealed game of meaning' (Telotte 2015: 162). However, this is further encouraged through the obvious inclusion of recycled footage. It is not just visual discrepancies that reveal the recycled moments: the original sources of the most prominent examples of spectacle, including *Flight to Mars* (Selander 1951) and *Lost Continent* (Newfield 1951), are widely known and relatively easy to access online, and the footage can therefore be relatively easily identified. Furthermore, the same footage from *One Million B.C.* has appeared in at least eight other films, including *Horror of the Blood Monsters* and the prehistoric sexploitation movie *One Million AC/DC*. In each case the footage is presented as new, with no acknowledgement of its recycled nature and, in the process, creates an unintentional intertextuality that is likely made easier to identify as a result of contemporary viewing conditions. This may, in part, help us understand their cult appeal; by using the same footage, the films invite 'comparison, connections, and linkages with other films' (Mathijs and Mendik

2008: 3) and open up the possibility for fans to demonstrate their subcultural capital through their ability to identify these intertextual moments.

Recycled footage appears sporadically throughout *Robot Monster* and has a rather loose and inconsistent relationship with the narrative. The footage is presented as new and claims to show evidence of an apocalyptic *future*. There is an inherent contradiction here, however, because the images are easily identified as recycled from a decade-old film depicting a *prehistoric* Earth and, consequently, are clearly oriented to the past in terms of both content and origins. The film begins by introducing two young children, Johnny and his sister Carla, having a picnic with their mother and older sister in an inhospitable, rocky ravine. After Johnny meets two archaeologists in a nearby cave – Bronson Canyon, a location that provides its own intertextual potential through its repeated appearance in tens, if not hundreds, of film and television productions – the family have a post-lunch nap. Waking before his mother and sisters, Johnny decides to explore the area. He re-enters the cave and a flash of stock footage lightning, negatively exposed and accompanied by the sound of static, knocks him over. Johnny lies unconscious while a ball of light – most likely another stock image – explodes. The shot abruptly cuts to footage from *One Million B.C.*, showing a tegu and an alligator fighting; the latter has a fin attached to its back, indicating it is meant to be understood as a dinosaur. In the subsequent thirty seconds, the fight takes precedence, interrupted only by a brief shot from *Lost Continent* of two stop-motion triceratops sparring. The recycled sequence signals a shift in the narrative: when Johnny wakes up, the cave is now inhabited by Ro-Man, and the world appears to be significantly altered. The archaeologists are now part of Johnny's family, while the rest of humanity, with a handful of exceptions, has been wiped out by the alien robot. It is only in the film's final moments that everything taking place after Johnny hit his head is revealed to have been a dream.

The efforts to create a connection between the recycled images and the surrounding narrative context are minimal here. Nevertheless, because the scene signals a shift from the film's initially established temporality into the dreamscape of Johnny's unconscious, we might be willing to overlook the spatial and temporal discontinuity. It is not clear, for example, if Johnny has witnessed the fighting 'dinosaurs', because no spatial relationship is established through editing or cross-cutting; there are no reaction shots and the events that we witness here are not subsequently acknowledged by any of the characters. This early instance of recycled footage in *Robot Monster*, therefore, demonstrates how loose the film's relationship between spectacle and narrative can be. Although the recycled images can retrospectively be understood as tenuously connected to the plot – we can infer that they represent the destruction wreaked upon Earth by the alien invaders – they primarily represent a moment in which the narrative is temporarily abandoned in place of spectacle. However, because of the recycled nature of these visual attractions, this is not simply an example of spectacle overwhelming the narrative, but of old, recycled images superseding and intruding on the new content.

Elsewhere, World War II and atomic bomb footage, as well as shots possibly taken from other movies, serve as illustrations of the destruction that Ro-Man has caused on Earth. In contrast to the previous example, these recycled images are relayed via a rudimentary wooden frame that serves as a viewing screen. Framed within a frame, the images are precisely what they appear to be: a visual record of past events, re-presented in a new context, that viewers, along with the characters who serve as the diegetic audience here, are invited to recognise *as images*. At one point, for example, Ro-Man transmits a series of stock shots to the small group of survivors, while informing them that, if they want to know what has happened to the other humans, they must watch the footage. Here, the recycled footage is kept at a distance: it is part of the diegesis but depicts events from a different moment in space and time. The footage also provides some visual spectacle that is nevertheless situated within its new narrative context; presented without irony or commentary, the scenes of war and destruction are relevant but non-essential and, ultimately, their strength as images is less because of their new context than their inherent, original meaning.

The most prominent recycled sequence occurs towards the end of *Robot Monster*, just before Johnny wakes up and realises that the terrible events – including the death of both his younger sister and himself – were a dream. The alien authority Great Guidance, displeased with Ro-Man's identity crisis caused by an unexpected and endearingly human infatuation with Johnny's older sister, unleashes recycled chaos on the world from the safety of his spaceship. 'I shall release our cosmic tube rays . . .', he rants, causing stock lightning to strike, followed by more shots of stop-motion dinosaurs from *Lost Continent* and the brief appearance of an armadillo with horns, '. . . from which will spring prehistoric reptiles to devour what remains of life'. On cue, the two stop-motion triceratopses have a brief fight with each other, and one knocks down a tree. No devouring takes place. Great Guidance continues to narrate events, declaring that 'psychotropic [?] vibrations will smash the planet Earth out of the universe', while *One Million B.C.*'s tegu-alligator-dinosaurs resume their fight. The alien leader releases a ray that appears to cause a recycled earthquake, and the scene fades away as Johnny wakes from his dream.

For these sequences to be accepted as new, original and unique to *Robot Monster*, the audience must neither identify the images as recycled nor recognise their original meaning. However, although the images are explicitly referred to in the narrative through Great Guidance's dialogue, little effort is made to visually integrate them. Even the accompanying dialogue is barely effective because the dinosaurs do not really appear to be acting in accordance

RECYCLED FOOTAGE

Figure 4.3A–F Recycled scenes of spectacle as the Great Guidance unleashes his fury, before Johnny wakes up from his dream, *Robot Monster* (Tucker, 1953).

with Great Guidance's wishes. The alien's comments, meanwhile, suggest that efforts are being made to adapt the new narrative to justify the old footage – by, for example, explicitly referring to 'prehistoric' creatures – rather than recontextualising the recycled images. Contra to the avant-garde principles of ironic decontextualisation, we see efforts to conceal the recycled nature of the images and, by extension, to justify the scenes as the film's primary spectacle. Despite the clear lack of visual or aesthetic continuity, the emphasis on narrative relevance through dialogue indicates an effort to minimise the negative effects of relying on pre-existing materials by presenting the attractions as an integral and inevitable part of the new film.

It is also worth briefly comparing *Robot Monster*'s recycled and original spectacle. As in other badfilms, the mise-en-scène is threadbare, the lack of money is evident throughout, and there is often little of visual interest on display. There are few examples of original spectacle in *Robot Monster* – or, even, of *attempted* original spectacle. Indeed, the film's theatrical poster brazenly displays an artist's rendering of crumbling buildings, lizards and dinosaurs fighting – none of which were conceived for this film specifically. This further demonstrates the ways in which old footage is flagrantly presented as new and suggests an implicit acceptance of these recycled sequences as the film's main attractions. One scene in *Robot Monster*, however, does suggest an attempt to create original spectacle. The family are made aware of two surviving scientists who plan to take life-saving serum to a space platform orbiting Earth. Ro-Man contacts the family via the viewing screen, where they watch recycled images of a rocket launching while Ro-Man provides some expositional information. The scene changes to show a small spacecraft flying in a circle accompanied, illogically, by the sound of an airplane. Although it may initially seem that this is the rocket we just saw being launched, the dialogue reveals that it is meant to be identified as the space platform itself. The family are then ordered to watch as Great Guidance fires a cosmic ray that causes the rocket to explode. He then turns his attention to the space platform, still flying wildly in a circle around the screen. The scene is negatively exposed, and the object explodes. Just before it does, the smoke that inexplicably features in the 'space' scenes clears enough to reveal a person, dressed entirely in black, holding the miniature prop.

There are several significant problems with this scene, which contribute to its narrative incoherence as well as its ineffectiveness as a visual attraction.

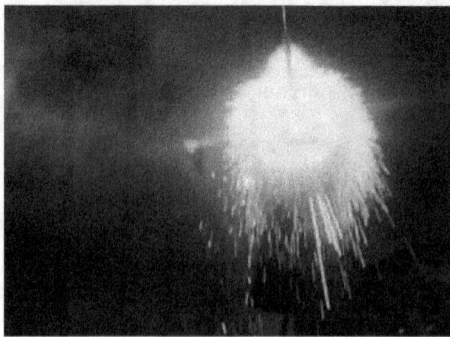

Figure 4.4   Note the man holding the 'space platform', visible in the bottom right-hand corner, *Robot Monster* (Tucker, 1953).

The images themselves are entirely unconvincing, while the space platform's rocket-like appearance is particularly jarring and unnecessarily complicates identification of it as distinct from the actual rocket that also features in the scene. Given that the events could have easily – and, arguably, more effectively – been relayed through dialogue alone, it appears that the intention here is to provide a moment of original spectacle, justified through the narrative but failing absolutely, with even the illusion of the 'special effect' obliterated by the accidental exposure of the person holding the spacecraft prop. This original scene thus exposes both the film's threadbare budget as well as the inept and unsuccessful efforts to produce spectacle that is unique to this film rather than poached from an existing source. Although the recycled attractions disrupt *Robot Monster*'s aesthetic coherence and share only a tenuous connection to the surrounding narrative, the decade-old footage is still of higher quality than the new footage and reveals larger production values than any of Tucker's efforts. Using recycled footage in this way can negatively impact the new film, therefore, not just through its unintended visibility as recycled, but by providing a standard that is comparatively more impressive and, given the typical production contexts of badfilms, difficult if not impossible to replicate.

Arguably, just as *Robot Monster* exploits recycled footage as a source of spectacle, so too does *Glen or Glenda*; yet the footage is (re)presented in markedly different ways that result in different interpretations. Thus, we need to be careful to avoid making blanket claims regarding how pre-existing footage is used in badfilms, and how it may be best understood. *Robot Monster*'s appropriation of visual attractions from previous feature films does not invite the same polysemous potential, even when footage from various sources is united through montage. Instead, the footage is minimally recontextualised and largely retains its original meaning. In other words, the purpose of the recycled footage appears more explicit in *Robot Monster* and, by originating within a previous narrative and now inserted into a new narrative, does not particularly invite us to look for any deeper or hidden significance in the way in which *Glen or Glenda*'s recycled sequences seem to do. *Robot Monster*'s use of pre-existing footage, therefore, is more representative of recycling practices within badfilm, whereby the footage fulfils two main functions: first, to serve the narrative; and second, to provide moments of spectacle rooted within the narrative, which the filmmakers would otherwise be unable or unwilling to produce themselves, due to budget, time, ability, ambivalence, or a combination of all four.

Exploring recycling practices in badfilms encourages us to reflect on intentionality that, in all its inherent ambiguity, can reveal itself in many different ways. It can be tempting to attribute intentionality to artistry but, as I suggested in Chapter 2, such an attribution risks denying or ignoring the possibility of other motivating factors, such as the intention to make money, or even to simply complete a film and release it to the public. By unwittingly enabling us to look beyond the narrative to the film's construction, badfilms can remind us that production contexts often hindered the creation of original spectacle, or necessitated films to be churned out quickly, cheaply and with minimal resources or effort (see Flynn 1975; Schaefer 1999; Davis 2012). The exploitation of recycled footage, particularly when it is not acknowledged and even presented as a film's unique selling point through promotional materials, as *Robot Monster* does, suggests a certain degree of resourcefulness, pragmatism and ambivalence that claims of artistic intention may not fully take into account.

The failed concealment and subsequent visibility of recycled footage, especially when exploited for its spectacular content, exposes the audacity of the people responsible, who blatantly present old images as new and fail entirely in their ability to do so convincingly. Of course, not all forms of recycling are inherently bad; as with any other formal or aesthetic decision, execution is key. Considering *Robot Monster*'s recycled footage, Telotte identifies a distinction between brief shots, such as the rocket's launch, and the longer sequences poached from *One Million B.C.* and elsewhere: in his view, the former works to 'support the narrative', whereas the latter is 'ill-fitting' (2015: 165). This suggests that, when recycled shots do not draw attention to themselves, they can be considered a more acceptable and appropriate cinematic device. Conversely, when recycled footage provides the primary and most successful examples of spectacle, but its recycled status is unacknowledged, it clashes against both 'mainstream' and avant-garde style, demonstrating the failure to achieve the coherent, consistent aesthetic and narrative style that characterises the former, as well as the inability to provide the interpretive, often ironic, potential of the latter, despite its visibility.

Nevertheless, blatant attempts to pass off recycled footage as impressive, new spectacle provide viewers with an opportunity – and even a reason – to look beyond the diegesis to the film's construction. These appropriations are typically not acknowledged in badfilms, and their 'success' depends on the audience not acknowledging them either. However, when recycled footage is ineptly and inadequately integrated into new productions, it is often difficult, if not impossible, to *not* recognise the inconsistency and aesthetic disparities. Subsequently, badfilms can provide opportunities to consider the multiple failures that are likely to have contributed to this viewing position, including: failure to adequately integrate footage from multiple sources; failure to provide original spectacle; and failure to achieve aesthetic or narrative coherence.

Finally, it is also worth noting that, even when recycled footage does not encourage any significant interpretive potential, it can still provide certain cultish pleasures through its intertextuality. The repeated appearance of *One Million B.C.* in later movies, for example, unites otherwise unrelated films through their appropriation of the same film, reminding us that not only are badfilms rarely made in isolation, but they often also implicitly speak to and about Hollywood. These films attempt to replicate the style and content of 'good' (or, at least, 'better') mainstream cinema, while simultaneously hoping we will not recognise the duplication. This provides certain investigative pleasures for badfilm fans seeking to identify the source of the recycled footage, to find those connections between films and to better understand their (usually unacknowledged) place within wider film culture and history.

5. BAD ACTING AND THE CULTIFICATION OF BAD ACTORS

As we have seen in previous chapters, badfilms are characterised by incompetence and failed intentions. They are 'objectively bad' (Hoberman 1980); our identification of failure does not need to constitute a value judgement based on subjective taste. Nevertheless, once incompetence is identified, how we respond to it is necessarily subjective and, I suggest, inevitably influenced by other information available to us. We can consider the implications of this through an examination of bad acting and the potential cultification of bad actors. In general, ineptitude can be 'more confidently demonstrated than other types' of badness (MacDowell and Zborowski 2013: 17) and, for reasons discussed below, it often seems that we can be particularly confident in our identification of inept acting. However, cultification can complicate notions of 'good' and 'bad', with the latter having the potential to be re-evaluated positively as an *alternative* form of presentation.

To some extent, this seems to evoke the spectre of 'so bad it's good'. Certainly, there are similarities in the way in which bad performances, like badfilms, can be re-evaluated as good experiences – ineffective acting can be unintentionally comedic, for example. Nevertheless, objectively bad acting, supported by extra- and intertextual information, can at times be read as good, with goodness here even unironically referring to the qualities of the performance itself. Bad acting can, for example, expose the effort behind the performance and encourage a more sympathetic approach to both actor and character. Because bad acting reveals the work of acting, it has the potential to collapse the boundaries between actor and character, unintentionally encouraging us to look beyond the latter to the former. The complex interactions between actor, text, character and viewer can be further complicated by the cultification and changing reputations of certain bad actors. When this happens, distinctions between 'good' and 'bad' acting collapse. Characteristics of 'good' acting, such as authenticity and realism, can emerge through bad acting, albeit in unintended ways. The potential for objectively bad performances to be re-evaluated as 'good' poses something of a challenge to claims of 'objective badness' and draws attention to the fact that all performance – good, bad or unremarkable – may be subject to various interpretations.

This chapter examines the characteristics of bad acting, drawing on a range of textual and other evidence to propose a means of understanding subsequent cultification and re-evaluation – or lack thereof. Badfilms expose failure in multiple ways: individual elements fail, and they fail to support one another. The following analysis acknowledges the impact of other filmic failures on acting, showing, for example, how bad sound and editing can expose and exacerbate the badness of an individual's performance. Extratextual information, meanwhile, can alter our perception of otherwise 'objectively' bad acting. Pragmatically, when faced with such overwhelming incompetence, we often draw from whatever knowledge we have that might help us make sense of what we are experiencing. We rarely watch any film in isolation and should, therefore, be mindful of the ways in which our identification, interpretation and evaluation of incompetence may be influenced, either positively or negatively, by other factors.

Analysing Screen Performance

It is only relatively recently that efforts have been made within the academy to pay more attention to the work and craft of acting and screen performance. Given that movie stars are 'among the most fascinating and idolised figures in virtually any society' (Lucia and Porton 2006: 1) and star studies has a long and rich history in film studies, the lack of critical consideration for acting itself can seem surprising. There are several possible explanations for this. Historically, the actor and the work of acting have not been viewed as synonymous. As promoted by the press and the studios during Hollywood's heyday, there may be a tacit assumption that 'good' actors, and stars in particular, have an innate talent for performing. Their ability to portray an authentic, coherent and complex character – usually understood to be the primary aim of screen performance in narrative cinema – is taken to occur naturally, needing only to be supported appropriately by other formal elements such as mise-en-scène, editing and sound design.

Conversely, scholarship has traditionally tended to favour formal film techniques other than the work of film actors and the qualities of screen performance, suggesting an underlying assumption that performances are primarily constructed in the editing room, rather than by the actor on screen. It can be difficult to separate a performance from other aspects of the film, while 'objective' analyses of acting can be complicated further because 'extratextual information often colours audience responses to performance' (Baron and Carnicke 2008: 67). There are even challenges involved in delineating between actor and character; the two are 'inextricably intertwined' (Klevan 2005: 4). Rather than consider these as obstacles to conducting analyses of screen performance, however, I suggest that acknowledging the complex interactions between text, viewer, actor and character can open new possibilities for detailed examination of how they work together to develop, or limit, the potential for cultification and re-evaluation of otherwise 'objectively' bad acting.

It may appear that screen performance does not necessitate detailed analysis in the way in which other formal film elements such as sound or editing do. Lucia and Porton suggest that part of the reason why acting has received so little critical attention is due to a belief that we are 'all more or less adept at observing and emotionally deciphering the smallest physical gestures, facial expressions, body language, speech patterns, voice quavers or inflections' (2006: 1) and therefore do not need to be familiar with acting or film technique to recognise and appreciate a 'good' performance. The prevalence of discussions of screen performance in fan-authored literature supports this claim. Logically, if we accept our natural ability to identify a 'good' performance, this recognition must extend to 'bad' acting also. Acting is the focus of close to half the categories in *Son of Golden Turkey Awards* (Medved and Medved 1986), which range from the 'worst performance by Ronald Reagan' (1986: 29–37) to the 'worst performance of a Nazi mad scientist' (1986: 119–28). The Golden Raspberry Awards feature 'worst' actor and actress categories each year (see Wilson 2005), which are often directly linked to the 'worst film' nominees – this implies connections between actor, character and other formal failures that are discussed in more detail below. More recently, Michael Adams (2010) and Rob Hill (2017) have both included acting as one of the categories by which they 'rate' bad movies, with the more visible and obviously excessive bad performances often considered to contribute positively – if we might describe it as such – to the film's overall potential as a source of pleasure, entertainment or unintentional humour.

Before going further, it is worth considering what is typically meant by 'good' and 'bad' acting. Underpinning much of the literature by fans, filmmakers and scholars is an acceptance that the ultimate goal of an actor is 'to portray with all your ability and sincerity a character, a *person*, with all your heart and soul' (Wood 1998: 10; emphasis in original). The widespread, often tacit acceptance of naturalistic acting as the preferred style in American narrative cinema indicates a general belief that an actor should aim to create a fully rounded, coherent character with the same depth and complexity as any 'real' person would have. If the actor is understood to have '"become" the character' (Heath 1981: 28) and the construction of the character is invisible (Dyer 1998 [1979]: 100), then the performance is usually considered successful. Good acting is thus typically described using terms like 'believable', 'realistic', 'truthful', 'sincere' and 'authentic' (for example, Baron and Carnicke 2008: 18), while, in contrast, bad acting is often evaluated as 'wooden', 'stilted', 'hammy' or 'overacted', with judgements formed on the basic that 'the performer "was obviously acting" and was therefore unbelievable' (Heath 1981: 31). This suggests an assumption that, like continuity editing and other formal conventions associated with classical narrative cinema, the work of the actor – the construction of the character – is concealed when successful and unintentionally exposed when not.

It should be pointed out, however, that these assessments exclude the possibility that a performance may be intentionally 'visible'. Andrew Klevan suggests that 'good' performance is 'about taking full advantage of "ontological equality", synthesising with the world of the film' (2005: 5). Rather than dismissing a performance for being obvious, we can consider its appropriateness and coherence within the diegesis. Although Paul McDonald argues that intentionality is irrelevant to the study of film acting, because 'it does not matter how the details got there, only that they are there and seem significant' (2004: 32), any evaluation based on the visibility of a performance invites consideration of appropriateness, which in turn raises the spectre of intentionality once again. As I have noted previously, the vast majority of the badfilms discussed in this book appear to be aiming to replicate and conform to the standards of classical narrative cinema; it is through the acceptance of this as the intended style that many comparative claims of failure are based. *Glen or Glenda* is the most obvious exception but, even then, its pseudo-documentary format still depends on naturalistic, unobtrusive and believable screen performances to assist in its presentation of events as inspired by and reflecting the 'real' world. Anecdotal information indicates that authenticity was a motivating factor behind the casting of real transvestites as extras (Weiss, in Grey 1992: 43). Wood also reportedly found creative ways to elicit believable reactions from the cast, including redressing the set without the actor's knowledge to encourage a more realistic expression of surprise (Evelyn Wood, in Grey 1992: 46). This, as well as Wood's own writing on acting (1998), supports the notion that visible acting is not typically the intended outcome of either the performers on screen or the director overseeing the films now considered to be among the 'worst of all time'.

Screen performances do not emerge in isolation and are impacted by other filmmaking decisions. Patrick McGilligan argues that a 'great' actor needs a '"great" character [. . . and] a "great" role in a "great" script' (2006: 36–39).

Naremore proposes, meanwhile, that measuring the effect of performance is problematic because the medium 'allows for so much manipulation of the image, throwing the power of "conducting" meaning into the hands of a director' (1988: 26). For example, the excessively choppy editing in *Manos: The Hands of Fate*, discussed further in Chapter 6, does not adequately remove 'dead' time within individual shots and, in the process, fails to support already bad performances. One scene early in the film, in which the police stop to speak to a couple of teenagers making out in their car, illustrates this well. A long second passes before the shot cuts from the policeman telling them to move along, to a closeup of the unnamed girl (played by Joyce Molleur), who looks nonchalantly in the opposite direction, fluffs her hair and finally responds. Suddenly adopting an irritated expression, she gripes: 'Why don't you guys leave us alone?' She looks at the policeman, then, appearing confused, lowers her gaze, then looks back at the policeman before the shot changes again. The combination of close-up shots and awkward editing exacerbate Molleur's unconvincing performance by failing to correct her badly timed delivery and drawing attention to the artificiality of the exchange.

The actors' performances on screen are similarly impacted by other formal elements in *Manos*. The lack of synchronised sound, for instance, appears to motivate certain framing decisions that can negatively influence our understanding of, and engagement with, the performances. It can be difficult to identify the actors' expressions, for example, because they are frequently framed in ways that conceal their faces. Conversely, reaction shots are frequently prioritised over shots of characters speaking, to avoid the need to synchronise voice to moving lips (see Chapter 3), but in the process expose the actors' inability to display appropriate emotional responses. Nevertheless, we must be careful to not simply explain away all performative failure in *Manos* and elsewhere as a consequence of other filmic elements. Rather, it is possible to 'illuminate [the] actor's contribution to films by demonstrating that framing, editing, and production design do not *do all the acting* in screen performance' (Baron and Carnicke 2008: 17; emphasis in original). Molleur's awkward delivery and seemingly unmotivated facial gestures may be emphasised through the editing, for example, but the actions she has chosen to perform in this scene would be inappropriate, irrespective of how they were framed.

In general, it seems likely that the restrictive conditions in which badfilms are made will impact the actors' ability to meet the standards and expectations of 'good' acting. Conversely, it is precisely because these films were low-budget, often independently produced and usually situated within 'low' cultural forms like horror, science-fiction, pornography and exploitation, that they attracted novices, amateurs, non-unionised actors and wannabes whose talents (or lack thereof) are visible for all to see. Their acting failures are then exacerbated by incompetence elsewhere in the filmmaking process. If we accept that clever camerawork, editing and direction can make '"bad" actors appear "good"' (Heath 1981: 28), it presumably follows that the opposite is also true. Jackey Neyman-Jones, for example, recalls the lack of support offered to the cast of *Manos* and says that, as a first-time director learning on the job, Warren 'left the actors to their own devices in figuring out how to play the part [...] Hal is waiting for someone to do something and everyone else is waiting for Hal to tell them what he wanted them to do' (2012b). These must have been particularly challenging and unhelpful conditions for the actors, who would likely have benefited from more time for rehearsals, the opportunity to do more than one take and, particularly, guidance and support from more experienced colleagues. Thus, the contexts in which these films were made undoubtedly contributed to and increased the likelihood of technical and aesthetic failure across all aspects of production, including performance.

Cult Stardom, Badness and Excess

Although many actors in badfilms have little or no notable cult reputation of their own, some can be considered cult stars. When cultified actors feature in badfilms, their presence can add value beyond the more general pleasures of identifying failure. They can be a reason to find and watch films that are obscure and may be difficult to access. A cult star can also add critical cultural value to bad movies, positively affecting the films' wider reputation and status. Furthermore, cult appreciation can alter the reception and evaluation of a performance, and a more sympathetic interpretation and re-evaluation of what might objectively be considered a 'bad' performance can be enabled by drawing on a range of textual, intertextual and extratextual information. In many ways, the methods by which this re-evaluation takes place is not dissimilar to how certain badfilms become cultified as, for instance, 'so bad they're good'.

Cult stardom and 'mainstream' stardom share certain characteristics but are differentiated by others. Of course, it is possible to argue that 'all stars have developed a cult following' through their ability to provoke 'desire, adoration, identification, sometimes impersonation' (Sexton and Mathijs 2011: 76). In this sense, the cult star can be understood as an actor whose stardom is only appreciated within a relatively small subculture and who lacks 'mainstream' recognition (Hills 2013: 21). However, Hills also suggests that the processes associated with cult stardom are 'strongly linked to subcultural audience discernment, recognition and valorisation rather than marketing-led or industry/PR-related constructions' (2013: 22). Whereas 'mainstream' stardom is typically associated with a specific mode of production, whereby the star is manufactured on- and offscreen, cult stardom is more dependent on the activity of fans; it is largely constructed in reception. In part, this is because cult films, and particularly badfilms, frequently lack the industrial resources and/or motivation to cultivate stars. With the cult reputation of the badfilms discussed in this book typically not developing until several decades after their initial release, there were fewer opportunities for the actors to hone their cult credentials, even if they had recognised a benefit of doing so. Indeed, several of the actors who featured in them had died before gaining any notable cult status.

Death, perhaps 'more than any other factor, has contributed to many a cult reputation' (Sexton and Mathijs 2011: 79; see also Brottman 2000), but also has the potential to stifle or limit cult affiliation by preventing the actor from participating in their own cultification. Death alone – even an untimely one – does not guarantee cult star status. Nevertheless, when considered in tandem with other qualities associated with cult stardom, an unusual or tragic death can undoubtedly enhance an individual's cult status. Knowledge of John Reynolds' death by suicide at the age of twenty-five, a month before the premiere of *Manos*, encourages a more sympathetic re-evaluation of his sole onscreen performance as Torgo, the Master's caretaker. Torgo is a lecherous yet reasonably tragic character. He is mistreated by his Master, denied the opportunity to have a girlfriend of his own and eventually cast out from the satanic sect after having his hand burned off in punishment for insubordination. He runs away and is never mentioned again, thus offering an open-ended conclusion and inviting speculative readings of the character's fate.

Torgo, as legend goes, was originally intended to be a satyr (Brandt 1996). Onscreen, the only evidence of this is his strangely misshapen knees, the result of homemade prosthetics that appear to severely impact his ability to walk comfortably. This contributes to, but does not entirely explain Reynolds' awkward movements, which are emphasised in scenes requiring him to complete otherwise simple activities, like collecting luggage from the car boot or even just standing up. Even when not moving, he portrays Torgo as though he is constantly uneasy: it is a particularly twitchy performance, characterised by strange tics, hand gestures and staggered mannerisms. Torgo also appears to be perpetually under the influence of mind-altering substances: this is not acknowledged within the text itself, but anecdotal information confirms that Reynolds was using drugs prior to and throughout filming (Brandt 1996; Neyman-Jones 2012b). The distinction between character and actor thus collapses; we watch Torgo but appear to also gain an insight into Reynolds' mental state. Whether the character is considered authentic, believable, coherent or realistic becomes less relevant than this perceived insight into the actor himself. By failing to fully embody the character, the performance – and the performer – is exposed. Reynolds' cult reputation, therefore, is based on a combination of various textual and extratextual elements that work together to construct an overwhelmingly sympathetic reappraisal of an otherwise bad performance. Such is the strength of his reputation that an (unsuccessful) campaign took place in the 1990s to get him a star on the Hollywood Walk of Fame in recognition of his only onscreen appearance.

Although these observations suggest that cult is 'inescapably part of the discourse of reception studies', it is still pertinent to see 'if it is possible to find textual evidence for cult affiliation' (Smith 2013: 109). As Smith and others (for example, Sexton and Mathijs 2011: 82–84) have noted, certain performance traits can be identified as likely contributors to the development of an actor's cult star status. These are often linked to claims of visibility and quality – or lack thereof. Steven Rawle suggests that cult performers can be distinguished from non-cult performers by their 'transgression of performance norms, of realism, or simply of notions of "goodness"' (2013: 127). Cult stars, he argues, demonstrate what he calls 'idiolect', an 'identifiable collection of physical and vocal performance traits that are defined and [. . .] appropriable, imitable, ironic, or excessive' (2013: 127). This is also applicable to the cultification of badfilms themselves; as Sconce notes, it is through the excessive visibility of cinematic failure that the paracinematic audience can foreground 'structures of cinematic discourse and artifice so that the material identity of the film ceases to be a structure made invisible in service of the diegesis, but becomes instead the primary focus of textual attention' (1995: 386).

In terms of performance, therefore, the visibility of bad acting can, on occasion, help badfilm fans identify certain characteristics that encourage cult affiliation and sympathetic re-evaluation. Cult stars are appreciated in this way for their apparent distinctions, notably 'special commitment [and] excessive charisma' (Nicanor Loreti, quoted in Hills 2013: 24), and they 'tend to represent narratives of graft and entrepreneurial spirit – having to take the work that's going' (Hills 2013: 26). It is not just the visibility of a bad performance that can encourage cult reputations, but also the effort that such visibility seemingly exposes. The reappraisal of an actor's seemingly bad performance is particularly likely when its badness suggests effort disproportionate to the role being portrayed. Just as some bad filmmakers are viewed sympathetically because of their apparent determination to complete their film against all odds, irrespective of the many limitations and challenges they face (for example, Sconce 1995; Juno and Vale 1986; Hoberman 1980), certain performances seem to elicit sympathy and appreciation for similar reasons. Excessively bad acting can reveal the actor's attempt to construct a character, however inept or ineffective the result, and the visibility of the effort itself can encourage an alternative approach to evaluation.

From Bad to Good: Cultifying the 'Has-Been'

Several badfilm actors once enjoyed relatively substantial mainstream success but, in later years, found that their star reputation had faded. These are the 'has-beens' (Weldon 1983: xii; Brottman 2000: 109); typically, older stars who are 'past their prime'. The ability to recruit former stars such as John Carradine, Lon Chaney Jr, J. Carroll Naish and Boris Karloff could be considered casting coups for independent filmmakers such as Wood or Al Adamson. The inclusion of a star – a recognisable name to include in promotional material – can draw audiences, in part, because they imply above-average production values and a certain standard of entertainment (see Dyer 1998 [1979]: 11). The involvement of a has-been certainly adds cultural value to a badfilm, providing a further reason to watch and re-watch, while also potentially making the film itself more visible beyond bad movie subcultures. By constituting part of the actor's wider filmography, and sometimes even gaining significance as the 'last' appearance of a faded star, these badfilms become part of wider cinematic canons. For the has-beens, however, their appearance in badfilms can draw attention to their age and declining health, as well as the uncomfortable realities of the downward trajectory of their career. This can create tensions between their original star image and their current position within the industry and serves as a bittersweet reminder that even stars are, ultimately, human.

Independent, low-budget films in the 1950s and 1960s offered a refuge for actors who had previously enjoyed some degree of success but, for any variety of reasons, now found that they had fallen out of favour with the more 'legitimate' film production outfits. These conditions encourage cult affiliation; stars can develop cult reputations 'after they have faded from the mainstream' (Sexton and Mathijs 2011: 81). Of course, the extent of their 'mainstream' visibility varies. Some of Ed Wood's regular collaborators, such as Lyle Talbot and Kenne Duncan, had long, successful careers prior to their involvement with Wood, but are more accurately described as character actors than major stars. Whereas contemporaneous audiences may well have recognised them, any recognition today is likely limited to cult viewers who primarily know them through their association with Wood.

It is perhaps unsurprising that the has-been is often subject to more sympathetic evaluations than the unknown actors, or even the films in which they appear. Such readings are encouraged by the wealth of extratextual information and the intertextual potential that open up due to a more accessible back-catalogue of films with which to draw comparisons. Extratextual information can help to transform a has-been's objectively bad performance into a subjectively 'good' one. Note that 'good' here does not necessarily refer to all the criteria for good acting as they are typically understood. The performance may still appear to be inappropriately visible, drawing unwarranted attention to the work of acting, but can work to construct a more direct relationship between viewer and actor. The informed viewer may be able to also identify moments of perceived honesty, truth and authenticity within and beyond the performance. Through a combination of textual and extratextual factors, performances that expose the (failed) attempt to embody a character can be understood to also expose the 'truth' of the actor's graft and effort.

The has-been offers potential for a deeper understanding of both the actor and the conditions under which their performances are produced, but the performances themselves tend to encourage sympathetic readings, particularly when the actor's hardship and continued professionalism is evident. David Konow, for example, acknowledges that 'many horror actors on their last legs *still gave it all they had, even if it was for low-budget films*' (1998: 78; emphasis added) and recalls an anecdote about Karloff on the set of one of his final films, in which the actor 'was bound to a wheelchair and needed a respirator but when the director called, "Action!" he willed himself out of the chair, hit his mark and said his lines' (1998: 78). Similarly, Sam Sherman remembers Chaney Jr on the set of *Dracula Vs Frankenstein* (Adamson 1971). Chaney, suffering from advanced throat cancer, played the role of a mute henchman and was 'constantly tired [. . . and] had to lie down between takes [. . .] he knew he was dying and he wanted to die'. Sherman acknowledges that these were 'not the elements that make for great acting in a movie! And yet [. . .] he did bring pathos to the character' (Sherman, in Konow 1998: 77). Thus, extratextual information can be used as a way of understanding the performance, looking beyond the character to the actor instead. As Sherman's comments suggest, success or failure is evaluated less based on whether the actor embodies the character, but on the perceived evidence of the actor's graft, effort and dedication to the craft, despite the obstacles in their way. By drawing attention to the work of acting and the context in which the performance was produced, the distinction between actor and character collapses, and both are approached with a certain degree of sympathy that is not often extended to the film itself.

'I WILL SHOW THE WORLD THAT I CAN BE ITS MASTER!': BELA LUGOSI, CULT STAR

Cult stardom, like 'mainstream' stardom, involves a duality between actor and character and invites certain extra- and intertextual possibilities. Bela Lugosi's collaborations with Ed Wood offer a means to explore the implications of this further. In particular, Lugosi's role in *Bride of the Monster* provides an opportunity to investigate the re-evaluation of a 'bad' performance through the acknowledgement of star reputation, revealing how his often inappropriately excessive, visible style of acting can be read positively as evidence of the actor's effort and sincerity. Director and co-writer Wood consciously evokes the spectre of Lugosi's previous roles, encouraging intertextual readings that, in the process, draw attention to his leading actor's physical frailty and age. This does not appear to be the intended outcome: the film, and Lugosi's role in it, both suggest a lack of adequate acknowledgement of the time that has passed since the star's heyday. For the informed viewer drawing on exegetic material to inform their interpretation, however, connections can be made between the actor's offscreen hardships and the character's onscreen presentation.

Bride of the Monster occupies an interesting position in the wider badfilm canon: although a shoddy picture, it is nevertheless one of Wood's more competent films – not good, necessarily, but comparatively better than others. Rodney Hill suggests, for example, that it 'bears few remarkable qualities, aside from the star presence of Bela Lugosi' (2015: 181). Lugosi features in two of Wood's other films, *Glen or Glenda* and *Plan 9*, and it is notable that the three films in which the actor and filmmaker collaborate are both Wood's best-known works and his most notoriously bad movies. However, *Bride* lacks the excessive incompetence and general 'weirdness' of the other two and, comparatively, can appear relatively conventional. Nevertheless, I suggest technical incompetence is on display throughout the film, such as poorly integrated recycled footage, the entirely unconvincing giant octopus prop and the stilted dialogue that so often epitomises a Wood-authored script. Notably, the film's failings were identified at the time of release, with critics deriding it as 'singularly crude and tasteless [. . .] horror fiction at its lowest level' (Anonymous author 1956: 75). It is interesting, however, that Hill explicitly identifies Lugosi's presence, suggesting that the actor's reputation – cult or otherwise – is such that it adds value to an otherwise seemingly unremarkable movie. Indeed, even in 1955, critics speculated that 'the only conceivable reason for production is the Bela Lugosi name in the horror market', while also decrying the actor's performance as 'histrionics [. . .] reduced to the ridiculous through over-direction' (Whit 1955: 22).

Bride follows a fairly typical 'mad scientist' narrative, with Lugosi playing Dr Vornoff, a man exiled from Europe and now living in America where he continues his atomic experiments in secret. The film works as an homage to the horror films of the 1930s that Wood watched when growing up. This rather positive description, however, perhaps reveals my subjective appreciation here; the film could just as easily be disparagingly referred to as a cheap imitation, arriving two decades after the genre had fallen out of favour. *Variety*'s contemporaneous review, for instance, describes it as a 're-hashed version of a story that was old-hat years ago' (Whit 1955: 22). Hill's suggestion that *Bride* appears to be an effort to 'recreate the kind of motion picture that might have starred Lugosi twenty years earlier' (2015: 180), meanwhile, evokes ideas of the film as a star vehicle. Lugosi had enjoyed critical and commercial success when making films for Universal in the 1930s but – limited by a thick accent and hampered by a series of poor management choices, financial difficulties and a debilitating addiction to methadone – his career moved from the major studios to Poverty Row and, eventually, the independents and Ed Wood. Although prolific in the final decades of his life, Lugosi had little opportunity to demonstrate any range or scope with the roles he was offered. He became known for his 'strange mannerisms [. . .] that were regarded as perfect for his performance of Dracula, but soon came to be seen as artificial, repetitive and affected in other roles' (Jancovich and Brown 2013: 254). Towards the later part of his career, Lugosi was increasingly associated with a 'form of camp of which critics were highly critical' (2013: 245). Typecasting encouraged repetitive performances that negatively affected how Lugosi was viewed as an actor.

Although Dr Vornoff was allegedly written specifically for Lugosi (Wood, quoted in Grey 1992: 67), it offered little opportunity for the actor to expand his range and instead works to reinforce his existing (faded) star persona. To paraphrase Umberto Eco (1985 [1984]: 10), Vornoff is not *one character*, but Lugosi's *characters*. This is the actor's final speaking role and, for the informed reader, carries with it some degree of déjà vu. A mad scientist whose henchman Lobo (played by former wrestler Tor Johnson) ultimately causes his demise, Vornoff appears to have psychic and hypnotic abilities that, illogically, work whether his victim is present or not. This serves as an homage to – or imitation of – Lugosi's previous role as voodoo master Murder Legendre in *White Zombie* (Halperin 1932), although the attempted synthesis of science and the supernatural clashes uncomfortably. Certain formal techniques are also exploited so as to encourage viewers to recall Lugosi's earlier roles: the repeated focus on Lugosi's eyes and hands are reminiscent of his performance as Dracula, but this had already been rendered ineffective through repetition by the 1940s and was largely ridiculed by critics (Jancovich and Brown 2013: 254). It appears that Wood's efforts to remind viewers of his leading man's star reputation through formal devices were misguided, as they merely drew attention to those qualities of Lugosi's performance that were subject to criticism, not praise.

Lugosi's posthumous cult star reputation, however, has developed largely because of, not despite, the contemporaneous criticisms. Typecasting has enabled more comparative, intertextual evaluations of his performance, while his 'hammy' acting is now celebrated not as a failure but as an '*alternative* form of acting that contains more personality than many more respectable performances' (Sexton and Mathijs 2011: 82; emphasis in original). Even the way in which his work ethic is understood has shifted dramatically. Whereas critics in the 1930s and 1940s 'condemned' Lugosi in part for his apparent disdain for the films he appeared in (Jancovich and Brown 2013: 254), now he is praised for his dedication, consummate professionalism and graft. Bill Warren's comments typify how Lugosi is written about today. He uses extratextual information to explain and implicitly justify the actor's appearance in 'truly dreadful' Ed Wood movies (2010: 136). Lugosi's unconventional acting is acknowledged positively by Warren, who also praises his work ethic: his 'rich, sometimes ripe, performances were for years wasted on shoddy films' (2010: 135) and, irrespective of the film's quality, he 'gives his all, of course' (2010: 136). This revisionist approach indicates not only how an actor's reputation can change significantly over time, but also highlights the inherent subjectivity of performance evaluation, whereby motivated fans draw on a range of textual, intertextual and extratextual evidence to support their positive interpretation.

Physically, Lugosi in *Bride of the Monster* is a shadow of his former self, a fact made painfully clear in the film itself. In a moment that entirely collapses the distinction between actor and character, several of Lugosi's publicity photos feature as part of a dossier supposedly collected on Vornoff. This allows for comparison between the actor at the peak of his career and physical health, and now, irrespective of the viewer's knowledge of his previous movies. Aged seventy-two at the time of filming, Lugosi entered rehab shortly after shooting completed. His age and gaunt appearance are obvious, but not supported by the script. Vornoff is presented as strong, powerful and virile: for example, he expresses sexual interest in Janet, a woman many years his junior. His response to Lobo's disobedience, meanwhile, invites the viewer to identify him as an imposing presence despite his obvious physical weakness. Lobo is a far more visually impressive character, but appears fearful of Vornoff, who cows him into submission through violence. However, while it might initially appear that Lugosi's portrayal of Vornoff is inappropriate due to the failure to acknowledge the actor's (and, by extension, character's) visible physical limitations, the informed viewer can look beyond the character and, seemingly, gain insight into Lugosi's mental state at the time. Wood recalls Lugosi having a conversation with a fan after a screening of *Bride* in which he said, 'I'm 71 [sic], but the brain, the brain, it never feels that you're old. Only the body looks old, but never the brain. The brain is young, then the body is still young, like a young man' (quoted in Grey 1992: 72). Thus, rather than deride Lugosi's overly exuberant performance in *Bride* as evidence of his 'hammy' (bad) acting, it can be celebrated as evidence of the actor's unwillingness to conform to societal expectations of old age.

Certain moments in *Bride of the Monster* can be positively interpreted as signifiers of the actor's life, rather than of the character. In particular, a monologue delivered by Vornoff during a conversation with his former colleague Professor Strowski (George Becwar) gains new significance in the context of Lugosi's life and has subsequently become one of the most iconic scenes in the film. The dialogue in this scene seems pertinent to both actor and character, enabling the informed viewer to make positive connections between Lugosi's onscreen performance and his offscreen life. Hence, the performance takes on new meaning and can be re-evaluated, with emphasis placed on Lugosi's apparent sincerity and authenticity. He might not necessarily embody the character in a way that makes the acting 'invisible' but nonetheless seems to

Figure 5.1 Publicity shot of Bela Lugosi featured in *Bride of the Monster* (Wood, Jr, 1955).

authentically embody the emotion motivating the character at certain points. In moments like these, Lugosi's performance can thus be appreciated, not for its perceived incompetence, but because of the 'genuine pathos' (Adams 2010: 64) that it inspires.

The scene in question sees the men sitting opposite each other in comfortable chairs beside the fireplace, with the setting and framing suggesting a cosy domestic space. Symmetry in the mise-en-scène emphasises the contrast between the actors' depiction of their characters. Becwar's performance is animated: he moves his hands, leans forward in his chair, bows and raises his head. Perhaps surprisingly, given his reputation for overacting, Lugosi remains almost entirely motionless throughout the exchange. Vornoff is dressed in loose black clothing that mostly conceals the actor's gaunt frame and draws attention to the few parts of his body – his hands and face – that can be seen. The minimalist mise-en-scène, use of close-ups and lack of physical movement offers little to distract from Lugosi's exaggerated, overly emphatic performance, encouraging us to focus on him and him alone. Vornoff remains still as Strowski begins to explain his reason for visiting but reacts defensively to the reminder of his former life, asserting that, despite being exiled from his homeland and classed as a 'madman, a charlatan, outlawed in a world of science', he is now 'all right'. Listening intently, Strowski explains that their government now wants Vornoff to return home to Europe. Lugosi's expression changes to one of surprise. Raising his eyebrows in response, he begins to speak. 'Home?' he asks, before lowering his head and shaking it gently as a poignant musical score is introduced. Lifting his head, he blinks as though on the verge of tears and says: 'I have no home. Hunted. Despised. Living like an

Figure 5.2   Dr Vornoff declaring his intentions to 'conquer the world', *Bride of the Monster* (Wood, Jr, 1955).

animal!' Clenching his fist in his lap, he becomes more animated and defiant, raising his voice as he declares: 'The jungle is my home. But I will show the world that I can be its master! I will perfect my own race of people. A race of atomic supermen which will conquer the world!' Punctuating his final claim, Lugosi raises his clenched fists to the sky before lowering them to rest casually on the chair's armrests, his face lighting up in a self-satisfied smile.

Lugosi's performance is notably visible here: he delivers the absurd dialogue in an overstated manner, emphasising certain words in the speech and emphasising claims with exaggerated, dramatic facial expressions that contrast with Becwar's more neutral, naturalistic performance. Visibility often implies inappropriateness, which in turn suggests badness. The scene, however, can be positively interpreted in relation to Lugosi's life, allowing for a more positive re-evaluation of his 'objectively' hammy acting through identification of the actor's sincerity and authenticity. This reading is supported by extratextual information. By this stage, Lugosi had suffered a major decline in his career and health and had been almost entirely abandoned by the 'mainstream' film industry. For example, actor Paul Marco recalls that, when attempts were made to use *Bride*'s premiere to raise money for Lugosi's medical treatment, not even Universal was willing to donate (quoted in Weaver 1988: 254). For the informed viewer, therefore, this scene seems to reveal a personal truth: Lugosi mourning the loss of his 'home' in the industry, then defiantly informing those who had rejected him that he, like Vornoff, is 'all right'. In this way, the cult actor's onscreen persona becomes an extension of his actual life (Sexton and Mathijs 2011: 84), and we have an opportunity to look beyond the character to recognise a 'truth' about the actor. As a has-been, a faded star, Lugosi's animated performance serves as a reminder of the qualities that were once lauded, with the emotional transition from sadness and self-pity to confidence and defiance seeming to be a sincere reflection of Lugosi's own outlook on life. Despite being cast out by Hollywood, he continued working until his death in 1956.

Using *Bride* as evidence, we can consider the extent to which the qualities of Lugosi's performance support his posthumous status as a cult star. It is quite easy to empathise with Vornoff, despite his villainy, because of Lugosi's charismatic, dynamic portrayal of the character. Lugosi imbues Vornoff with life and vitality through his exaggerated, expressive performance. While this clashes somewhat with his obvious physical frailty, the contrast can be read as a positive, admirable character trait while simultaneously inviting us to look beyond the frame to the actor himself. Lugosi's enthusiastic performance indicates effort, which in turn appears to confirm the romantic idea of the actor as a consummate professional, putting everything into the role and treating it with a degree of dignity and respect that one might not expect from a former star now appearing in a film of such obviously poor quality.

It should be noted, however, that not all bad performance can be re-evaluated in such positive terms. Indeed, even in *Bride* certain moments can present a challenge to this form of positive appropriation. Whereas scenes like the one discussed above suggest a synthesis between character and actor, others seem to expose a disconnect. For example, although the film's climax sees Vornoff subjected to his own experiments and transformed into an 'atomic superman', thereafter he is presented as vulnerable, confused and passive. Lugosi's performance in the film's conclusion is inappropriate and unsupported by other formal elements, such as framing and editing that all draw attention to his failure to embody the character's newfound strength and power. His visible, hammy acting is harder to re-evaluate here: were we to read Lugosi's performance in the film's conclusion as evidence of his life, it would only reveal the weakness and confusion of a frail old man. Unsurprisingly, moments like these tend to go unmentioned in fan-authored analyses.

All of this raises a paradox of certain forms of cult performance: on the one hand, it is entirely possible to describe Lugosi's performance in *Bride* in negative ways, pointing to its frequently inappropriate visibility, his theatrical, exaggerated reactions and 'hammy' style. On the other hand, however, it is equally possible to identify moments in which the performance nonetheless seems to *also* be truthful, authentic, sincere and believable. These are all descriptors of 'good' acting, although they reveal themselves in different ways. A bad performance can be 'authentic' precisely because it reveals the work of acting – it allows us to look beyond the character to the actor, and to recognise their sincerity and effort. This latter approach is made possible primarily through an interpretive framework that combines textual, intertextual and extratextual evidence to collapse the distinction between actor and character and construct a cult star instead. Significantly, positive evaluation does not negate identification of badness, but works alongside it: Lugosi's performance is objectively bad, because it is inappropriately visible, *and* it is good, because its inappropriate visibility reveals authenticity in unintended ways.

'She Couldn't Even Scream and Make It Convincing': Bad Actors in Cult Movies

With regard to the films discussed in this book, arguably only a small proportion of the people who appear in front of the camera have developed any notable cult reputation, and fewer still could be appropriately or productively labelled as cult stars. Although the relatively recent academic interest is welcome for 'bringing discussions of film acting, performance and the self-representation and construction of films stars' personae into the field of cult film studies' (Egan and Thomas 2013: 5), approaching acting through the lens of stardom risks excluding analysis of the performance qualities of those who appear in cult films but, through a lack of visibility or appropriation, cannot be considered cult stars.

Badfilms of the 1950s and 1960s are filled with unknowns: people whose acting 'career' is limited to a single performance or, possibly, a handful of films that may be obscure and difficult to access. These unknowns tend to comprise actors who lacked the talent, longevity or industrial connections to establish any notable reputation or cult affiliation, and whose performance style is perfunctory at best, but not necessarily excessively and visibly bad enough to be distinctive or memorable. On occasion, the films themselves further ensure this anonymity. Most of the characters in *Monster A-go Go*, for example, cannot be attributed to any specific actors because the film's credits are incomplete. The cast of the prehistoric sexploitation film *One Million AC/DC* are listed on IMDb, but they also remain effectively anonymous, because so few have specific roles attributed to them. Alternatively, actors may choose to use pseudonyms, or may be deliberately omitted from the credits due to the kind of role they are required to fulfil. Tom Mason is not listed in *Plan 9*'s credits, for example, despite his frequent (and highly visible) appearances as a body double for Lugosi. Despite the substitution being entirely unconvincing – Mason is taller and far younger than Lugosi – his name is omitted from the credits in an attempt to conceal his onscreen contribution.

All bad acting exposes the artificiality of the character and the work of acting, but this visibility does not inevitably result in the re-appraisal of performance that cultification encourages. As we have seen in the case of Lugosi above, performances that reveal some form of excessive badness – usually identified as over-acting, exaggeration and 'hammy' or 'camp' style – are more likely to be re-interpreted in sympathetic ways because they appear to indicate effort.

In contrast, performances that seem to expose a lack of effort are harder to re-evaluate in sympathetic ways and tend to receive more criticism. Although these 'flat' performances reveal the actors' failure to embody a character in ways that are just as obvious as those seen in 'hammy' performances, they rarely invite the same kind of positive interpretation.

However, it is also important to consider other information that we might use to inform our interpretation of a performance or group of performances. Generally, the lower the cultural value of the films, the less information – from full cast lists to production notes and any other extraneous material – is likely to be available. Thus, extratextual and intertextual information have a significant impact on the way in which a viewer might recognise, receive and respond to a performance. For instance, we can confirm Mason's involvement in *Plan 9*, not just through the visual disparities within the text, but also through the copious exegetic material surrounding the film, including the contributions from his widow, Margaret Mason, in Grey's biography on Ed Wood (1992). We can also locate him in another Wood film, *Night of the Ghouls*, where he is credited. Although these two minor roles in two unsuccessful films barely qualify him as a cult star, they do allow for some cult affiliation that is less easily established when there is a lack of adequate information. Accepting, therefore, the premise that 'textual evidence of cult performance may be seen, in part, to [be] determined by extra-textual factors' (Smith 2013: 109), we can examine how, or if, cult reputation can develop *without* extratextual information or knowledge of other factors that could assist in re-evaluating or appropriating a bad performance. The question then becomes: can bad actors develop cult reputations when viewers must base their appraisal primarily, or even exclusively, on the text itself?

With this in mind, *Orgy of the Dead* (Apostolof as AC Stephens, 1965) offers a useful case-study. It certainly has the credentials to qualify as both a badfilm and a (relatively minor) cult movie. The incompetence and cheapness of this 'bargain-basement striptease show masquerading as a movie' (Wilson 2005: 264) is evident throughout, from the discontinuity between day and night shots in the post-credits sequence, to the artificial cemetery set, to the awkward dialogue and the absurd addition of a Wolfman and Mummy, who are apparently intended as some form of light comic relief. Much of its reputation arguably stems from its status as an 'Ed Wood film' (see Bartlett 2019b), due to his involvement as screenwriter. There is, however, limited information available regarding the film's production context or its on-screen 'talent' beyond some brief anecdotes in Rudolph Grey's biography of Ed Wood (1992: 129–30). Although it appears that most of the actors who appear in *Orgy* also featured in a handful of other, lesser-known sexploitation movies, the quantity and quality of biographical information about them which could be used productively to inform interpretations of their performances is negligible. Any cult reputations that do develop, therefore, can be judged to be based on, at most, a combined evaluation of actor and character.

As the female protagonist in *Orgy of the Dead*, Pat Barringer (listed as Pat Barrington) might appear to be one of the more likely candidates for cultification, if such a status could be achieved by bad acting alone. She makes her film debut here, playing two characters – one disguised by a blond wig and gold body paint – and this remains her best-known performance. This, however, is less because of her specifically than the film's minor cult status through its connection to Wood. Little is known about Barringer. According to her co-star John Andrews, she 'thought she was going to be a big fucking star. And she couldn't even scream and make it convincing. She couldn't do shit' (quoted in Grey 1992: 129). The stardom she allegedly believed she deserved never arrived. Instead, she toiled on the sexploitation circuit for four years before returning to her previous life as an exotic dancer and model. Although it is not possible to confirm or deny Andrew's claim regarding Barringer's career aspirations, his assessment of her acting is supported by filmic evidence and may seem to suggest a lack of effort on her part. This, in tandem with an absence of extratextual information, works to limit the potential for cultification, despite the visible, overwhelming failure of her performance.

Barringer plays Shirley, whose boyfriend Bob (William Bates) is seeking inspiration for his latest horror novel. After a car accident, the pair find themselves in an old cemetery, where dead women are being resurrected to dance for the sexual gratification of the Emperor (Criswell), leader of the undead. The film's narrative content is particularly sparse, serving primarily to offer justification – however tenuous – for the lengthy, tedious dance sequences that make up about half of the film's ninety-minute runtime. After the couple are captured by the Wolfman (John Andrews) and the Mummy (Louis Ojena), they spend the remainder of the film tied to posts and forced to watch the dancers. This results in an odd, and oddly invisible, situation in which Barringer-as-Shirley watches herself perform one of the routines, the Gold Dance.

As Shirley, Barringer's role primarily requires her to convey fear in response to her surroundings, and to squabble with Bob, whom she blames for their predicament. She is demonstrably incapable of accomplishing either to any satisfactory degree. Her performance is often characterised by inertia. While 'good' actors tend to invent actions or business even when the script does not explicitly require it (Naremore 1988: 42–43), Barringer's lack of action when she is visible in the background, for example, suggests she only 'activates' her performance when it is necessitated by the camera's gaze on her specifically. Even then, her attempts to portray emotion are never believable. She is wooden throughout and frequently misses her cues. As Andrews notes, Barringer's screams are particularly unconvincing – although given his equally ludicrous and misjudged werewolf howls, he might be better served assessing

Figure 5.3   Shirley (Pat Barringer) screaming, *Orgy of the Dead* (Apostolof, 1965).

his own acting ability, or lack thereof. When the Emperor acknowledges the Wolfman's apparent interest in Shirley, Barringer screams in response – a high-pitched shriek that lacks any emotional authenticity. Moments later, when the Emperor suggests she might become a 'reward' for the Wolfman and Mummy, her second scream is so similar to the first that it could be mistaken for a repeated shot. Repetition confirms what is already so apparent: these are clearly not expressions of genuine terror. Further compounding the lack of believable emotion in her performance, elsewhere in the film – including the shots preceding and following her screams – she frequently appears bored and detached. Despite stating on several occasions that she is 'frightened', there is rarely any sense of underlying emotion motivating her dialogue or physical gestures. It is all too easy to interpret this negatively as a lack of effort, as evidence that she is simply 'going through the motions' by doing the bare minimum.

Barringer regularly reveals her acting limitations, but other formal aspects of *Orgy* also contribute to, and exacerbate, her demonstrable failure. Wood's screenplay, for example, provides scant material for her to work with. Shirley is constructed as helpless and passive, simultaneously blaming Bob for the situation in which they find themselves and relying on him to get them out of it. The character's emotional responses are illogical and incoherent. In a single exchange with Bob, for example, Shirley vocalises concern, then fear, then informs her boyfriend that she hates him. There is no immediate motivation behind these fluctuating emotions, while Barringer's indifferent performance ensures the transition is even more difficult to understand. Elsewhere, dialogue actively undermines her performance. After the couple have been captured and tied up, they discuss their predicament. As Shirley stands, staring impassively,

Bob urges her to stay calm, noting that 'panic won't do us any good'. Later, he tells her not to change her expression 'too much' so that their captors will not notice his escape attempts. The advice is patently unnecessary, given Shirley's perpetually blank expression, but the irony seems unintended – the accidental consequence of a script that mistakenly assumes a minimum of competency from the actors.

Barringer has more opportunities to (fail to) demonstrate her acting ability than most of the other women who feature in *Orgy of the Dead*. Although women appear onscreen for the majority of the film's runtime, they serve primarily as visual pleasure (Mulvey 1975) clearly intended for a primarily male audience. Ten dance routines occur, each vaguely themed around some aspect of the resurrected women's lives. Characterisation is entirely dependent on costuming, some rudimentary props and the briefest of introductions by either the Emperor or his sidekick, the Black Ghoul (Fawn Silver); the dancers themselves have no opportunity to portray their apparently tragic characters with any depth whatsoever. The credits – which list the roles as 'Skeleton *Dance*', 'Hawaiian *Dance*' and so on – explicitly prioritise the performances as spectacle, indicating the insignificance of these women as actors or characters. Additionally, their routines are regularly undermined by other formal incompetence. The women's heads are regularly cut out of the frame, for example, while at other times the camera's gaze drifts away, focusing instead on inanimate props like a skull in the Dance of Skulls. The smoke machines, used excessively throughout, frequently obscure the dancers during their routines, at times completely concealing them from view.

Accepting McGilligan's claim that actors require, in part, good scripts and roles in order to be good themselves, it appears that the most these women can hope to achieve is to provide erotic spectacle. Although formal decisions outside the actors' control do not support the performances in *Orgy*, if eroticism is the intended result – as the film strongly suggests it is – these women fail utterly and completely, independent of other technical failures. Indeed, demonstrable incompetence elsewhere in the film, such as preposterous dialogue and the Wolfman's and Mummy's ridiculously cheap costumes, can serve as a welcome distraction from the tedium. Rob Craig asserts *Orgy* 'falters miserably as narrative melodrama, *and also fails* as prurient erotica' (2009: 217; emphasis added), while Michael Adams describes it as 'borelesque' (2010: 69), directly correlating badness (being boring) with the film's presentation of erotic spectacle (burlesque). The dance routines, lacking any notable choreography, are dull, repetitive and uninteresting. They are often awkwardly, self-consciously delivered, suggesting a dual lack of effort and ability; the women seem ambivalent about the quality of their performance. The badness of the dancing is further emphasised by cutaways to the male characters, who invariably appear either apathetic or disgusted. If even the

Emperor and Bob – two apparently virile, heterosexual men – are unimpressed, who are we to disagree?

Orgy of the Dead's status as a badfilm is, of course, not contingent on any single failure, but the demonstrably bad acting is undoubtedly a significant contributing factor. However, with one notable exception (discussed below), the vast majority of the people responsible for the obviously inept performances have not been cultified in the way in which the film has. In this sense, they have failed not only to fulfil their onscreen responsibilities effectively, but also to evince the kind of performative badness that might encourage re-evaluation. While the performers' bad acting is evidence of the failure that has led to the film's cultification, at the same time the failed erotic spectacle for which they are responsible is simply boring, limiting *Orgy*'s instrumental and alternative potential as an object of fun. Their inept, seemingly half-hearted efforts are monotonous and tedious, inducing a kind of stasis as we are left waiting for something – anything, good or bad – to break the boredom and potentially entertain us again. Indeed, a 'fan's cut' of *Orgy* (available on YouTube at the time of writing) has removed the lengthy striptease sequences, reducing the film to about half its original runtime and, arguably, increasing its watchability by at least that. Consequently, however, the dancers have also been entirely excised and denied the opportunity for evaluation in *any* form.

Notably, the lack of extratextual information about *Orgy*'s actors further limits the potential to re-evaluate their performances by identifying, for example, biographical or other offscreen insights. Although the acting is visibly, demonstrably bad and draws attention to the work of acting, it lacks the qualities or supporting evidence that might enable a closer relationship to be forged between actor, character and viewer. If we knew something about these women – their lives, their potential hardships, their (failed) aspirations – perhaps we would be able to identify some unintended 'truth' within their performances. Conversely, maybe it would simply confirm Andrews' remark about Barringer's career aspirations and expose an unattractive mix of arrogance, self-entitlement and delusion. Certainly, the lack of effort suggested – rightly or wrongly – by her wooden performance could support such a reading. Nevertheless, the point is that this can *only ever be* speculative because we do not have the resources to support any reading that attempts to look past the character to the actor.

Appearing in a cult film, therefore, does not guarantee cult status. Cult films can work with and without cult stars (Hills 2013: 34); one does not necessitate or require the other. As Peary implies when he distinguishes between 'cult movie stars (and stars of cult movies)' (1991: 15), however, there is a certain amount of subcultural visibility that is gained by featuring onscreen in a film that subsequently develops a cult reputation. Yet, this is negligible for the majority of actors who appear in badfilms. Most do not fit either of Peary's categories – they feature in badfilms, but they are not 'stars' in any sense of the word. As the previous discussion of John Reynold's reputation indicates, an actor requires neither a leading role nor a lengthy career to be appropriated as a cult star. Rather, it appears that this cultification is more predicated on their ability to evince a memorable (and, preferably, memorably weird) performance and our ability to relate this, somehow, to some aspect of their offscreen life. These conditions simply do not exist for many badfilm actors.

'I Am Criswell': Cult Actors, Stars, Personalities?

In contrast to the other actors who feature in *Orgy of the Dead* – and who benefit from more screen-time – only one has any notable cult reputation separate from their performance in this film. Hack radio psychic and regular Wood collaborator Criswell receives top billing as the Emperor. *Orgy* begins with him rising from a coffin to repeat the introductory monologue from *Night of the Ghouls* almost verbatim, indicating one of the ways in which Criswell's role invites intertextual readings (see Bartlett 2019b). He also introduces himself as Criswell, despite being billed as the Emperor and being cast in an otherwise conventional character role. In this way, the distinction between actor and character collapses and is further complicated by Criswell also being a stage persona, writer and showman; it is unclear where the line is between Criswell-the-character and Jeron Criswell King, the man behind the character.

Criswell enjoyed a certain level of fame while alive, due to his outlandish predictions about the future and his various media appearances, but his cult status following his death in 1982 was solidified through his work with Ed Wood. He is by no means a 'star' in the traditional sense, having appeared in only three films, none of which received favourable reviews or notable box office receipts. In *Plan 9 From Outer Space*, he appears in the pre- and post-credits sequences, where he explicitly replicates the 'Criswell predicts' segment of the television show he presented on a local Los Angeles station, playing a semi-diegetic, semi-omniscient narrator and uttering the now-infamous opening lines that originated on his television show but have since become permanently and irrevocably linked to cult's most notorious bad movie: 'Greetings, my friend. We are all interested in the future, for that is where you and I are going to spend the rest of our lives'. Although it is obvious that he is reading his lines, this is somewhat acceptable in *Plan 9* because they are delivered in the style of a news anchor. In *Ghouls* and *Orgy of the Dead*, Criswell's dependence on cue cards is far more distracting, serving as a constant reminder that the characters he is portraying have not emerged 'naturally' but are constructed. Criswell's utter failure to meet even the most basic requirements of an actor – to remember and deliver his lines independently – exposes the work of acting, as well as his inability to complete that work to any appropriate standard.

Criswell's film appearances have ensured his cult star status, immortalising on screen his flamboyant appearance and the distinctive, authoritative yet strangely flat intonation of absurdly convoluted and poorly written statements. He delivers his lines with the flair of a radio presenter, while being seemingly incapable of supporting his vocal performance with appropriate physical gestures or facial expressions. The resulting performance style is simultaneously wooden *and* excessive. Criswell repeatedly collapses the distinction between actor and character in a variety of seemingly intended and unintended ways, such as exposing his inability to deliver even the simplest dialogue without assistance and using his own coffin as a prop in several of Wood's films. The textual, extratextual and intertextual weirdness associated with Criswell supports his cult status and ensures that he contributes 'mightily' to the 'startling wretchedness and camp appeal' of the movies in which he appears (Peary 1991: 121). His performances are poorly executed and the characters he portrays are never convincing, even when he is apparently playing himself. Nevertheless, it appears he acts 'as only *he* can' (Wilson 2005: 265; emphasis in original). Criswell is by no means a 'good' actor, but his performance style is such that it is now recognised for certain distinctive, memorable qualities that help to blur the lines between his onscreen acting and his offscreen persona.

Criswell's reputation indicates that cultification and the designation of someone as a cult star is not necessarily or solely because of acting or performance ability (or lack thereof). As explained above, bad acting and cult stardom are not synonymous, and the relationship between the two is complex, inconsistent and indefinite, often relying on extra- and intertextual evidence as much as textual evidence. Furthermore, as Criswell's reputation indicates, it is possible to gain cult recognition for reasons that may be supported by onscreen

Figure 5.4   Criswell rising from his coffin to introduce *Night of the Ghouls* (Wood, Jr, 1959).

appearances but are not necessarily the result of those appearances alone. Criswell constitutes a form of cult personality rather than a cult actor specifically, with the former suggesting a broader understanding of an individual's cultification that could also extend to members of the film crew, for example. Indeed, there appears to be a tendency among fans to seek out and celebrate those involved in production far more than those who feature onscreen. Only one actor is interviewed in Juno and Vale's book, *Incredibly Strange Films*, alongside nine filmmakers, while the subjects of Tom Weaver's numerous interviews comprise writers, producers, directors and make-up artists far more than actors (Weaver 1988; 1994; 1996). When actors are interviewed, questions often focus on their experiences of working with specific filmmakers or other cult personalities rather than their own performances. This suggests that production details and behind-the-scenes insights hold more cultural value for many badfilm fans, who can then use this information as a way of understanding wider issues such as authorship.

It is, therefore, necessary to examine this concept of the cult personality further, with particular consideration of how, or if, onscreen performance impacts the development of cult reputations. Typically, the media personality is assumed to 'perform (what the audiences sees as) themselves, the more seamlessly, the better' (Turner 2004: 15). In terms of cult personalities such as Criswell, however, it is more often through the *failure* to successfully play someone else that the person is exposed. In *Orgy of the Dead*, despite the role requiring Criswell to play the Emperor, he appears incapable of submerging his 'public identity completely in the role' (Turner 2004: 15) and thus unintentionally 'eliminate[s] the distance' between his performance and himself (2004: 15). With badfilm fans regularly seeking out extratextual information as a way of understanding and, implicitly, explaining such evident failure onscreen, it is likely that there already exists a proclivity towards blurring the line between actor and character, which is made easier through bad acting.

Offscreen, Onscreen: Cult Stardom and the Director-Actor

It can be difficult to untangle an individual performance from other formal elements of a film, such as editing and screenwriting, while also not denying the actor's authorship by assuming that a performance is primarily constructed in the editing room. Badfilms can offer a way of avoiding these potentially conflicting approaches to performance because of the multiple on- and offscreen roles performed by many individuals: several badfilm directors act in their own movies, for example. Recognition of this often requires some extratextual knowledge, as many of these actor-directors perform under a pseudonym, possibly in an attempt to suggest that the film was a larger production than it actually was. Vic Savage (Arthur Nelson White) is both director and protagonist in

The Creeping Terror, for instance, while director Harold P. Warren is credited as Hal Warren for his leading role as Michael in *Manos: The Hands of Fate*. Arch Hall Sr performs under the pseudonym William Watters in *Eegah* and *Wild Guitar* (both 1962), while directing the former and producing the latter as Nicholas Merriweather, possibly with the aim of not only concealing his multiple roles on- and offscreen, but also to avoid claims of nepotism through his casting of Arch Hall Jr, his son, as the lead in both films.

Cult fans can demonstrate their subcultural capital through their ability to identify the director onscreen, as recognition requires a 'cultural effort from the viewer' (Mathijs 2013: 147). Mathijs argues that director cameos also 'add pleasurably intertextual and reflexive dimensions to a movie' (2013: 146) by drawing attention beyond the frame, even briefly. Although the examples in the previous paragraph are less cameos than prominent, even leading roles, directors appear onscreen in a variety of roles, some more easily identifiable than others. Al Adamson, for example, has cameos – all uncredited – in at least six of his own productions. Although most visible as the antihero in his last feature *Night Train to Mundo Fine*, Coleman Francis appears at least once in all three directorial efforts; his wife and sons also feature on screen, most prominently as the hapless Radcliffe family in *The Beast of Yucca Flats*. As I have discussed elsewhere (Bartlett 2019b), Ed Wood appears onscreen in perhaps eight directorial features, in a variety of roles comprising cameos, uncredited roles and leads. Identification of some of these onscreen contributions is dependent primarily, if not exclusively, on extratextual information and anecdotes. It is not clear from the text itself, for example, whether he is the voice heard over the radio and the 'Man holding newspaper' in *Plan 9 From Outer Space*, as currently listed on IMDb, or whether Paul Marco is accurate (quoted in Weaver 1988: 247) when he recalls Wood acting as a stunt double for the leading women in *Plan 9* and *Night of the Ghouls*. Indeed, it is not particularly unusual for the director to feature onscreen in an entirely 'invisible' role: allegedly, the gorilla characters in *The Mighty Gorga* and *The Beast That Killed Women* were each portrayed by the films' respective directors, concealed entirely beneath costumes. Unlike the director cameo as discussed by Mathijs, there is little evidence to suggest that the viewer is meant to recognise the director onscreen in any of these roles; rather, they appear more indicative of a resourcefulness necessitated by production contexts. Nevertheless, even the possibility of these being a form of 'concealed' director cameo can encourage inter- and extratextual readings that can affect how the film, and the director, is understood.

To various degrees, directors such as Adamson and Francis have gained cult reputation and status that has likely been enhanced by their onscreen appearances, irrespective of any specific performance traits. Examining Wood's status as a cult filmmaker, for instance, illuminates the relationship between acting and cultification. Aside from the previously mentioned 'cameo' appearances, Wood appears as the lead in two films with notable autobiographical implications, *Glen or Glenda* and *Love Feast* (Robertson 1969, also released as *The Photographer* and *Pretty Models All in a Row*). In the former, under the pseudonym Daniel Davis, he features opposite his then-girlfriend Delores Fuller and draws direct inspiration from his own life and experiences as a transvestite. For the informed viewer, this extratextual information ensures that the performance can be understood as honest and brave, particularly given the time-period in which it was made, and it is typically received sympathetically.

The lack of consideration for the quality of Wood's performances in these films is notable, however. For example, remarks about the 'sincerity' within *Glen or Glenda* (Adams 2010: 61) instead suggest that Wood's ability to authentically portray Glen is due to the role reflecting his own life, rather than his success as an actor. In this instance, extratextual information works to conceal and undermine the work of the acting itself. As William Routt points out, literature on Wood inevitably devotes a 'considerable amount of space' to extratextual, biographical information (Routt 2001: 2), which is used to inform readings of the films. This information then seems to legitimise readings that collapse the distinction between actor and character. Routt suggests that, in the case of Wood, the 'badness of the life is taken as evidence for the badness of the work' (2001: 2). Yet, the reverse is also true: the authenticity of his performance is taken as evidence of the reality of his life. Glen – and, later, Mr Murphy in *Love Feast* – appears to offer the informed viewer a glimpse into Wood's life, into his personality and his hardships (Bartlett 2019b). However, there seems to be an implicit acceptance underpinning these readings that, because he is a bad director, editor and screenwriter, Wood must also be a bad actor and that his portrayal of Glen (and Mr Murphy) is only successful because he is merely 'playing himself', rather than evincing any particular acting ability. Wood's cultification, therefore, is not necessarily the result of his acting, although it is undoubtedly enhanced and supported by his onscreen appearances. His reputation – his status as a cult personality – originates offscreen, in his life and his filmmaking.

As I have noted already, the more information a viewer has at their disposal, the more likely they are to use it – either consciously or not – to support specific readings or analytical approaches. Relatively speaking, there is considerable information available about Ed Wood, including, but not limited to, personal writing, anecdotes from family, friends and co-workers, some academic scholarship and around fifty years of fan-authored literature. This can be, and often is, used to evaluate his prominent onscreen roles in sympathetic ways, drawing on extratextual and biographical information in particular. In contrast, there are far fewer opportunities to approach other directors' onscreen performances in similar ways, even if the motivation or desire to do so existed. Unlike Wood, the acting roles fulfilled by other badfilm directors

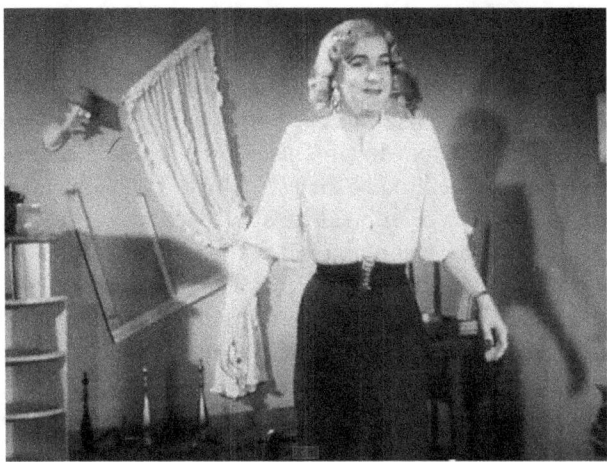

Figure 5.5 Edward D. Wood, Jr, as Glenda, *Glen or Glenda* (Wood, Jr, 1953).

tend to comprise fictional characters within entirely fictional narratives and, as a consequence, seldom invite biographical readings. Instead, the failure of a director-actor's performance can draw attention to failures in other areas of production, which can in turn be used to further support their broader cult reputation and status as a bad filmmaker.

The decision to take on multiple roles, both in front of and behind the camera, can have direct implications regarding a director's ability, authorial control and competence. It is harder to excuse bad acting as the result of external factors such as editing or direction, for example, when the actor is also responsible for multiple aspects of the film's production. Who else but Hal Warren can be blamed for his utter inability to portray doomed husband and father, Michael, in a sympathetic manner in *Manos*, when he is the film's writer, director and producer as well? Anecdotally, Warren believed that the character gave him the opportunity to play a 'hero and a good guy' (Neyman-Jones 2013), but through his performance Michael appears unnecessarily aggressive, callous and domineering. However, any possible claim that Warren's acting was undermined, altered or misrepresented due to failures in other aspects of production, such as scriptwriting or direction, would do little except to draw attention to his other failures. Thus, responsibility for the performance, when considered either in isolation or in relation to other formal elements, falls squarely on him: he is the one who wrote the repetitive, nonsensical script that fails to construct interesting, complex characters; he has failed to direct his cast appropriately; his own inexperience has meant that he could not offer adequate guidance to his equally inexperienced crew; and he has failed to support his own performance or conceal his own errors.

A director's decision to appear onscreen can also suggest a certain amount of hubris. While it is possible – even likely – that dual roles were necessitated by the meagre production contexts in which these films were made, there also seems to be an underlying assumption that taking on multiple duties is easy, somehow, or that acting does not require any particular skill or effort. Ray Dennis Steckler, who tended to use the pseudonym Cash Flagg for his onscreen roles, appears to have been ambivalent about acting and the skill involved. His comment that it is 'easy enough to act in a film when you're the director' (quoted in Juno and Vale 1986: 47) dismisses the potential conflict that may arise when trying to juggle multiple responsibilities and suggests that he considered his performances to be largely successful. This opinion does not seem to be widely shared, but his onscreen appearances nevertheless contribute to his reputation as a cult auteur. Michael Sauter's description of Steckler/Flagg as a 'schlockmeister who's not afraid to be *in front of* the camera when he makes a fool of himself' (1999: 309; emphasis in original), and Juno and Vale's ironic observation that he makes his 'weird, individual and radi[c]al films [. . .] that much better' (1986: 56) by appearing onscreen in them indicates that he is thought of as a filmmaker and director first, and actor second. In this way, his onscreen roles can be read as further evidence to support a cult reputation based primarily on his apparent 'individual visual and quirky originality' rather than any specific performative traits or qualities.

Arguably, this approach works in Steckler's favour. There is limited evidence of 'quirky originality' in his performances. This is particularly evident in his most widely known badfilm, *The Incredibly Strange Creatures Who Stopped Living and Became Mixed Up Zombies!!?* in which he plays doomed protagonist Jerry. The character appears to be intended as a charismatic rebel, but Flagg's performance frequently appears half-hearted, with the effect being that Jerry emerges less as a countercultural hero than an unsympathetic layabout. He seems to sap energy instead of exuding it and appears bored by life instead of invigorated by it, in direct contradiction of the character's explicit claim that he believes that the world is 'here to be enjoyed, not to make you depressed'. Although it seems that we are meant to align ourselves with Jerry, Flagg's performance, which is alternately unremarkable and inappropriately visible, regularly limits our potential to do so. This suggests an inherent failure – a clash between the intended and actual presentation of the character – that is central to identifying the performance as bad. It is an unmemorable performance, one that seems characterised by apathy. At best, it seems to confirm Steckler's ambivalence towards acting; he considers it to be 'easy' and therefore not requiring any particular effort.

As *Incredibly Strange Creatures*' tragic protagonist, Jerry should elicit sympathy. He is constructed as a free spirit, a young man in the prime of his life who becomes a victim, forced to commit murder against his will and, finally,

BAD ACTING

Figure 5.6 Jerry (Cash Flagg) as a mixed-up zombie, *The Incredibly Strange Creatures Who Stopped Living and Became Mixed-Up Zombies!!?* (Steckler, 1964).

transformed into a mutant. Flagg's ineffective performance, however, limits our ability to engage with the character as apparently intended. The apathy and lack of effort that Flagg evinces further limits the potential for the performance to be reappraised or celebrated for its idiolect; neither the character nor the actor portraying the character are memorable or distinctive. While visible acting may be re-evaluated and cultified because it can reveal an actor's graft or dedication, the lack of consistent commitment to the role makes it difficult to reappraise Flagg's performance, or to celebrate him as a cult star who is 'giving it his all'. Consequently, we can consider whether there are other ways in which the performance can be re-evaluated so that it becomes significant or meaningful.

Steckler's status as a cult auteur is based primarily, but not exclusively, on his offscreen duties. Like other badfilm auteurs, his involvement across a range of aspects of film production support claims that his films are evidence of an individual vision. His onscreen appearances, therefore, can provide further evidence to support his wider cult reputation. However, the extent to which his cultification can be understood as the result of any particular performance traits or acting ability is less clear; Steckler is a cult personality, but this does not necessarily mean that Flagg can be appropriately described as a cult actor. It is notable, for example, that he features in Danny Peary's influential book *Cult Movie Stars*, but equally significant is the way in which Flagg is described therein (1991: 187): the entry is entirely devoted to anecdotes about the exploitation tactics employed by Steckler to promote *Incredibly Strange Creatures*, and a brief list of the various roles he played on- and offscreen. There is no mention of any specific performance qualities or characteristics.

To sum up, examining the reputations of badfilm director-actors invites reflection on the relationship between cultification, stardom and acting, and indicates that cult personalities can develop irrespective of the performance traits that often underpin the celebration of specific actors as cult stars. In the case of Cash Flagg, the qualities of his performance are less significant to Steckler's cult status than the fact that he 'stars' in cult movies; therefore, performance qualities can draw attention beyond the frame, beyond the character, to the director. This extratextual knowledge can also be used to further evaluate the filmmaker's success or failure across a range of aspects of production, to support or challenge claims of authorship, for example, or to provide further evidence of their attitude, entrepreneurial spirit or graft, which in turn can encourage certain cult reputations. Although the characters that Flagg plays offer little in the way of biographical potential, as some of Wood's onscreen performances seem to do, they nevertheless offer the investigative pleasures of identifying the director onscreen and serve as further textual evidence to support and reinforce the director's status as a cult personality.

As noted previously, bad acting and cult stardom are not synonymous. However, if we accept that cult film stardom can develop due to the potential alternative pleasures of 'seeing the acting happen', it is worth reflecting on the relationship between bad acting and cultification. Exposing the work of acting can result in a collapsing of distinction between actor and character, whereby the failure to appropriately embody a character distracts from the diegesis and draws attention beyond the frame instead. Although we should not assume that all performance intends to be 'invisible', this is nonetheless the dominant approach and typically appears to be the aim of the performances discussed here. Certainly, the critical response to a performance can be affected if a disparity is identified between the intended outcome and the actual result, which can unwittingly draw attention to the (failed) art and craft of acting itself. Like other formal elements, when there is an identifiable gap between the desired standard and the achieved standard, bad acting draws attention to the non-diegetic elements of the film and reminds us that we are watching a constructed performance.

The form in which the badness of that performance reveals itself, however, directly impacts the actor's potential cultification. Flat, half-hearted, lacklustre performances characterised by a lack of excess often prove more difficult to re-evaluate and celebrate as an alternative form of acting: it is harder to celebrate the actor's effort when it is not obvious. In contrast, the excessive visibility of a hammy, over-acted performance can invite cult re-appraisal by suggesting a form of authenticity and sincerity not necessarily intended by the actor; a truthfulness that exposes the work of the performance, rather than conceals that work behind a character. Failure to appropriately embody a character can create a stronger connection between actor and viewer by removing the obstacle that character represents. In turn, this can help to create the conditions that enable an objectively bad performance to be transformed into one that is subjectively appreciated, collapsing the distinction between 'good' and 'bad' in the process.

6. THE POTENTIAL PLEASURES OF BAD EDITING

While it is possible to identify 'objective' badness to the extent that we can persuasively argue the appearance of the failed attempt to achieve a certain outcome, there will always be an element of subjectivity in our subsequent response to that badness. Despite the term 'so bad it's good' implying that watching certain badfilms is a 'good' or pleasurable experience, we cannot assume that enjoyment is the inevitable consequence of experiencing excessive, demonstrable failure. However, although I am hesitant to suggest anything so rigid as a consensus on which films are described as 'so bad they're good', it does appear that some films are more widely accepted for their potential to elicit positive experiential responses than others. Recognising this distinction opens up the possibility to consider whether we can identify textual evidence for these receptions.

This chapter examines bad editing and indicates how we might account for the frequency by which certain badfilms are identified as 'so bad they're good', while others tend to elicit feelings of boredom and tedium. As I demonstrate, these different responses can be understood in relation to editing. For example, visible cuts and unpredictable yet seemingly unmotivated editing choices can result in an odd, consistently inconsistent style that both focuses attention on the diegesis and, paradoxically, distracts from it. This highly visible yet inappropriate editing can encourage a more active spectatorial position: establishing spatial, temporal and other connections becomes a task for the viewer, who has to 'fill in the gaps' and try to find a way of making sense of what is unfolding before them. The ambiguous ways in which space, time and narrative are presented thus invite particular interpretive possibilities that can encourage recognition of, and positive responses to, badness through their inherent inconsistency, unpredictability and weirdness. Conversely, when editing is functional and unremarkable rather than excessive, it can negatively impact viewer engagement, producing a form of *anti-pleasure* experience. With the cuts themselves offering little of interest, there is nothing to distract from badfilms' shoddiness, their poorly constructed narratives and their ineffective spectacle. This chapter, therefore, indicates some of the ways in which we might account for the different experiential pleasures – or lack thereof – of badfilms. Here, I propose that, although appreciation is necessarily subjective, a closer examination of bad editing can help to understand the textual features that encourage some badfilms to be celebrated as 'so bad they're good' and others to be cultified in different ways, as 'just' bad.

Badfilm Editing Practice

The lack of information regarding badfilm editing means that identifying possible intentions behind decisions – or even who the decision-maker was – can be particularly challenging. It is possible, however, to make an educated guess regarding the possible aims of the editors, by placing badfilms within their historical-cultural context and acknowledging the general conditions in which they were made. The films discussed throughout this book were made at a time when classical continuity was the dominant form of editing practice in narrative cinema, particularly in the US. Although some 'maverick' filmmakers were beginning to challenge established editing conventions (LoBrutto 2009: 45), the radical visibility of New Hollywood style had not yet emerged, and there is no notable evidence to suggest that the people responsible for badfilms were purposefully deviating from 'mainstream' practices. Furthermore, given that badfilm fandom only really emerged in the late 1970s and early 1980s (Sconce 2019: 668–69), there was neither much motivation to intentionally appeal to a specific taste sensibility that had yet to gain any visibility, nor clear financial benefit to making a film that flouted conventions through a deliberate reproduction of 'bad' style. The production conditions, demonstrable lack of effort or care in other aspects of production and the historical context in which these films were made all serve to support readings of unconventional editing style as accidental and unintended, rather than consciously radical or transgressive.

Like other formal devices, editing may be affected by the material poverty and restrictive working conditions that contribute to, and often exacerbate, badfilms' demonstrable failure. This is particularly pertinent here, because editing has the potential to correct and conceal mistakes that arise in production (Orpen 2003: 116), yet this potential is rarely realised in the films discussed in this book. Instead, bad editing draws attention to the many issues throughout the filmmaking process and adds new problems to existing ones. Looking beyond the text could offer a way of understanding the motivations behind editing decisions, but this approach is limited due to the scant information regarding either the people responsible for editing the movies, or the details of their working conditions. Furthermore, even when such information does exist, it is not necessarily reliable or complete. However, by drawing on the information we do have, as well as comments from established film editors in relation to what they consider to be 'best' practice, it is possible to get a sense of the challenges that badfilm editors faced and the ways in which they might have attempted to navigate those challenges.

In a *Cineaste* special issue (2009), several editors were invited to discuss the nature of their work. Their descriptions of both the desired working conditions and the temperament best suited to the work of editing offer a sharp contrast to what is known about badfilm production context and the people involved, suggesting that failure was often likely, if not inevitable. For example, several comment on the benefits of having enough time to complete the work and maintaining a sense of perspective (for example, Squyres, in Chew et al. 2009: 60) and note that editing can be a long, even tedious process. Having enough footage is also important: the fewer options the editor has, the less chance they have to address issues such as bad performances or discontinuity, making it more likely that these will remain in the finished film. Maintaining some distance from production is helpful, meanwhile, as it can allow editors to act as mediators between 'the director's vision and what's really on the film' (Heim, in Chew et al. 2009: 57). Given that there are no 'hard and fast rules' of editing (Orpen 2003: 116), it is unsurprising that several remark on it being a largely intuitive process, with decisions made as much on 'gut instinct' (various, in Chew et al. 2009: 59) as on intellectual choices regarding narrative clarity and dramatic or emotional emphasis. Thus, to be successful, editors need to have an 'eye for detail' (Hutshing, in Chew et al. 2009: 57) and a sense of 'drama and storytelling' (Coates in Chew et al. 2009: 57), with the qualities most desired including patience, sensitivity and the ability to draw on a wide range of knowledge and experience.

In contrast, the filmmakers responsible for making what are now referred to as badfilms were typically working in impoverished conditions and lacked time, money, experience and/or expertise across all aspects of production. Reshoots and multiple takes were generally kept to a minimum due to budgetary constraints, limiting the options available to the editors, who themselves often lacked the technical understanding to mitigate against the challenges they faced. It is notable, for instance, that several of the most notorious badfilms were either the first or the only production on which the editor(s) worked. Neither Thomas Casey nor Alex Ameri, the editing supervisors for *Monster A-go Go*, had any previous experience. *Eegah* was Don Schneider's first foray into editing; he followed this up with *The Incredibly Strange Creatures Who Stopped Living and Became Mixed Up Zombies!!?* two years later. Elsewhere, filmmakers juggled multiple roles and responsibilities, including directing, editing, writing, producing and acting. As well as creating an environment in which the editor might lack the critical distance to be able to recognise and address flaws in the work, this can suggest a rather cavalier attitude towards the expertise required to complete each job effectively. Taken together, then, these conditions do not appear conducive to best editing practice. Although limitations can encourage filmmakers to find creative solutions to problems – something that badfilmmakers have been celebrated for (for example, Juno and Vale 1986: 5) – it seems reasonable to suggest that these same limitations will also affect their ability to do so effectively.

When available, extratextual information and other trivia about badfilm production contexts, the people involved and their working conditions may offer a means for understanding and explaining their demonstrable incompetence and inherent weirdness. We can positively interpret their unconventional, inconsistent style as a product of circumstance, or as evidence of creativity or resourcefulness. However, even widely circulated trivia can be incorrect or misleading, while the films' credits and the memories of those involved are not always reliable. For instance, although Coleman Francis is listed as the co-editor of his directorial debut *The Beast of Yucca Flats* – discussed further below – his involvement is disputed by the film's producer and regular collaborator Tony Cardoza (quoted in Weaver, n. d.) who instead attributes the work to himself and two others. Similarly, writer-director Ed Wood is listed as the editor in *Plan 9 From Outer Space*'s opening credits. If correct, this would constitute his first attempt at editing, but his contributions have been disputed, and at least two more people may have been involved (Grey 1992: 85, 203). Thus, we must be mindful of possible inaccuracies in anecdotal and other information used as supporting evidence, particularly when attempting to assign responsibility to specific individuals, or explain or justify ambiguous formal decisions.

As I have noted elsewhere, auteurism regularly underpins badfilm appreciation. The emphasis on certain filmmakers as bad or accidental auteurs can work to downplay the possible contributions of others, or even deny them altogether. For example, although Wood typically delegated editing to others, spatial and temporal discrepancies in his directorial efforts continue to be read as evidence of *his* inability to 'master the basics of continuity, screen direction, or the construction of cinematic space' (Sconce 1995: 387). Much of the positive re-evaluation of Wood as both a cult auteur and an 'accidental artist of the avant-garde' (Hill 2015: 173), meanwhile, rests on the unconventional style of *Glen or Glenda*, discussed in Chapter 4. That film's experimental approach to editing and narrative construction is consistently attributed entirely to Wood;

I have yet to find any mention of the film's editor, 'Bud' Schelling, in either fan-authored or academic literature on the film. *Glen or Glenda* appears to be his only known foray into film production of any kind. He remains largely invisible, unmentioned and unacknowledged. It seems likely that we will never know the extent of his contribution to, or possible artistic/creative influence on, *Glen or Glenda*'s experimental approach to storytelling and cinematic construction.

In addition to ambiguities regarding the extent of individual involvement in editing decisions, the editing process itself is rarely discussed by the filmmakers responsible for badfilms. This can suggest a certain ambivalence towards the art and craft of editing. So irrelevant is the editor, apparently, that they are entirely absent from the opening credits of several of Larry Buchanan's Azalea films, for example. This has the effect that, for anyone lacking the extratextual information confirming his various contributions as director, producer and editor (Buchanan 1996: 78), the credits suggest *Zontar: The Thing from Venus, Curse of the Swamp Creature* and *In the Year 2889* (Buchanan 1967) were simply not edited at all – no one can be held responsible. This also works to downplay the value and significance of editing by effectively denying its contribution to the film as a finished product. Conversely, however, we can find remarks that suggest some filmmakers were overly confident in the potential for editing to correct errors and address issues that arose during filming, and that they believed it was 'always' possible to fix mistakes through 'montage and cut' (Sherman, quoted in Konow 1998: 81). Yet even when the possible benefits of editing appear to be recognised in principle, too often it seems that the filmmakers were either unable or unwilling to create the conditions that would enable these to be put into practice effectively.

Analysing Editing

Editing is often an elusive aspect of the filmmaking process and can be difficult to discuss in isolation from other elements of film form. The classical continuity system typically intends for editing to go unnoticed. Motivated by 'narrative clarity and dramatic emphasis' (Dancyger 2011: 267), classical continuity editing works to conceal the constructed nature of the diegesis, enabling action to unfold in a way that is not confusing or disorienting for the viewer. As a result, we are often 'faced with the paradox that many effective cuts are effective precisely *because* they are not noticeable' (Orpen 2003: 4; emphasis in original). Although this could suggest that a 'bad' edit is a visible one, Orpen argues it is more useful to consider 'good' and 'bad' editing in terms of whether it is 'appropriate' or 'inappropriate' (2003: 116). With the majority of the films discussed in this book being rooted in narrative cinema, we can examine whether the editing works to support or distract from the narrative content and the viewer's potential emotional engagement and then judge its success or failure to achieve narrative and/or aesthetic coherence in a manner that seems appropriate and justified. Dancyger suggests that, if the editing draws 'unnecessary attention' to itself, it indicates the filmmaker's and editor's failure to 'present the narrative in the most effective possible manner' (2011: 371). Rather than to approach editing through the lens of visibility/invisibility, it is more productive to acknowledge that whether the editing is visible – the viewer notices the cuts themselves – is only important insomuch as this visibility can be accepted as consistent, necessary and appropriate to the film.

In many ways, editing works (or does not work) not in isolation, but in relation to the viewer. There is a 'complicity in the making of films' (Fairservice 2001: 8); as viewers, we know that we are watching a construction. Classical continuity works to limit this, encouraging us instead to focus on narrative development and emotional engagement, effectively aiming to conceal the construction entirely, and our acceptance of this impacts our wider approach to cinema. We 'assume' consistency and coherence because our prior knowledge of filmic conventions lets us form strong expectations about what shot will follow the one we are seeing (Bordwell and Thompson 2017: 236). Conversely, this suggests that we do not expect inconsistency and incoherence, and our prior knowledge of filmic conventions are likely to make the experience of unexpected inconsistency particularly jarring. Although there are no hard and fast rules of editing, there 'do appear to be cuts that "work" – where the conceptual, graphic and rhythmic gears of each shot mesh perfectly and "invisibly", and other cuts which don't – where those gears jam up against each other and disorient the audience' (Murch, in Chew et al. 2009: 55). The editing in badfilm fails – and becomes visible – because its unconventional style is inappropriate; it becomes an unavoidable distraction that dismantles the illusion of the diegesis, disrupts narrative coherence and limits the film's immersive potential.

Of course, classical continuity is by no means the only form of editing. Just as not all bad editing is inherently visible (as I will discuss later in this chapter), visible editing is not inherently bad and can produce positive, pleasurable effects. Presenting the diegesis in ambiguous ways invites active engagement, encouraging the viewer to adopt a more interpretive framework so that they can fill in the gaps themselves. Taking an active role in meaning-making in this way can be a pleasurable experience (see Vernallis 2001: 32). Badfilms can encourage similar responses, while also activating a heightened awareness of cinematic construction by drawing attention to structures that would normally remain concealed. At the same time, visible editing draws attention to film style, which can itself produce pleasurable effects. For example, Orpen discusses the radically visible editing style adopted by Jean-Luc Godard and other French new wave filmmakers, who deliberately flouted conventions and consciously broke the rules, noting the 'pleasure of [*A bout de souffle*, Godard 1960], pleasure of its rapidity, of its energetic jump cuts, of the unpredictability of editing, of its movement' (2003: 64). As I demonstrate below, these characteristics can emerge through failure also, and closer examination can help to understand why certain badfilms appear to be more likely to elicit pleasurable responses than others.

On the surface, therefore, there appear to be similarities between the kind of 'bad' editing consciously adopted by Godard and other avant-garde filmmakers, on one hand, and the editing in badfilms, on the other. At the very least, both seem to carry the potential effect of distancing the viewer from the film, defamiliarizing the content and offering the possible pleasures of more active engagement. Nevertheless, there are notable differences in motivation, intention and outcome. Counter-cinematic style is understood to be a 'strategic intervention' in which innovations are self-consciously employed (Sconce 1995: 384) and internally consistent. The editing in *A bout de souffle*, for example, 'jettisons the conventions of continuity editing but [...] is not baffling [and] leaves certain questions open without frustrating us' (Orpen 2003: 64). In contrast, badfilms 'rarely exhibit such pronounced stylistic virtuosity as the result of a "conscious" artistic agenda' (Sconce 1995: 384–85) and are regularly baffling, frustrating, illogical and incoherent. This is in part, I suggest, because we do not expect films that appear to be rooted in narrative cinema to present their narratives in such distracting, distancing, inconsistent ways. We do not expect to have to work so hard to make sense of the story presented to us. Furthermore, failure reveals itself in a myriad of ways, meaning that badfilm style is regularly illogical and incoherent, thereby presenting a particular challenge for interpretation and meaning-making.

It is worth noting at this point that cultified badfilms come with their own 'baggage' – it seems likely that contemporary viewers will be aware of their reputation and status as badfilms. Therefore, we might argue that incoherence is expected. However, while a contemporary viewer may well be expecting 'bad', visible and even inappropriate editing when watching canonised badfilms, I suggest that this does not make them any less of a jarring, disorienting experience. Conversely, because our identification of editing technique is constantly developing, contemporary audiences can 'quickly get accustomed to even very aggressive editing styles, rendering them "invisible" if the style is implemented consistently, and, most important, well' (Squyres, in Chew et al. 2009: 56). Editing techniques that were once startlingly obvious (visible) due to their novelty may be rendered invisible through repetition and familiarity. Although this suggests that contemporary viewers may be less likely to recognise the unconventional editing in badfilms altogether, this is evidently not the case. The editing in films such as *The Skydivers*, *Plan 9*, *Manos: The Hands of Fate* and *Monster A-go Go* is still disorienting and draws attention to itself through its inability to convey time, space or narrative progression coherently. The inconsistency of the editing, meanwhile, implies a lack of intention and suggests that whatever is motivating specific decisions, it is something other than the pursuit of a conscious style. Thus, even when we expect the editing to be bad, it still reveals itself to be inappropriate.

By exposing the film's constructed nature, bad editing can limit the immersive potential of the film and, instead, draw attention to other aspects of the film that are typically concealed in 'good' movies. It can point to certain modes of production, for example: shooting out of sequence; creating composite settings from unrelated locations; using body doubles. The creation of a diegesis through a combination of recycled and new footage, discussed in Chapter 4, can only be successful if the audience does not notice (or is willing to overlook) the aesthetic discrepancies between the various pieces of footage and is either able to recognise an acceptable relationship between the action(s) contained within the shots, or understands that they are *meant* to notice the disparity through the film's internal acknowledgement of the same. Bad editing, therefore, can provide viewers access to a more critical awareness and understanding of editing in general. As Sconce argues, badfilms can expose 'usually invisible codes organising the narrative' (2003: 21), with incompetent editing offering the potential to highlight, among other things, the formal devices of continuity that tend to be concealed in 'good' films. This is possible, I suggest, because badfilms offer us the opportunity to recognise both the intended effect (continuity) and the failure to achieve that effect and, in the process, can provide access to, and more critical awareness of, devices and formal technique of editing that 'good' films deny us.

In addition, examining editing in badfilm can offer a means of understanding the potential for pleasure – or not – that these films offer. Different forms of bad editing have different experiential value and produce different effects. Positively, the seemingly unintended visibility of editing can draw attention to the film's construction and style in disorienting, unexpected ways. In the process, it activates new interpretive possibilities and heightened viewer awareness. This can help to account for the pleasurable/enjoyable experience of badfilms with a reputation for being 'so bad they're good'. Conversely, examining other forms of less visible bad editing provides a way of understanding why some badfilms produce a kind of *anti-pleasure experience*, one that is characterised by tedium, boredom and despair. Of course, our response to any film – good, bad or otherwise – will always be inherently subjective. Nevertheless, as I demonstrate through the case-studies below, it is possible to identify some of the formal characteristics of badfilms that encourage certain responses over others.

Pacing and the Potential Pleasures of *Manos: The Hands of Fate*

Badness is evident even in the title of Harold Warren's sole foray into filmmaking – *Manos: The Hands of Fate* literally translates as *Hands: The Hands of Fate*. The title encapsulates the film's failures: it is infuriatingly repetitive. Actions and dialogue are repeated, then repeated again. Attention repeatedly returns to an entirely irrelevant subplot involving two teenagers making out in a car, who are repeatedly interrupted by the same policemen. The Master's brides repeatedly squabble with each other, verbally and physically. The film's jazz score is repetitive. The film begins and ends with car journeys that involve different characters but suggest that they will all suffer the same fate. Despite being only seventy minutes long, *Manos* seems to only have the narrative content for a film half that length. It ought to be a tedious, boring viewing experience, and in some respects it is. Yet, it is also so formally bizarre and disconcertingly fragmented that it can also be an unexpectedly enjoyable experience. Despite its repetitiveness, *Manos* is thoroughly disorienting and entirely unpredictable.

Manos tells the tragic tale of a vacationing family who accidentally encounter a satanic cult residing in an isolated farmhouse. It was shot in colour, predominantly at night on location in El Paso, Texas, over the course of six months and on an estimated budget of only $19,000. Although briefly mentioned in some early fan-authored literature (Weldon 1983; Juno and Vale 1986), its reputation as a badfilm was cemented when it was shown on *Mystery Science Theater 3000* in 1993. Since then, it has been firmly positioned as one of the 'worst films of all time', with all the perks – documentaries, biographies, Blu-Ray releases and so on – that such a status typically entails (see Barefoot 2017: 1–3). This interest has also led to more information about *Manos*' production being available, primarily through the recollections of the surviving cast and crew, which can offer apparent insights into the motivations behind the film's bizarre style. Warren's alleged refusal to shoot more than two takes of any shot meant that the editors had fewer options to correct errors, while it seems likely that framing and editing decisions were motivated at least in part in a (largely unsuccessful) attempt to conceal dubbing. The jerky, repetitive and frequently unmotivated cuts, meanwhile, are typically explained by the decision to shoot *Manos* with a camera that could only record a maximum of thirty-two seconds of footage at a time (Robert Guidry, quoted in Brandt 1996). As discussed below, however, this is directly contradicted by the film itself. As always, we must be careful when using anecdotes – particularly those recalled years after production – to explain or rationalise a film's failure.

Although the credits list James Sullivan and Ernie Smith as *Manos*' editors, Jackey Neyman-Jones, who played young Debbie, alleges that post-production was completed in a single six-hour session by Warren, Robert Guidry and Bernie Rosenblum, using the local television station's equipment (2012b).

Whoever was responsible for *Manos*' editing, they wholeheartedly failed to achieve any sense of coherence. Cuts are frequent but unpredictable, and they regularly fail to conceal errors in other areas, such as unconvincing acting and poorly dubbed dialogue. The presentation of space, time and narrative action is fragmented and disorienting. However, by unintentionally foregrounding the formal aspects of the film's construction, the editing distracts from the banality of the repetitive story. At the very least, *Manos* is disorienting enough to maintain our interest. Its unpredictability draws attention away from the film's lack of action or character development, and its demonstrable badness has the potential to become unintentionally comedic. This is, I suggest, in part because of the twitchiness of *Manos* that is caused by a contrast between a lack of movement *during* shots and constant, seemingly unmotivated shifts in camera angles *between* shots.

An early sequence is a good example of this. Having lost their way, Michael, his wife Margaret, daughter Debbie and the family's pet poodle arrive at a desolate farmhouse. Although shot on location, no establishing shot of the building is provided, but the lower portions of some whitewashed walls can partially be seen in the background as the family drive past. Having stopped the car, Michael looks beyond the frame and remarks that 'this place' was not there earlier. Margaret suggests that they can ask someone for directions and comments that there is someone at the door. As she says this, the shot changes to a very brief, extreme close-up of a new character; we subsequently learn that this is Torgo, the caretaker. An unnecessarily long take follows, showing the mundane action of the car weaving its way up the driveway. Cut to Torgo again, as the camera awkwardly zooms in from medium shot to a close-up of his face, then back to Margaret, looking horrified. The implication, then, is that the shots of Torgo represent Margaret's point-of-view, but it is impossible to get a coherent sense of the spatial relationship between the characters. Michael parks the car, and the family get out; cut to Torgo, who introduces himself. Although the subsequent conversation indicates that the various characters are sharing the same space, the editing and framing continues to suggest distance and separation. The exchange is presented almost entirely through a series of close-ups, with each person kept isolated from one another within the frame. Only in the final moments are the characters all shown together, but this occurs too late to establish their proximity to each other in an effective or appropriate manner.

The unconventional editing in *Manos* constantly dismantles and fragments space and time, resulting in a particularly disorienting viewing experience. There is no consistency in the way in which characters are framed and no obvious motivation for many of the cuts and shifts in perspective. Nevertheless, despite the meagre plot, the film's pace appears brisk. The incoherent presentation of diegetic space and time results in 'mental hiccups' (Pepperman 2004:

8; Orpen 2003: 60), whereby the viewer's eyes respond to the movement of the image onscreen without their brain comprehending it at the same speed. We are constantly presented with new information but given neither the narrative substance nor the visual continuity that might enable us to register its significance. Few of the shots in the above-mentioned scene contain shared visual markers that might help us understand the space, for example. Torgo is presented in particularly ambiguous, confusing ways. He is shown from all angles: in close-up directly facing the camera; in profile with a doorframe and white wall behind him; in opposite profile, with foliage in the background. These disparate views are never adequately unified into a single, coherent space. Space is fragmented and presented in illogical, confusing, bewildering ways. This, however, suggests a possible explanation for *Manos*' ability to be entertaining rather than tedious. Unifying the space becomes a task for the viewer and, by focusing our attention on the film's construction rather than its content, the incoherent editing distracts us from the narrative inertia.

This sequence typifies the conflict between *Manos*' narrative content and its construction. Shots are short and cuts frequent, implying a quick pace, but much of the scene comprises 'dead' time. For instance, a thirty-second section features five individual close-ups during which no one speaks. Although the characters are presented in ways that suggest reaction shots, nothing has occurred for them to react to. There is an uncomfortable intimacy in these shots, which focuses attention on the actors as they appear to mutely stare at one another, as if waiting – like us – for someone to break the silence. It is moments like this, perhaps, that cause Juno and Vale to claim the editing in *Manos* is '*leaden* [. . .] If the actors have difficulty remembering their lines, the camera stays on them until they do – no matter how long it takes!' (1986: 204; emphasis in original). However, this misrepresents the characters' relationship with the camera, which does not *wait* for them to speak, but repeatedly shows them *not speaking*. Furthermore, although Juno and Vale suggest that *Manos* is 'completely devoid of Hollywood influence or conventional filmmaking technique' (1986: 204), the film is constructed in a way that indicates an awareness of editing conventions like shot-reverse-shot, as well as inept efforts to replicate them. The authors' mischaracterisation of *Manos*' editing inadvertently supports Orpen's assertion that 'it is usually impossible to remember [editing] correctly after viewing a film' (2003: 11). It is clear, however, that, even if specific editing choices are difficult to remember accurately, the *effects* of editing and the film's bizarre style are indeed memorable; the sense of disorientation and bewilderment remains.

Trivia regarding the camera's limitations appear to offer some rationale for *Manos*' unconventional editing style: the frequent cuts are the unavoidable consequence of shooting with a camera that can only capture thirty-two seconds of footage at a time. However, at least two shots in the film far exceed

Figure 6.1A–D   Torgo (John Reynolds), shown from different angles, *Manos: The Hands of Fate* (Warren, 1966).

this alleged maximum. One occurs roughly thirty minutes in, when Michael leaves the farmhouse to search for Torgo in the desert. When they meet, Torgo knocks Michael unconscious, and a washed-out, poorly lit shot lasting over ninety seconds follows, showing Torgo dragging Michael to a post and tying him up. Another notably long take also features Torgo, showing him getting woken by his Master. Again, this seems to emphasise the character's physical hardship, staying fixed on him for eighty seconds as he attempts to stand up. The film's pacing abruptly shifts from rapid to excruciatingly slow. These extended shots reveal how awkward and strenuous Torgo's movements are, and we have no choice but to watch his efforts because there are no cuts. Whereas other characters are shown in quick, constantly changing close-ups that distract and disorient through the 'mental hiccups' that they engender, these uncompromising long shots thus invite us to forge a different relationship with Torgo by emphasising – in painfully prolonged detail – his physical exertions.

Although the existence of these shots contradicts Guidry's anecdotal information about production, they are distinctly part of the film. They are not recycled footage, for example, and there is no evidence to suggest that they were filmed by anyone other than Warren and his crew. The aesthetic badness evident in these moments is consistent with the rest of the movie, from the lack of camera movement during the shot, to the washed-out cinematography and bad lighting. The only explanation, therefore, must be that the trivia so often used to understand *Manos*' unconventional editing is not wholly accurate. Oddly, this discrepancy has not been acknowledged elsewhere, despite badfilm fans often demonstrating a sophisticated awareness of formal construction and close attention to detail. Perhaps this is simply another example of 'trash' criticism, whereby an amusing anecdote is prioritised over accuracy, but it could also point to the challenges of remembering editing correctly; the incoherent, fragmented style that characterises the majority of the film is so disorienting that it overwhelms everything else.

Few of the formal elements in *Manos* are effective, but the editing is one of the more disturbing, confusing aspects of the film. Although editing has the potential to correct mistakes and provide continuity, these benefits are not utilised here. 'Dead' shots, serving no apparent purpose other than to extend the film's running time, are prevalent, while the absence of establishing shots and over-reliance on close-ups result in a particularly disorienting viewing experience. Throughout the film, action is mismatched across shots, insects fly across the camera and at one point a clapper board is clearly visible. The sound editing is poorly judged also, with dialogue badly and obviously dubbed. In a notorious sequence featuring a brawl between the Master's wives, abrupt cuts occur mid-sentence, while at other times characters are shown speaking, but no words are heard. A sudden cut on action – likely two takes of the same shot – results in one wife apparently finishing her sentence without moving her lips. Not only have the filmmakers failed to conceal the numerous issues with which they were confronted in production, but they also create further problems through inept editing decisions.

Manos' editing, therefore, is demonstrably bad and inappropriately visible, but it is also a key reason for its reputation as 'so bad it's good': the constant cuts and unmotivated shifts in angle and perspective result in a 'comic surrealism' (Adams 2010: 92). It presents its diegesis in ways that are never effective, and the illusion of the filmic world is obliterated. The 'mental hiccups' resulting from cuts without apparent purpose are indicative of its spatial and temporal incoherence. We are kept in a state of constant confusion, bombarded with new visual information but not provided the opportunity to orient ourselves, or the characters, within the space. Nevertheless, there is an oddly consistent inconsistency to *Manos* – it is consistently disorienting and tells its repetitive story in awkwardly repetitive ways. It is unsurprising that it gained its reputation on *MST3K*, or that it became a benchmark by which subsequent films were evaluated by the show's writers. With more cuts comes more opportunity for discontinuity, more likelihood of exposing other formal failures, more chance for a distraction from the plot's banality. Given that badfilm fans seek out evidence of failure that can be ironically appropriated and/or unironically appreciated for the unintended comedy it provides, *Manos* offers a wealth of opportunity for both.

Bad Editing and the (De)Construction of Space and Time

As the analysis of *Manos* indicates, there is a correlation between inappropriately visible editing and the potential viewing pleasures of badfilm. The excessive incoherence, visual discontinuity and ambiguously motivated cuts and shifts in perspective invite an unusual viewing position marked by an unusual combination of alertness and detachment: bad editing can simultaneously draw attention to the films' formal elements while limiting the possibility of narrative immersion. Even considered in relation to other badfilms, *Manos'* 'hopelessly fragmented' editing (Barefoot 2017: 2) stands out as particularly inept. Rob Craig suggests 'no other film ever made looks even remotely' like *Manos*; it seems to be 'unique' even within the context of badfilm (Craig 2015: 140). However, I suggest that the fragmentation of cinematic space and time, and the sense of disorientation it engenders, is a relatively consistent characteristic of badfilms. There are many different ways to fail, and each failure reveals itself in different ways. Yet, conversely, the effects of failure often share more similarities than differences. As a result of obvious, unintended visual and aural discrepancies, the construction of filmic space and time is emphasised, and the artifice of the diegesis is exposed. Of course, continuity and 'invisible' editing are not always the intended result; editing can deliberately present spatial and temporal relations in more 'ambiguous and uncertain' ways (Bordwell and Thompson 2017: 226), encouraging more active viewer engagement in the process. Nevertheless, badfilms are typically assumed to have 'aspired to Hollywood standards but failed miserably' (Barefoot 2017: 6), and their inconsistency and incoherence do not suggest a conscious rejection of cinematic style. Rather, discontinuity is equated with incompetence, the unintended consequence of a lack of knowledge, ability, understanding and/or effort.

Badfilms can encourage active viewer engagement: trying to make sense of them becomes a task for the viewer. Yet, their ambiguous presentation of space and time poses a particular challenge for interpretation and meaning-making, precisely because it so often seems to be accidental. In addition, although Pepperman argues that 'few people watch films with an interest in post-production possibilities; and fewer inexorably take note of "misses" –

and "near-misses" – occurring on screen' (2004: 114), discontinuity is often obvious in badfilms. One does not need to be proficient in the technicalities of editing to recognise blatant errors such as a mismatching between day and night shots. We do not need expertise to recognise a discrepancy in *Robot Monster* when Ro-Man is blatantly incapable of tying newly-captive Alice up, yet she appears fully bound in the next shot. Through their failure, badfilms draw attention to the 'misses' – they are unavoidable. As a result, their excessively visible discontinuity unwittingly encourages a heightened awareness of cinematic construction that, in itself, can be a quite satisfying, even pleasurable, experience.

The badness of *The Beast of Yucca Flats*, for example, is not due to any one aspect of formal or technical failure, but arises from a combination of multiple failures, each one exacerbating and compounding the badness of the others. Its incoherence, however, can be understood to constitute a direct consequence of bad editing that imposes discontinuity onto an inherently coherent space. Due to the film's sparse narrative content, anything of interest – if it is to be found at all – must be located elsewhere. *Yucca Flats*' fragmented, illogical and entirely incoherent presentation of geographical space thus offers a distraction from its other, more 'boring' and unremarkable qualities. This discontinuity can be attributed to failures in editing specifically, given that the film is shot almost exclusively on location, on the Sierra Highway in Saugus near Los Angeles. Discontinuity is particularly evident in a sequence in which one of the characters, Hank, is mistaken for the Beast and repeatedly shot at by patrolman Jim from an airplane flying above. The sequence appears to intentionally invite intertextual readings; relatively limited cultural capital is required to recognise it as an homage to (or rip-off of) one of cinema's most enduring and iconic action sequences, the crop duster scene in *North by Northwest* (Hitchcock 1959). In the process, *Yucca Flats* invites comparisons between the two films and aligns itself with classical Hollywood cinema, creating a categorical context in which Francis' debut emerges as the clear loser.

Rapid editing is employed in this action sequence and, despite some brief shots explicitly indicating Hank and Jim's proximity to one another, it is almost impossible to establish a consistent sense of the spatial relationship between the characters. The potential for comprehension is shattered by the overwhelming discontinuity. The landscape is dismantled completely, its fragmentation emphasised by the frequent aerial shots that variously depict flat farmland, giant rounded rock formations, desert landscapes and undulating hills, none of which seem to relate coherently to one another, despite being edited together to suggest a single, continuous action sequence. The editing does not propose that Hank was chased for such a distance that he travelled from farmland, over rocks, to a nearby desert. Although this, arguably, would have been entirely possible using the footage collected in production, the

Figures 6.2A–E Bad editing obliterates the natural logic of the landscape, *The Beast of Yucca Flats* (Francis, 1961).

various landscapes are instead intercut together. The result is baffling, and the natural logic of the space collapses to such an extent that it 'verges on surrealism [. . . and] reaches new heights of incoherence' (Warren 2010: 97).

However, *Yucca Flats* not only draws attention to its post-production failures here, but also hints at production conditions – notably, the decision to film only on weekends over the course of a year (Cardoza, quoted in Weaver, n. d.). The fragmented landscape depicted in the film, therefore, points to the failed attempts to combine footage shot in a context whereby space, but not time, is shared. In this sequence, the location's natural geography – the real and logical spatial relationship between the various places – is obliterated through the editing, which is wholly ineffective. The motivations behind these editing decisions remain ambiguous. Arguably, had the various shots not been cut up, they would have retained their spatial logic. Yet, the decision was made to disassemble the footage, with the subsequent reassembling completed in particularly inept ways. We can infer the intention to reproduce a famous cinematic moment and the attempt to create suspense and tension, but recognition of the former only renders this scene more incompetent through comparison, while any potential to achieve the latter is obliterated by the extreme disregard for visual continuity. For example, how can we care about Hank's wellbeing when we are unable to ascertain the danger in which he actually finds himself? Technical incompetence overwhelms the possibility of narrative engagement and instead draws attention to the film's construction. In the process, however, it rewards close attention, enabling the observant viewer to recognise that the visual incoherence is the result of splicing together individually coherent moments. We can start to separate the different shots, which were likely filmed on separate occasions over *Yucca Flats*' year-long schedule: the plane; Hank running along a path; Hank climbing over rocks; the farmland location where the plane makes its 'near-miss' with Hank in the scene's concluding moments.

Of course, cinematic space can be presented in ambiguous ways without being inherently confusing; ambiguity can be appropriately and effectively used to 'stir our imaginations' (Bordwell and Thompson 2017: 259). This points to the possible interpretive pleasures of unconventional, bad editing. When temporal and spatial discontinuity seems to be unmotivated and accidental, as is so often the case in badfilm, our imaginations are 'stirred' because of the confusion caused by the resulting ambiguity. Discontinuity invites us to attempt to locate meaning ourselves; lacking a clear explanation for the resulting incoherence, we are encouraged to adopt creative interpretive frameworks. This, in turn, can offer a positive distraction from the banalities of the narrative by, for instance, shifting focus from narrative deficiencies that might be 'boring' to the inconsistent and unpredictable formal devices through which that narrative is relayed. The following example develops this concept further.

Contradictions of Space and Time in *Plan 9 From Outer Space*

Like *Manos* and *Yucca Flats*, *Plan 9* regularly displays an extreme disregard for spatial, temporal and narrative continuity. This often appears to be the result of misguided faith in the ability of editing to conceal and correct issues that arise in production. *Plan 9*, like several other badfilms, attempts to tell an ambitious story, one that likely could never be adequately depicted given production conditions and the restrictions necessitated by the film's budget. Wood attempts not just a science-fiction/horror narrative (which already carries the expectation of otherworldly, futuristic spectacle) but a full-scale alien invasion story. In many ways, *Plan 9* is quite a dense film: it features a wide array of characters and vaguely interrelated storylines, and although much of the action appears to be localised, it also depicts seemingly connected events occurring around the country. The voice-over narrator (Criswell) provides additional exposition that tends to contradict, or at least complicate, our understanding of what is happening. Although material poverty is evident throughout, it is one of Wood's more 'expensive' films: its estimated $60,000 budget is three times that of *Jail Bait* and *Glen or Glenda*, and only $10,000 less than *Bride of the Monster*. *Plan 9*'s status as the 'worst film of all time' may be debated, but it is certainly one of Wood's more obviously inept movies and is notable for having become 'badfilm's equivalent of *Citizen Kane* as an inventory of characteristically paracinematic stylistic devices' (Sconce 1995: 388). Nothing seems to work: the acting varies from wooden to histrionic; the aliens' plan is ludicrous and nonsensical; the dialogue trite and contradictory. Even the most 'effective' moment – a newly reanimated Inspector Clay (Tor Johnson) rising from the grave – is followed by 'one of the least convincing model shots in movies' (Routt 2001: 7). *Plan 9* is a 'movie of pure effect' (Routt 2001: 1), whereby our attention is constantly – yet seemingly unintentionally – drawn away from the narrative to its construction. Despite presenting itself as a conventional narrative film prioritising dramatic action and emotional engagement, we are constantly reminded that we are watching a movie made of disparate, unrelated parts.

Plan 9's most obvious continuity errors include mismatches between footage filmed on location and on a sound stage, apparent discrepancies between day and night, the unconvincing integration of stock footage and the use of a body double – chiropractor Tom Mason – in original scenes supposedly featuring Lugosi, who appears briefly in footage filmed for another purpose prior to his death. The disorienting effects of bad editing are apparent throughout, although the causes of such disorientation have not always been identified correctly. Discrepancies between day and night are primarily the result of certain shots being filmed on location during the day and others being filmed on a sound stage with a black backdrop suggesting night, but they have been misinterpreted as Wood's apparent inability to adequately process day-for-night shots in post-production (Medved and Medved 1980: 206; the different locations are not acknowledged by others, although the clash between day and night has been – see Warren 2010: 667; Adams 2010: 66). Thus, the blatant visual discrepancies are evidence of both temporal and spatial discontinuity, drawing attention to specific conditions of production as well as the spartan minimalism of the studio set.

Discontinuity exists not just in the cuts, but also in the screenplay itself, as can be seen in an early sequence. The Old Man (Lugosi) and a small group of mourners are attending a funeral service. This is one of the few shots in which Lugosi actually features and was filmed on location in a small cemetery in Sacramento (Wood, in Grey 1992: 78). Over the images, which lack diegetic sound, Criswell's voice-over narration reports that it is the '*sundown of the day*, yet also the sundown of the Old Man's heart'. As the funeral attendants leave, two men walk over and remove their jackets, while Criswell ominously notes that 'it was as the gravediggers *started their task* that strange things started to take place'. The bright sky is clearly visible, suggesting that, if Criswell is indeed the omniscient narrator as which he is presented, it must be late afternoon, with sunset presumably approaching. The next shot, inferred as parallel action through the voice-over's comments, reveals the exterior of a plane (likely stock footage) in flight, again in broad daylight. Inside the cockpit, the pilot and co-pilot are engaged in conversation, during which one mentions it is 'fifteen to four'. Considering the preceding scene, this seems to confirm that the action is occurring in the afternoon. However, this is immediately contradicted during a radio call to the control tower below, when the co-pilot remarks that 'it wouldn't surprise me if he [the control operator] was asleep, *this time in the morning*'.

Almost immediately, therefore, *Plan 9*'s temporal continuity has been compromised. The apparently 'omniscient' narrator contradicts the accompanying visual evidence, while characters create further confusion by explicitly stating a time of day that does not correspond coherently with any of the other information we have been provided. The misinformation in the opening minutes of *Plan 9* hints at Wood's inability to structure the film coherently or logically, while also seeming to confirm claims regarding his erratic writing habits and ambivalence towards proofreading (various in Grey 1992: 139–41). Conversely, the sequence is largely edited in line with classical continuity, employing devices of parallel editing and following conventions by including establishing shots followed by interiors and/or close-ups. While discrepancies in the script and contradictory visual evidence make it impossible to establish any logical sense of time, other editing techniques suggest attempts to conform to the standards of narrative cinema that were prevalent at the time.

The scene continues with a sudden burst of light emanating from beyond the frame. Apparently, something has caused the plane to sway wildly: the pilot and co-pilot grasp onto their meagre props and a typically 'other-worldly' sound of rushing air accompanies the image. The pilots look stage right. Cut to an apparent point-of-view shot revealing the cause of the commotion – a UFO, hovering over a painted, day-time backdrop (see Chapter 2). An air steward appears in the cockpit to enquire what has happened and remarks that is unlikely the passengers were disturbed because they are 'asleep', her comment seeming to then agree with the co-pilot's – and not the voice-over narrator's – timeframe. The UFO continues its journey, travelling left to right across a series of shots towards a graveyard. Oddly, this sequence suggests a significant passing of time as well as space, due to the changing backdrop. After clearly showing the UFO against the cloudy, day-time background, it comes to hover above a graveyard – what appears to be a real location with the flying saucer superimposed over it. Through this shot's position in relation to the preceding scene, we might infer that this is intended to be the graveyard of the opening shot, but there are no shared visual markers to confirm this. As the UFO hovers above gravestones and tombs, stars are visible in the night sky. These shots – seemingly combining stock footage, real locations, studio sets and miniature models – are edited together in such a way that it appears the UFO has covered an expanse of both time and space, having travelled such a substantial distance that night has fallen before it has reached its destination. Importantly, we are able to arrive at this interpretation due to Wood's general adherence to classical continuity style and, in particular, the 180-degree rule – the spaceship follows a logical path, its journey easy to understand as it moves from one shot to the next, from one side of the screen to the other. In the process, it draws attention to the visual discontinuity between the shots, thus drawing attention to the composite nature of the sequence.

Problematically, however, this apparent ellipsis is immediately contradicted by the next scene, which returns to the gravediggers as they continue their work. This confirms that everything we have seen since the gravediggers first appeared onscreen is parallel action that has occurred in a relatively short time-span – the men have not even completed their task when the UFO lands. It is also notable that, despite the apparent size of the spaceship in relation to the graveyard as shown in the preceding shots, the gravediggers appear unaware of any intrusion, creating further uncertainty regarding the UFO's location in relation to the characters. A lack of shared visual information within the various shots means that the space – spaces? – is ambiguous. Further confusing matters, the gravediggers continue to work in broad daylight, with no indication that 'sundown' is approaching. Thus, by arranging the shots in sequence, the editing strongly implies that we are meant to recognise a spatial and temporal relationship between the gravediggers, the plane and the UFO. Simultaneously, however, this is challenged by the visual discontinuity within the shots and further confused by character dialogue.

A noise alerts the gravediggers, who look up from their task. Cut to a brief shot of a graveyard, resembling neither the space in which the funeral occurred nor where the spaceship apparently landed, again in daylight. Spooked by the noise, the men decide to leave. They walk along an overgrown path, evidently a real location, still bathed in sunlight. Cut to what can only be retrospectively identified as a medium-long shot, showing some bare branches and the edge

Figure 6.3A,B Suggesting shared space through editing, *Plan 9 From Outer Space* (Wood, Jr, 1959).

of a building of some sort, set against an entirely black backdrop. It is hard to establish a sense of scale in the shot – the building comprises a blank wall and a plain pitched roof, so could be of any size – or any logical spatial connection between the shots, although their arrangement suggests that we are meant to recognise them in relation to one another. Character action within the shot also indicates shared space: the gravediggers glance right, subtly shrug their shoulders and continue walking. The shot returns to the ambiguous structure, as a woman, who is listed in the credits as the Vampire Girl but also identified by the voice-over narrator as the Old Man's recently deceased wife, emerges from behind the building. Finally, we can understand the shot's scale, revealing the building to be only slightly taller than the woman, and in a subsequent scene we can infer this to be the impossibly sized crypt where the Old Man is buried after his untimely death.

As the scene reaches its conclusion, it is once again possible to identify an attempt to adhere to classical continuity editing and present these two visually dissimilar and unconnected spaces as a unified whole. Cross-cutting is employed as the sequence switches between the gravediggers and the woman. The gravediggers walk along the path. The woman turns and begins to walk towards the camera. The gravediggers continue walking; a split-second before the shot changes again, it is barely possible to see one appear to startle at something before him. The cut occurs too soon: we are not given time to fully recognise and register this action, which could have helped to ascertain a connection between the characters. The woman, still framed in medium-long shot, comes to a halt behind some barren branches and raises her arms. Screams emanate from somewhere beyond the frame. Cut to black.

In the absence of shared visual markers to establish a temporal relationship between the various shots, it falls to sound and editing to create a connection. Both appear to ask us to accept this as a unified space, one in which the innocent gravediggers are in grave peril and, as is confirmed in a subsequent scene, meet their untimely, tragic deaths as a result of this terrible encounter. Yet, the entire sequence presents time and space in particularly ambiguous, confusing, contradictory ways. Through the editing, connections are implied between everything that has occurred since the initial funeral scene; the characters' lives are all intertwined, and everything seems to be happening in a space intended to be recognised as a unified, and relatively small, whole – later, in an uncanny twist of fate, it even transpires that the pilot lives next door to the graveyard. Thus, we can identify the intention here: not to draw attention to visual discontinuity, but to suggest temporal and spatial unity. In terms of the narrative, this is a significant sequence, one filled with information and action that establishes and motivates much of the rest of the film's story but, despite the apparent intention to foreground the plot, the extreme visual discrepancies and sheer incoherence of the sequence is utterly distracting. The film does not even allow for the suspension of disbelief, because the images it presents are so drastically different, the spaces are so incoherent and the timeframe is impossible to establish in any logical, rational way. With all the onus being placed on the viewer to try to make sense of what they have been presented with, engagement with the actual narrative content is necessarily side-lined.

Discontinuity is a key characteristic of badfilms, and rarely seems to be intended. Thus, the discontinuity in *Plan 9* as a result of bad editing is extreme, but not particularly unusual: space and time are regularly presented in inconsistent, illogical, incoherent ways, dismantling and disassembling the films into disparate parts. In *Plan 9*, the explicit references to time made by the voice-over narrator and various characters suggest the intention to establish the setting in an easily digestible manner, but the contradictory information only confuses. This is not only evidence of ineptitude but of carelessness: surely the discrepancies ought to have been noticed during the editing process. Yet they remain, with no obvious attempt to correct them. Furthermore, the incompetent editing also accidentally exposes the film's construction, revealing techniques that are common across all film production but typically concealed in 'good' films, such as shooting out of sequence or creating composite settings from multiple locations.

Notably, in many ways, *Plan 9*'s editing – in terms of the cuts themselves – is reasonably conventional and largely adheres to the conventions of classical continuity. The visual discrepancies, however, cannot be concealed simply through editing unrelated shots together. Rather than presenting a unified space, the audacious editing dismantles and fragments the space. It is hard to imagine anyone watching *Plan 9* without feeling utterly disoriented. Even Rob Craig concedes that the film's editing could result in the viewer feeling 'completely bewildered' due to the various shots within scenes apparently 'taking place on entirely different planes of existence' (2009: 152). By editing the film in largely conventional ways but without adequately acknowledging the blatant visual inconsistencies between shots, the film's narrative, spatial and temporal incoherence is amplified, not concealed. Individually, each shot may be entirely functional and capable of relaying information in an appropriate manner; together, they work to expose each other's failures. Thus, the editing becomes visible despite its adherence to conventions that are designed to work 'invisibly'. In the process, *Plan 9*'s other limitations and weaknesses – its material poverty, reliance on recycled footage and shoddy screenplay – are also exposed, and our attention is drawn away from the diegesis to its inept construction.

The sheer obviousness of visual discrepancies and narrative illogic as a result of inept, ineffective and inappropriately visible editing also effectively serve as distractions from other, less interesting moments in the films. The above-mentioned sequence in *Yucca Flats*, for example, is memorable in part because of its incoherence, but also because it is a rare example of excess in an otherwise minimalist film. We can foreground the incoherence of *Plan 9*, effectively downplaying – as I have surely done in my analysis – the numerous, forgettable scenes in which characters have mundane conversations or stalk barren graveyard sets. In the process, it is the excessive moments that are emphasised; moments in which the most abject examples of failure create the most bizarre effects.

In this way, then, we can reflect on the potential pleasures of badfilms and, in particular, the relationship between excessive failure and enjoyment. The sheer obviousness of visual discontinuity and narrative illogic effectively serve as a distraction from other, less interesting moments. On the one hand, bad editing is inappropriately visible and unintentionally compromises our ability to focus on, or respond emotionally to, the narrative content. In the process, however, it allows us to consider the film as a construction, with everything that this entails. Through this seemingly contradictory state of distraction and attention, a new relationship is forged between viewer and text, one that cannot intentionally be easily reproduced. We are presented with a challenge: to find a way of rationally explaining – even 'solving' – what is ultimately an irrational, illogical, incoherent text. Not everyone will necessarily accept the challenge, of course, and even those who do will probably find that their efforts are largely futile. Nevertheless, through this more active viewer engagement, it seems more likely that we will find – somewhere, even for a brief moment – something that is sufficiently weird and disorienting to also be (weirdly, we might say) enjoyable.

Editing, Narrative and the Anti-Pleasures of Badfilms

As the previous examples indicate, watching badfilms is often a disorienting experience, one that places the responsibility of making sense of the filmic world onto the viewer, typically with little or no chance of success. Attempts to analyse badfilms rationally tend to reveal their irrationality, but there is potential pleasure to be gleaned in the effort, the attempt itself. The ambiguity of badfilms makes them particularly malleable and open to interpretation, while their 'silliness', trashiness and low cultural status means that we do not necessarily feel the weighty critical burden of taking them seriously: we can have fun with them. Nevertheless, badness does not reveal itself only through the distracting visibility of ineffective shot transitions or inappropriate cuts. Narrative incoherence is as much a marker of badness as the many strange, inconsistent and inappropriate deviations in style. Editing is, at its core, 'about storytelling' (Pepperman 2004: 2), with the aim of classical continuity editing in particular being to 'tell a story coherently and without distractions' (Orpen 2003: 16). The cuts themselves do not need to be distracting to dismantle narrative coherence. As the previous case-studies have demonstrated, when editing is excessively visible, it can serve to unintentionally distract from narrative banality, which in turn can encourage a more positive reappraisal and cult appreciation for both film and filmmaker. Conversely, editing can be entirely functional and still utterly fail to present the narrative in a coherent, dynamic or interesting way, with the added 'problem' being that now there is also nothing to distract from these narrative deficiencies.

The badfilms discussed throughout this book tend to be viewed within the categorical context of narrative cinema, but they often have markers of exploitation, too (see Chapter 4). For example, badfilms are full of 'padding' (see Schaefer 1999: 68), moments that extend the runtime but seem to offer little else of interest. Deviations from the main plot – in particular, relatively lengthy scenes of ineffective spectacle – are typical, disrupting the narrative flow and affecting pacing. The dance routines interspersed throughout *Incredibly Strange Creatures*, for instance, do not provide adequate spectacle to distract from their lack of narrative purpose. Similarly, we could consider the mundane 'attractions' of lengthy, repetitive scenes of anonymous, semi-naked characters engaging in pedestrian activities such as playing volleyball in dull nudie-cuties such as *The Beast That Killed Women* or *Nude on the Moon* (Wishman 1961), or any depiction of unerotic writhing around in softcore sleaze pictures. As others have suggested, Ed Wood's later pornographic pictures fail to provide the entertainment of his earlier badfilms, due to the dominance of boring scenes intended to incite erotic pleasure. For Sconce, *Glen or Glenda* is an 'extraordinary document of cinematic possibility', while *Necromania: A Tale of Weird Love* (Wood 1971) is 'unbearable' (2019: 667). Conversely, comments by both Joe Blevins (2013) and Rob Craig (2009: 242–51) suggest that there is a lot within *Necromania* that could appeal to Wood fans, if the explicit sexual content were removed and the film recut with a stronger emphasis on plot and dialogue (see also Bartlett 2019b). Blevins even declares it to be 'one of the most quotable films in the entire Wood canon' (2013). As noted in Chapter 5, *Orgy of the Dead* has already received this treatment through a 'fan's cut' that removes the film's lengthy striptease sequences in order to emphasise the narrative qualities of Wood's screenplay. Although we can rightly point out that such scenes cannot really be 'padding' because erotic spectacle is the primary aim and the central priority of the film, their ineffectiveness makes them monotonous and tedious, inducing a kind of stasis as we are left waiting for something – anything, good or bad – to break the boredom and entertain us once again.

It would be misleading to suggest that watching badfilms is to be constantly overwhelmed by excessive, obvious, incessant and – potentially – entertaining failure. Rather, badfilms are often marked by a strange combination of excess and inertia, with long passages of inaction punctuated by sudden, jarring deviations in style, tone, or narrative progression. It is little wonder that fan-authored badfilm literature tends towards synopsis-style criticism, with specific moments of 'interest' (typically, the most obvious and excessive moments of failure) picked out and discussed in more detail. 'These are the moments that make the viewing experience worth it!' these reviews seem to imply; your patience will be rewarded. Indeed, badfilms are often quite difficult to remember in their entirety. The various formal elements do not cohere together, as they do not work to support one another. Thus, badfilms are fragmented, and they are remembered (and misremembered) in fragmented ways also. We might not be able to recall the plots of badfilms such as *Blood of Ghastly Horror*, or *The Skydivers*, or *Night Train to Mundo Fine*, or *Dracula Vs Frankenstein* in any kind of coherent way – because they are not coherently presented to us – but the feelings of confusion and bafflement linger.

Badfilms are often characterised by a lack of spectacle, although fan-authored and academic literature tends to emphasise their more excessive moments of spectacular failure. The typically tiny budgets and restrictive production conditions simply did not allow for the kind of visual pleasures that their narrative and genre contexts imply. Of course, limitations can encourage creativity and, at the very least, the people responsible for the badfilms discussed in this book are resourceful and creative to the extent that they do not admit defeat or abandon the plan in favour of something less ambitious. Their solution, however, is often less evidence of creativity than functionality: what is the cheapest and easiest way of relaying necessary information, either visually or aurally, to the audience? Thus, when badfilms are not attempting to pass off recycled spectacle as new, for example, they are relying on character conversations to provide exposition instead. The tendency to have 'two people sit down and ramble on at one another' is not just a recurring feature of Ed Wood's films (Routt 2001: 10), but of many badfilms. Functional and effective, this device is remarkable only in its unremarkableness. The intention here seems so transparent, and its functionality is more difficult to re-evaluate or ironically celebrate as a result: we cannot appreciate unconventional, accidental deviations in film style when there is no particular evidence of style on display. Furthermore, the device has been explicitly recognised – by Larry Buchanan, no less – as bad. Buchanan describes what he terms the 'kitchen picture' as follows: 'a film of talking heads, wherein one player walks to the kitchen, pulls out a chair for a companion and utters the most damaging words in cinema, "Sit down, I want to talk to you"' (1996: 32). It is ironic, although unsurprising, that his films should employ variations on this trope so often, which is then accurately, according to his own claims, identified as evidence of failure.

Sometimes, bad editing is so excessively inappropriate, so audacious in its combinations of shots, that it can distract from other (narrative) failures and enable an alternative form of viewer engagement that prioritises construction and the identification of formal style. Other times, however, it fails not due to discontinuity between individual shots, but because of a more general inability to present action or narrative progression in an engaging, appropriate manner. Buchanan's Azalea pictures (see Chapter 2) often seem to encapsulate this. Their minimalism suggests a functional approach to production: do what is required, nothing more and nothing less, in the cheapest and easiest way possible. The result is perfunctory, uninspiring and more often seems to expose ambivalence rather than effort. As already suggested, even by Buchanan's own standards, his films fail. He also argues that 'tension is the absolute, indispensable ingredient in *every* film' (1996: 36; emphasis in original); yet his Azalea pictures are marked by a lack of tension. We can see the efforts, on occasion. By only offering tantalising glimpses of the titular monster in *Curse of the Swamp Creature*, for example, it appears that the intention was to build tension until the final reveal. This decision only exacerbates the feeling of (inevitable, some might argue) disappointment when we finally see the creature in all its ping-pong-ball-eyed glory. The result is an 'epic anti-climax [. . . and] the very essence of [. . .] failure' (Curran, quoted in Buchanan 1996: 98). Of course, it may be that the decision to keep the creature hidden for the majority of the film was motivated by a desire to conceal its underwhelming appearance for as long as possible. Nevertheless, the effect is the same: a lack of tension, and no satisfactory reward for our perseverance.

The Azalea pictures serve as a useful reminder that badfilms are not inevitably, inherently, 'so bad they're good' – they are not always enjoyable or pleasurable experiences. *Zontar: The Thing from Venus*, *It's Alive*, *Curse of the Swamp Creature* and *The Eye Creatures* are characterised by inertia. The films must be endured, and the lack of stylistic excess means that there is nothing to distract from the banality of the plot, the lacklustre performances, the material poverty visible in every scene. They are memorable only because of the strange amnesia they engender: it is surprisingly difficult to remember

Figure 6.4   The swamp creature reveals itself, *Curse of the Swamp Creature* (Buchanan, 1968).

anything notable about them, other than a lingering sense of boredom. The badness of Buchanan's films is less obviously excessive than, for example, Wood's 'more accessible' incompetence and constitutes a 'test of even the most dedicated paracinematic viewer's patience' (Sconce 1995: 390). With nothing to distract from the narrative and aesthetic minimalism, the Azalea pictures seem to stretch time 'into a tortuous infinity' (Curran, quoted in Buchanan 1996: 98). Their minimal functionality also limits their potential to be reinterpreted as an object of fun or, even, of fascination – they seem so obviously perfunctory that they cannot even be understood as curiosities. Even Buchanan's most vocal advocates, *Zontar* magazine's critics, acknowledge that there are few moments in any of his films that are 'even the slightest bit unintentionally funny' (Douglas St Claire Smith, quoted in Buchanan 1996: 119). As a result, their badness seems to reveal itself in ways that prohibit the pleasure that other badfilms offer; they are 'snoozers [. . .] that] all achieve the same level of boring badness' (Adams 2010: 297). This, in itself, is evidence of failed intentions. Although Buchanan appears to have somewhat embraced his status as a badfilm-maker, there is no evidence to suggest that he ever intended to make boring films, which is surely the most damning description of badness there is. Unsurprisingly, it is the more 'entertaining' bad movies that have been most sympathetically and enthusiastically appropriated.

The persistent descriptions of some badfilms as 'so bad they're good' indicate that some forms of failure offer more potential for pleasure than others. As discussed in Chapter 1, the 'so' in 'so bad it's good' indicates excess: technical failure is so visible, so obvious, so abundant. The badness in films such as the Azalea pictures, in contrast, is always visible and always obvious, but in repetitive, uninteresting ways. In this way, the badness itself fails, by failing to be excessive enough to be entertaining, or to even incite much curiosity. The functional competence offers less opportunity to recognise the apparently naïve artistic ambition that underpins other forms of badfilm appreciation. Instead, their badness is underwhelming, suggesting a basic ability to adhere to cinematic conventions with minimum effort or creative vision. In contrast to the examples discussed previously, the editing is largely unremarkable and uninteresting, and it rarely reveals unintended 'mental hiccups' or discontinuities that elsewhere provide a distraction from narrative inaction. Consequently, badfilms like Buchanan's fail to be effectively engaging enough to be considered 'good' *and* they fail to be excessively disorienting and weird enough to become 'so bad they're good'.

The cultification of badfilms such as Buchanan's Azalea pictures, I suggest, rests primarily on the anti-pleasure experience they offer. Characterised by tedium and inertia, they produce negative effects of terminal boredom and defamiliarisation and become a test of endurance. Yet, as Sconce argues, it is precisely because they are 'unwatchable for most mainstream viewers' that they have assumed an 'exalted status' among certain badfilm fans (1995: 390). Of course, just as badness reveals itself in different ways across different badfilms, the possible responses to badness are just as varied. Although the majority of fan-authored criticism of Buchanan's films appears to largely align with those of *Zontar* magazine's writers – at least to the extent that other criticism also discussed Buchanan's films in terms suggesting boredom, endurance and unrealised expectations – there are others who assert that the resulting viewing experience is still an 'entertaining' one (Craig 2007: 8). Nevertheless, I propose that there are still certain textual characteristics that can work to encourage particular responses to different kinds of badness; not all failure warrants or receives the same kind of appreciation (see Dyck and Johnson 2017: 290). Examining editing failures in badfilms provides a means of understanding the standards through which the distinction between 'good' bad movies (so bad they're good) and 'just' bad movies is established. This, in turn, presents an approach that allows for a more objective understanding of the textual features that encourage these various responses.

I have already suggested that recognising and appreciating badness often relies on the dual identification of both the attempts to conform to certain conventions of film style and the failure of such attempts. This identification implicitly assumes evidence of intention, with the filmmaker's efforts perceived to be evident and, ultimately, misguided. Bad acting can be cultified, for example, when it enables the viewer to not only 'see the acting happen' but to recognise this visibility as evidence of the actor's perceived commitment, dedication and charisma. It is possible to make similar assertions with regards to bad editing. It is more likely that films like *Manos*, *The Beast of Yucca Flats* and *Plan 9* have greater potential to 'entertain' through their inappropriately, excessively visible editing than *Zontar* or *Curse of the Swamp Creature*, which are functionally and unimaginatively constructed. In effect, the badness of films such as *Zontar* is neither excessive nor obvious enough to adequately distract from their cheapness, their underwhelming attempts at spectacle, their shoddiness and their lack of artistry. By failing to be engaging either intentionally through narrative action or unintentionally through stylistic incompetence, these films are neither good *nor* bad enough to be entertaining.

7. CONCLUSION: TAKING BADFILMS SERIOUSLY

> 'I've lived the Hollywood rat race and I've filmed in the Hollywood rat race. Check my films! And check some others! And then realise how easy it is to make a cheap picture and fail'.
>
> Edward D. Wood, Jr, *Hollywood Rat Race*

Failure is central to badfilm identification and appreciation: every poorly delivered line of dialogue, every unconvincing special effect, every incoherent plot development and every distracting moment of asynchrony and discontinuity exposes the failure to achieve even the minimum standards of cinematic representation. Badfilms are incoherent, inconsistent and frequently bizarre – not despite their demonstrable failure, but precisely because of it. Ironically, it is also because they are failures that some have gained cult success. The extent of this cultification varies from film to film and is dependent on a range of factors that have been discussed elsewhere in this book and are not limited to formal incompetence but must also take into account reception contexts – existing reputations, issues of access and availability, and so on. Nevertheless, there is a correlation between badfilms' failure and their cult success – the greater the evidence of the former, the more chance of the latter.

Accepting that badfilms are artistic failures, it can seem as though their value – if it is to be located at all – lies primarily, if not exclusively, in their ability to be appropriated as cult texts. The formation of a badfilm canon has established a hierarchy of failure, whereby the 'best' badfilms are those with the most evidence of failed intentions and demonstrable incompetence, and therefore have the most potential to be entertaining, enjoyable or otherwise pleasurable experiences. However, while not wishing to deny or refute their potential instrumental value as objects of fun, the value of badfilms can be located elsewhere also: in the failure itself. Because badfilms are incompetent, they allow us to recognise disparities between the attempts to achieve a certain outcome and the actual results, and thus draw attention to elements of production and formal construction that are ordinarily concealed in 'good' films. Their inept construction limits their immersive potential; in the process, the formal failures draw inappropriate attention to themselves, unwittingly encouraging an unusual viewing position marked by a combination of heightened awareness, critical detachment and, often, utter bewilderment.

Bewilderment, of course, does not necessarily equate to enjoyment or pleasure, but it does point to the unconventional and regularly baffling experience of watching badfilms. There is, I suggest, a difference between recognising failure and appreciating or valuing it; one does not necessarily ensure the other, and we should be careful not to conflate the two. At the very least, doing so risks limiting the films eligible for consideration (by assuming that only cultified badness has value) and therefore reduces the opportunities to consider cinematic badness outside cult contexts. Individual tastes determine our response to badfilms which, because of their inherent incoherence and inconsistency, are regularly ambiguous enough to allow for a range of possible readings (Bartlett 2019a). Badfilms can be appropriated as accidental art; read sympathetically as evidence of entrepreneurial graft and auteurist determination; rationalised as the seemingly inevitable consequence of particular modes of production; laughed at or otherwise enjoyed for the unintentional comedy that their failure engenders; or dismissed as 'trash' and acknowledged only because they represent one end of the quality spectrum. Reception is necessarily subjective, but all these responses (and there are surely many other possibilities) begin with the shared assumption and acceptance of the films' intrinsic, demonstrable, objective badness – of their failure. As demonstrated in Chapter 2, approaching badfilms from a position that addresses failed intentions thus provides a means of shifting the focus away from reception back onto the text itself and opens up new possibilities for further investigation.

The Badfilm Canon after 1970

The badfilms discussed throughout this book were made in the US during the two decades widely considered to be the 'golden age' of canonical badness. As noted in Chapter 1, the 1950s and 1960s presented the optimal conditions for independent, low-budget filmmakers to carve out positions for themselves on the fringes of Hollywood, while working under particularly restrictive conditions that made failure more likely. The subsequent cultification of films including *Glen or Glenda*, *The Beast of Yucca Flats* and *The Creeping Terror* indicates how their demonstrable incompetence and failure is not only identified but also celebrated and potentially valued. Because these films, among others, have been canonised as the 'worst of all time', they have helped to set the standards by which cinematic badness continues to be understood and evaluated. Thus, they provide particularly accessible and relatively widely available examples of failure, and they are worthy of further scrutiny, not least of all because they set the benchmarks for technical ineptitude.

Notably, far fewer films made after 1970 have secured their place within the badfilm canon. This suggests that there is a historical-cultural aspect to both identification of and cult appreciation for cinematic badness. As others (for example, Schaefer 1999; Davis 2012; Hill 2017) have noted, the film industry in the US underwent significant changes in the late 1960s and 1970s, which had a marked impact on the production, distribution and exhibition of low-budget, independent films. Sconce, meanwhile, traces the decline of the 'golden age' of canonical badness to the disappearance of particular modes of production that existed in the 1950s and 1960s but became increasingly rare in the 1970s, by which time the 'conditions conducive for producing woefully incompetent product [. . . had] all but vanished' (2019: 669). Technological advances and changing production contexts, as well as developments in the film industry more broadly, made the kind of naïve failure and demonstrable incompetence that characterises canonised badfilms less likely. For example, recycling and repurposing existing footage, discussed in Chapter 4, became less common, as did MOS shooting due to advances in sound technologies. As a result, Sconce suggests that 'enjoyably "bad" movies are now, more often than not, the product of atrocious scripts and terrible acting (aspects of film art that, as of yet anyway, have no technological fail safes)' (2019: 670). Adding to this, I suggest that material poverty – exposed through bad cinematography, cheap sets and shoddy special effects – also remains a key marker of contemporary canonical badness, while all badfilms are characterised by incoherence and failed intentions.

They may be less common, but contemporary canonised badfilms are frequently as demonstrably, objectively incompetent as the 'classic' badfilms from the 1950s and 1960s. They regularly share similar characteristics of failure – bad sound design, incoherent and distractingly visible editing, wooden and/or histrionic performances and ineffective spectacle. *The Room*'s numerous technical and formal failures have been detailed elsewhere (for example, MacDowell and Zborowski 2013; there are also many fan-authored reviews to be found online), but one particular moment that always stands out to me, although rarely mentioned elsewhere, occurs towards the end of the film. Having discovered that his fiancée has been cheating on him with his best friend, Johnny (Tommy Wiseau) flies into a rage and trashes his apartment.

Wiseau's performance here, as elsewhere, is highly visible, simultaneously excessive and flat, and produces unintentionally comedic effects. The dramatic musical score, which seems intended to emphasise and underscore the scene's emotional impact, only serves to highlight how absurdly overwrought Johnny's reaction is. Howling intermittently in apparent anguish, Johnny knocks fruit out of a bowl on the coffee table, before turning his attention to a tall candelabra behind the sofa. He kicks over some storage boxes and a small shelving unit, then dramatically sweeps several glasses and candles off the mantlepiece. In the process, he knocks over a framed picture that comes to rest *on the camera itself*. The fourth wall collapses; at the very point when we should be focusing our attention on Johnny, the tragic protagonist who has been lied to and betrayed by the people he cared for the most, the illusion of the film's world as a contained space is obliterated. It is a particularly jarring experience to become so suddenly and unexpectedly aware of the camera's physical presence within the diegesis. There is, however, no indication that we are meant to recognise it as such; rather, this is just one moment among many in *The Room* where formal failure limits the film's immersive potential and draws inappropriate attention to its artificiality and its inept, careless construction.

Other contemporary badfilms also expose incompetence in ways that, despite being made some fifty years later or more, are not dissimilar to the formal failures that characterise 'classic' badfilms. Thematically, there are some similarities between *Glen or Glenda* and *Ben & Arthur*, in that both are queer badfilms with seemingly noble intentions that nonetheless present rather regressive, problematic and stereotypical depictions of homosexuality. In the latter, Sam Mraovich – who receives eleven credits in the film's titles, including director, editor, producer and writer – plays Arthur, who wants to get married to his partner Ben but faces innumerable obstacles including legal restrictions, Ben's wife and Arthur's murderous, homophobic, religious fanatic brother. The film is shot on video, and its miniscule budget is apparent throughout. The church set, for example, is replete with fake stained-glass windows, a cardboard cross and a portrait of Jesus that, when viewed today, immediately invites comparison to amateur artist Cecilia Giménez' sincere but botched restoration of a fresco in Spain, which famously became known as 'Monkey Jesus' (see MacDowell and McCulloch 2019: 646).

It is, however, not just *Ben & Arthur*'s abject cheapness that makes it so bad; it is entirely incoherent. As Jim Vorel remarks, the film 'has an incredible way of randomly spiking up the intensity every once in a while without ever giving the viewer an understanding of what is about to happen. Stuff *just happens*' (Vorel and Lowe 2019; emphasis in original). Character actions are unmotivated and illogical – at one point, Arthur declares his intention to find a new job, but is subsequently shown searching for an apartment. His brother, Victor (Michael Haboush), is introduced shortly after, when Arthur turns up

Figure 7.1   Portrait of Jesus, *Ben & Arthur* (Mraovich, 2002).

at his house hoping to get a loan. Neither men recognise one another, but once Arthur establishes that they are siblings, Victor looks surprised and comments that they have not seen each other for seven years. Moments like this point to the inherent failure of the screenplay to establish any clear sense of continuity or logic, but also suggest a further inability on the part of those involved to recognise and/or correct the problems that surely must have been apparent during filming.

Ben & Arthur's failures are too numerous to list here; absolutely nothing whatsoever works in the way in which we might expect. Of note is a scene in which Arthur unsuccessfully auditions to be an exotic dancer, before being indecently propositioned by the club's manager. A generic electro score features in the preceding scenes, as Arthur phones various companies to enquire about their vacancies and then walks to his interview, but it ends abruptly once he enters the club. When the manager asks if he is ready to proceed, Arthur asks if he 'gets any music', to which the manager shrugs and tells him to 'just wing it, improvise something'. As Arthur performs his strangely interpretive routine in near darkness, the scene plays out in almost complete silence, accompanied only by ambient sounds produced by his movements and, occasionally, him singing under his breath. It is a truly bizarre scene, made all the stranger by the fact that a conscious decision appears to have been made to *not* include music, as indicated by the characters' conversation. Attempting to ascertain the intentions behind this aesthetic choice produces no satisfactory explanation: why include dance music in the preceding scenes, but not when the narrative actually requires it? What possible benefit could there be to have the characters draw attention to the lack of music and explicitly acknowledge its absence? What effect was the filmmaker attempting to achieve in the scene?

How are we, as viewers, supposed to respond to what we are experiencing here? It is impossible to rationally or logically understand the filmmaker's motivations in this moment, and the scene is rendered incoherent, uncomfortable and entirely ineffective as a result.

As I have noted previously, badfilms regularly speak to and about other films, through the intertextual readings they intentionally (or accidentally) invite. This is true also with regards to more recent entries in the canon. *Troll 2* (Fragasso 1990), for example, is entirely unrelated to *Troll* (Buechler 1986) and does not even feature the titular characters, but the connection is nonetheless strongly suggested through its presentation as a sequel. Johnny's pained declaration that his fiancée's actions are 'tearing [him] apart' in *The Room*, meanwhile, explicitly alludes to *Rebel Without a Cause* (Ray 1955). *Birdemic: Shock and Terror* (Nguyen 2010), discussed in greater detail below, pays tribute to *The Birds* (Hitchcock 1963), with a more explicit environmental message. *Ben & Arthur*'s concluding scene is a direct and blatant rip-off of the ending of *Scarface* (De Palma 1983), albeit now queered and with a particularly tasteless undertone of incestuous desire. Every time these films align themselves with conventional narrative cinema, they further expose their failure through the incompetent attempts to reproduce moments from more critically acclaimed and technically proficient films.

Significantly, these more recent entries to the badfilm canon have gained their reputation not solely due to their demonstrable cheapness, bad scripts and unconvincing acting, but because, like the most notorious badfilms of the 1950s and 1960s, they reveal many different kinds of excessive, obvious failure throughout. There are similarities in the interpretive strategies adopted by contemporary badfilm fans also: auteurism remains central to badfilm appreciation, for example, and filmmakers like Wiseau, Nguyen and Mraovich can be celebrated for their apparent determination to realise their artistic vision despite their demonstrable limitations or, alternatively, they can be derided for their hubristic aspirations to art. Sconce suggests that films like *The Room* are the 'exception[s] that prove the rule' (2019: 670), but surely at least part of *all* canonised badfilms' appeal is that they are exceptions. It is not enough for the films to be generally bad; they must be exceptionally awful. Furthermore, this 'exceptional awfulness' must be widely recognised and accepted for a film to gain a position within the canon – these are the films that have been cultified for their failure, but this does not necessarily mean that they are somehow the *only* films that are demonstrably, excessively, exceptionally incompetent. As Hill notes, there is always the potential to discover a previously 'unheralded gem' (2017: 14).

I have no doubt that there are plenty of films that comfortably meet all the criteria to be inducted into the badfilm canon, but for any number of possible reasons remain largely, if not entirely, unknown. The cult status of *Children of the Living Dead* (Ramsey 2001) is negligible, for example, but it is certainly a worthy candidate for canonisation. Unlike films like *Ben & Arthur* that can be described as 'vanity projects' created without 'any discernible demand in the marketplace' (Sconce 2019: 670), Ramsey's movie has strong associations with the 'professional' film industry. Made for around $500,000, it was produced by John Russo, who wrote *Night of the Living Dead* (Romero 1968) and Joseph Wolf, the executive producer of such films as *A Nightmare on Elm Street* (Craven 1984), and it was intended to be an official addition to the 'Living Dead' franchise. It is also one of the few contemporary badfilms to feature a recognisable star – special effects legend Tom Savini – although he is killed by a zombie fifteen minutes in and never mentioned again. The scant information regarding *Children*'s production context indicates that it was just as ramshackle and fraught with difficulties as many of those discussed throughout this book: apparently, Russo's original script was thrown out at the last minute and replaced by one written by Wolf's daughter Karen, an aspiring screenwriter, while director Ramsey regularly found himself at loggerheads with his producers, due to their alleged insistence on hiring friends as cast and crew, irrespective of experience or ability. The lack of cohesion between those tasked with making the film seems to have contributed to its onscreen incoherence and demonstrable failure, while also making it difficult to accurately ascertain who, if anyone, can be held accountable. In a lengthy response to a negative online review, Ramsey attests to the film's badness but largely absolves himself of responsibility, instead apportioning most of the blame to Karen Wolf, whom he describes as an 'untalented, inexperienced, uninformed [. . .] spoiled, immature, arrogant hack' (reprinted in Fawcett 2002) who imposed herself upon all aspects of production.

Children of the Living Dead's failure does not reside solely in the screenplay but can be located across all aspects of production. The opening sequence, featuring Savini as Deputy Hughes, is tinted blue; this appears to be less a consciously stylistic choice than an unsuccessful attempt to conceal a day-for-night shoot. Savini's dialogue is very obviously dubbed, with the blatant asynchrony serving to obliterate the 'illusion' of diegetic coherence, as discussed in Chapter 3. The film's temporal structure is nonsensical and features two significant ellipses – one of fourteen years and another of one year – that are announced through intertitles. As a seemingly unintended consequence, we are not introduced to the main protagonists until half an hour into the film. *Children of the Living Dead* does appear to be attempting to present a coherent, linear narrative motivated by the classical conventions of cause and effect, but it fails wholly and completely to achieve this in any acceptable manner.

Like so many of the canonised 'classic' and contemporary badfilms, *Children of the Living Dead* reveals its incompetence in numerous, varied and excessively obvious ways that are more than capable of producing entertaining or otherwise 'pleasurable' effects. It is a terrible film, but it is rarely boring. Its demonstrable failure and inherent incoherence draw attention away from the diegesis and towards its construction, encouraging more active viewer engagement in the process. It also regularly, if inconsistently, exposes the processes of filmmaking itself. For example, inept editing during a scene midway through the film produces a particularly disorienting effect. Matthew (Damien Luvara) has just purchased the land on which the town's graveyard is located, with plans to build a new car dealership. He goes to a diner for food and chats with the waitress, and future love interest, Laurie (Jamie McCoy) while she pours him a coffee. However, it appears that, in the attempt to reproduce the conventional presentation of the conversation through a shot-reverse-shot structure, the editing has failed to account for, or conceal, the actors' inability to maintain consistency between the dialogue they are uttering and the actions they are performing during those moments of dialogue. Their conversation contains a significant amount of exposition, but it is hard to concentrate on what they are saying because the scene is edited in such a way as to suggest Laurie fills his coffee cup, then removes it, proceeds to pour another cup, then wipes the saucer, refills the cup again and, for good measure, refills it one more time. Matthew is never shown drinking the coffee and, to add insult to injury, leaves the diner without having paid. Thus, just as inept editing disrupts the temporal and spatial structure of films like *Plan 9*, as discussed in Chapter 6, here the incompetent way in which different shots are stitched together distracts from the narrative content and exposes the failed attempt to maintain continuity, in particularly bewildering, unexpected and potentially entertaining ways.

The above-mentioned examples suggest that, although the potential for failure might have been lessened by technological developments and industrial advances, it has not been eliminated: it is always possible to fail to achieve the intended outcome. This is not to say, however, that the landscape in which contemporary badfilms are both made and received has not changed quite significantly. It seems likely, for example, that, as film production contexts change and the standards of cinematic representation expand, the ways in which failure might reveal itself could also change. Furthermore, whereas there was no particular audience for badfilms during the 1950s and 1960s – at least, none so visible that filmmakers might recognise the benefits of making deliberately bad movies – by the 1970s a cult audience was emerging and, as early as the 1980s, the 'taste for bad cinema had made it to the outer banks of the mainstream' (Sconce 2019: 668). Today, although badfilm appreciation is by no means ubiquitous, the concept that films – and other arts – can be 'so bad they're good' is widely recognised and accepted. This has several implications for badfilms and badfilm appreciation, some of which will be briefly outlined now.

The continued interest in badfilms, as well as the ongoing search for the 'worst movie of all time', has, in one sense, led to badness being commodified. This has meant wider access to, and wider availability of, films from the 1950s and 1960s that were largely ignored at the time of release and would quite possibly be 'lost' (or, at least, forgotten) were it not for their cultification. In the last decade or so, many of the more notorious 'golden age' badfilms have found their way online and are easily accessible on streaming platforms such as YouTube, for example. At the same time, continued interest in certain badfilm auteurs working during the 1950s and 1960s has resulted in documentaries and biopics (see Chapter 2), as well as DVD releases of previously inaccessible titles from their catalogues. For instance, it was widely believed that some silent outtakes were the only surviving footage of *Take it Out in Trade* (1970), one of Ed Wood's later directorial efforts, until cult film distributors Something Weird Video located a 16mm print; now the film is available on DVD and Blu-Ray. Indeed, many of the sexploitation and pornographic films to which Wood contributed are now relatively easy to access and typically marketed in ways that clearly capitalise on his notable cult auteur reputation, irrespective of the form or extent of his involvement – *The Big Box of Wood* (S'more Entertainment, 2011), for instance, contains a selection of Wood-scripted films alongside his later directorial efforts but declares them all to be 'Ed Wood films'. It is unlikely, for several reasons (see Bartlett 2019b), that any of Wood's later movies could threaten his earlier films' positions within the badfilm canon. Nevertheless, the ongoing cult interest has undoubtedly provided new opportunities to enhance our understanding of Wood and his career beyond the romantic, constructed cult 'character' of him as the 'worst director of all time'. Thus, there is always the potential to discover a new film or group of films that could, at the very least, expand our understanding of canonical badness.

The increased visibility of an audience for badfilms has also, inevitably, led to the production of intentionally bad movies. As noted in Chapter 2, filmmakers such as Larry Blamire play on the 'conventions' of badfilms, sympathetically recreating 'bad' style through consciously inept acting, deliberate discontinuity and so on, largely for comic effect. The success of films like *The Lost Skeleton of Cadavra* (Blamire 2001) and *Dark and Stormy Night* (Blamire 2009) as intentionally bad movies depends on the audience not only recognising the 'badness' as deliberate, but also relies on their awareness of a 'style' associated with canonical badness. Thus, intentionally bad movies can only be read as parodies or homages to badfilms if the filmmaker and viewer have a shared understanding of what constitutes cinematic incompetence. This suggests that, for all their weirdness, incoherence and inconsistency, there *is* a style associated with cinematic failure: badfilms are internally incoherent, but united through a strangely 'consistently inconsistent' style (see also MacDowell and Zborowski 2013: 21; Sestero 2013: 250), and it is possible to identify certain recurring characteristics associated with failure.

As discussed in Chapter 2, intentionality is central to badfilm identification and appreciation: claims of incompetence are based on the acceptance that there is a demonstrable gap between the intended effect, which was undertaken sincerely, seriously and in good faith, and the actual result. Recognition of this gap allows fans to read the films as, for example, accidental art or, more commonly, unintentional comedies. However, the contemporary media landscape generally has meant that the 'authenticity' of more recent badfilms can be difficult to ascertain. The general shoddiness of movies like *Sharknado* (Ferrante 2013) seems more the consequence of a general apathy towards aesthetic quality – Asylum, the company that produced it, caters primarily to 'certain audiences' desire for transgressive spectacle' (Hunter 2014: 483); as a result, their films do not particularly need to be 'good'. It is notable, however, that the later films in the *Sharknado* franchise are bigger budget and veer far more towards explicit parody but contain far less evidence of the aesthetic badness that had helped to secure the original's 'instant' cult status. This suggests that formal failure was less the result of incompetence or inability than a combination of ambivalence and budgetary restrictions.

The commodification of cult generally, and badness more specifically, has also led to some fans and scholars expressing doubts about the 'authenticity' and 'sincerity' of even the most firmly established, canonised badfilms. For example, Sconce says that, although *Birdemic* seems 'truly awful [. . .] in our current era of guerrilla marketing and internet buzz, who can know for sure?' (2019: 671). As I have discussed elsewhere (Bartlett 2019a; see also Hill 2017: 16), however, *Birdemic* is demonstrably, objectively incompetent. To interpret it as an intentionally bad movie would require accepting not only that everyone involved in production was 'in on the joke', but also that they were able to reproduce badfilm style *so* perfectly that it is read not as parody, but as pure, unintentional failure. This reading would suggest a particularly impressive level of sophistication and self-awareness on the part of the filmmakers, which, I suggest, is negated by the film itself, particularly when also taking into consideration its sequel.

Birdemic presents itself as a horror-romance with a serious environmentalist message regarding the dangers of global warning, but everything about it – including its terrible sound design, bad acting, incoherent editing and failed spectacle in the form of birds of prey who spit poison and explode on impact but are also very obviously barely moving GIFs – is overwhelmingly inept. Its sequel, *Birdemic 2: The Resurrection* (Nguyen 2013), arrived three years later and constitutes a blatant attempt to capitalise on the cult popularity of its predecessor. In this respect, its 'success' depends on its ability to 'replicate the "failure" of [*Birdemic*] and evince the same essential authentic sincerity' (Hunter 2014: 490). However, *Birdemic 2*'s sincerity is called into question because it merely replicates, repeats and exaggerates the original film's failure;

there is little evidence of any attempt to improve or do anything differently. To complicate matters further, not everyone agrees that *Birdemic 2* is a self-conscious but still inept attempt to reproduce the style of the first film: as many people seem to perceive its incompetence as sincere, as are those lamenting its lack of originality and its intentional badness. The film's mixed reception, therefore, points to the multitude of overlapping ways in which a film can fail; *Birdemic 2* is neither competent enough to be 'good' nor authentically bad enough to be appreciated in the same way as its predecessor. However, it also indicates the challenges of identifying intention when a bad filmmaker embraces their (unanticipated) cult status and serves as a reminder that we rarely view any film in isolation: for the informed viewer, the categorical context of *Birdemic 2* includes its predecessor, which encourages it to be read as a more self-conscious effort that intends not to be 'good' necessarily, but to be *cult* and, consequently, is a notably less 'satisfying' experience as a badfilm.

The Future of Badfilm Studies

Interest in badfilms – and bad films – continues to thrive within the academy and beyond, and the recent surge of scholarship indicates a range of possibilities for further investigation. The contributions by scholars including Barefoot (2017), Hunter (2019), Smith (2019), Johnson (2019) and Sconce (2019) point to several ways in which our understanding of cinematic badness and the badfilm canon can be understood and productively analysed and are most welcome. Notably, this contemporary academic work does not claim to provide the 'final word' on badness but, instead, aims to suggest 'steps in the right direction' (MacDowell and McCulloch 2019: 647). Likewise, I hope that this book will encourage further consideration of cinematic badness and all the complex, unexpected, disorienting, contradictory and downright bizarre ways in which it reveals itself.

As noted in Chapter 1, if failure studies are to constitute a viable critical approach, humility is required on the part of those conducting the study. Because of their demonstrable incompetence and potential for comedy, celebrating badfilms as objects of fun always carries with it the risk of *schadenfreude*. However, watching badfilms can be as humbling an experience as watching great films, albeit for different reasons: they remind us how easy it is to fail. As discussed elsewhere in this book, central to badfilm identification and appreciation is an acceptance of their serious intentions: that they were artistic endeavours undertaken sincerely and in good faith, that they take themselves seriously and want to be taken seriously. Their demonstrable incompetence, however, means that it is not possible to take them seriously as 'good' films, but we can, I suggest, take them seriously as *badfilms*. In this way, it is possible to acknowledge their potential instrumental value – their unintended success as cult texts – while also recognising that, because their failure cannot be consciously replicated, they have intrinsic value that extends beyond the ways in which they can be appropriated by cult audiences. Just as 'one need by no means attach the value of "good" to conventions in order to make a judgement of "bad" when they appear to be striven for and missed' (MacDowell and Zborowski 2013: 16), we do not need to make claims regarding the potentially 'good' or 'pleasurable' experience of badfilms in order to demonstrate their value as failures, or to legitimise them as worthy of academic investigation.

Shifting the focus back on to the texts and considering badfilms in terms of failed intentions provides new opportunities to expand the canon and to consider, for example, how failure is identified and potentially valued (or not) across other forms of cinema and within other national, historical, cultural and aesthetic contexts. As noted in Chapter 1, although the majority of films discussed throughout this book are canonical badfilms, I do not wish to claim that these are the 'worst' – or even the 'best-worst' – but rather that they have helped to set the standards by which contemporary badfilms are judged and, therefore, offer a productive means of investigating badness-as-failure that can also be applied to films beyond US-American productions from the 1950s and 1960s. It is also notable that academic work on these canonised badfilms is surprisingly sparse. Perhaps because their badness seems to be so overwhelmingly obvious and their positions as both cult films and canonised badfilms are so firmly established, it might appear as though no further consideration is required, or that nothing new can be revealed about them. Hopefully, the present study demonstrates otherwise and points to some of the ways in which we can develop our understanding of the canon, indicating the scope for further examination of the films – and filmmakers – within the existing canon.

Moreover, the badfilms of the 1950s and 1960s continue to have pedagogical value (see Sconce 2003) – perhaps even more so than the more recent entries to the canon in which authenticity can be more difficult to ascertain. Here, I can only speak anecdotally. Nevertheless, I have found that screening badfilms like *Plan 9 From Outer Space* and *Manos: The Hands of Fate* in cult and other film courses has produced interesting and perceptive discussions with my students, of failure, aesthetics and film form, as well as the value of these films as incompetent texts, including, but not limited to, their potential experiential pleasures. This suggests that these films' failed intentions remain as visible to contemporary viewers today, although the ways in which we might respond to those failed intentions are necessarily subjective and based on individual tastes: recognising failure does not guarantee a corresponding appreciation of it. Indeed, I wonder if viewing these historical badfilms in a contemporary context might enable some degree of critical distance and reduced expectations of their ability to be read as unintentional comedies, which in turn activates a more 'objective' approach to the various ways in which failure can be both identified and potentially valued.

Badfilms, I suggest, are intrinsically valuable because of their incompetence. Their incompetence makes them weird, and their weirdness makes them intriguing. Badfilms raise questions but rarely provide clear answers; they are incoherent, disorienting and confusing. However, it is possible to accept the consistent inconsistency of badfilm style and examine badness on its own terms. In this way, we can acknowledge that some badfilms contain some elements that 'work', as well as ones that do not, without undermining their value as incompetent texts. Our analysis can include awareness of the many ways in which badness can manifest itself, even within a single text, and the various possible ways in which badness may be interpreted and appreciated. Because badfilms are characterised by failed intentions, I suggest that they provide unique opportunities to consider not only how we identify failure and respond to it, but also how failure itself works.

BIBLIOGRAPHY

Adams, Michael (2010), *Showgirls, Teen Wolves, and Astro Zombies: A Film Critic's Year-Long Quest to Find the Worst Movie Ever Made*, New York: itbooks
Altman, Rick (1980a), 'Introduction', *Yale French Studies*, 60: Cinema/Sound, 3–15
Altman, Rick (1980b), 'Moving lips: Cinema as ventriloquism', *Yale French Studies*, 60: Cinema/Sound, 67–79
Andrew Klevan (2005), *Film Performance: From Achievement to Appreciation*, London: Wallflower
Anonymous author (1954), 'Robot Monster, U.S.A., 1953', *Monthly Film Bulletin*, 21:240, 180
Anonymous author (1956), 'Bride of the Monster, U.S.A., c.1954', *Monthly Film Bulletin*, 23:264, 75
Arthur, Paul (1997), 'On the virtues and limitations of collage [Transformations in Film as Reality (Part 6)]', *Documentary Box* #11. Available at: https://www.yidff.jp/docbox/11/box11-1-e.html [Accessed 13 April 2019]
Barefoot, Guy (2011), 'Recycled images: Rose Hobart, East of Borneo, and The Perils of Pauline', *Adaptation*, 5:2, 152–68
Barefoot, Guy (2017), *Trash Cinema: The Lure of the Low*, London and New York: Wallflower
Barker, Martin (2013), 'Embracing rape: Understanding the attractions of exploitation movies', in Feona Attwood, Vincent Campbell, I. Q. Hunter and Sharon Lockyer (eds), *Controversial Images: Media Representations on the Edge*, London; New York: Palgrave McMillan, 217–38
Baron, Cynthia L. and Sharon Marie Carnicke (2008), *Reframing Screen Performance*, Ann Arbor: University of Michigan Press
Bartlett, Becky (2015), 'How failure works: Understanding and analysing the characteristics of badfilm, 1950–1970', PhD thesis, University of Glasgow, Glasgow
Bartlett, Becky (2019a), '"It happens by accident": Failed intentions, incompetence,

and sincerity in badfilm', in Jamie Sexton and Ernest Mathijs (eds), *Routledge Companion to Cult Cinema*, Oxon; New York: Routledge, 40–49

Bartlett, Becky (2019b), 'Madman, genius, hack, auteur? Intertextuality, extratextuality, and intention in "Ed Wood Films" after *Plan 9 From Outer Space*', *Continuum* 33:6, 653–65

Begy, Jason and Generoso Fierro (2011), 'The design and speculative technology of MST3K: Joel Hodgson and Trace Beaulieu at MIT', in Robert Weiner and Shelley E. Barba (eds), *In the Peanut Gallery with 'Mystery Science Theater 3000': Essays on Films, Fandom, Technology and the Culture of Riffing*, Jefferson NC: McFarland, 184–96

Benshoff, Harry M. and Sean Griffin (2005), *Queer Images: A History of Gay and Lesbian Film in America*, Lanham, MD: Rowman & Littlefield

Berg, Charles Ramirez (2009), 'Notes on the emergence of failure studies', *The Velvet Light Trap*, 64, 101–2

Betz, Mark (2003), 'Art, exploitation, underground', in Mark Jancovich, Antonio Lazaro Reboll et al. (eds), *Defining Cult Movies*, Manchester: Manchester University Press, 202–22

Birchard, Robert S. (1995), 'Edward D Wood, Jr: Some notes on a subject for further research', *Film History*, 7:4, 450–55

Blevins, Joe (n. d.), 'Ed Wood Wednesdays', *Dead 2 Rights*. Available at: https://d2rights.blogspot.com/2013/09/you-know-what-this-weekend-would-be.html [Accessed 23 July 2019]

Blevins, Joe (2013), 'Ed Wood Wednesdays, week 21: "Necromania" (1971)', *Dead 2 Rights*. Available at: https://d2rights.blogspot.com/2013/11/ed-wood-wednesdays-week-21-necromania.html [Accessed 18 September 2020]

Bordwell, David (2006), *The Way Hollywood Tells It: Story and Style in Modern Movies*, Berkeley, London: University of California Press

Bordwell, David and Kirstin Thompson (2017), *Film Art: An Introduction*, 11th Edition, New York: McGraw-Hill

Bowen, Michael J. (2002), 'Doris Wishman meets the avant-garde', in Xavier Mendik and Steven Jay Schneider (eds), *Underground U.S.A.: Filmmaking Beyond the Hollywood Canon*, London, New York: Wallflower Press, 109–22

Brandt, Richard (1996), 'The hand that time forgot', *Mimosa*, 18, 35–38. Available online at: http://www.jophan.org/mimosa/m18/brandt.htm [Accessed 18 August 2019]

Brottman, Mikita (2000), 'Star cults/cult stars: Cinema, psychosis, celebrity, death', in Xavier Mendik and Graeme Harper (eds), *Unruly Pleasures: The Cult Film and its Critics*, Guildford: FAB Press, 105–19

Browne, Nick (1980), 'Film form/voice-over: Bresson's *The Diary of a Country Priest*', *Yale French Studies*, 60: Cinema/Sound, 233–40

Buchanan, Larry (1996), *'It Came From Hunger!' Tales of a Cinema Schlockmeister*, Jefferson NC: McFarland

Carter, David Ray (2011), 'Cinemasochism: Bad movies and the people who love them', in Robert Weiner and Shelley E. Barba (eds), *In the Peanut Gallery with 'Mystery Science Theater 3000': Essays on Films, Fandom, Technology and the Culture of Riffing*, Jefferson NC: McFarland, 101–9

Cartmell, Deborah, I. Q. Hunter, Heidi Kaye and Imelda Whelehan (eds) (1997), *Trash Aesthetics: Popular Culture and Its Audience*, London; Chicago: Pluto Press

Chew, Richard, Anne V. Coates, Alan Heim, Joe Hutshing, Walter Murch, Pietro Scalia, Arthur Schmidt, Thelma Schoonmaker, Tim Squyres, Christopher Tellefesen and Dylan Tichenor (2009), 'The art and craft of film editing', *Cineaste*, 34:2, 54–64

Chion, Michel (1999), *The Voice in Cinema*, edited and translated by Cynthia Gorbman, New York: Columbia University Press
Craig, Rob (2007), *The Films of Larry Buchanan: A Critical Examination*, Jefferson, NC; London: McFarland
Craig, Rob (2009), *Ed Wood: Mad Genius, A Critical Study of the Films*, Jefferson, NC; London: McFarland
Craig, Rob (2015), 'Manos: The Hands of Fate', in Andrew J Rausch and R. D. Riley (eds), *Trash Cinema: A Celebration of Overlooked Masterpieces*, Albany, GA: Bear Manor Media, 139–42
Crane, Jonathan L. (2000), 'A lust for life: The cult films of Russ Meyer', in Xavier Mendik and Graeme Harper (eds), *Unruly Pleasures: The Cult Film and its Critics*, Guildford: FAB Press, 89–101
Dancyger, Kenneth (2011), *The Technique of Film and Video Editing: History, Theory and Practice*, 5th Edition, New York: Focal Press
Danks, Adrian (2006), 'The global art of found footage cinema', in Linda Badley, R. Barton Palmer and Steven Jay Schneider (eds), *Traditions in World Cinema*, Edinburgh: Edinburgh University Press, 241–53
Dante, Joe (1966), 'Dante's Inferno', *Famous Monsters of Filmland*, 1966 Yearbook, 68–77
Davis, Blair (2012), *The Battle for the Bs: 1950s Hollywood and the Rebirth of Low-budget Cinema*, New Brunswick, NJ; London: Rutgers University Press
Doane, Mary Ann (1980), 'The voice in the cinema: The articulation of body and space', *Yale French Studies*, 60: Cinema/Sound, 33–50
Dombrowski, Lisa (2009), 'Fuller's most fascinating flop: *Park Row*', *Velvet Light Trap*, 64 (Fall), 81–82
Donnelly, Kevin J. (2014), *Occult Aesthetics: Synchronization in Sound Film*, Oxford: Oxford University Press
Dwyer, Tess (2014), 'B-grade subtitles', in Claire Perkins and Constantine Verevis (eds), *B is for Bad Cinema: Aesthetics, Politics and Cultural Value*, Albany, NY: State University of New York Press, 43–64
Dyck, J. and M. Johnson (2017), 'Appreciating bad art', *Journal of Value Inquiry*, 51:2, 279–92
Dyer, Richard (1998) [1979], *Stars*, London: BFI Publishing
Dykhoff, Klas (2012), 'Non-diegetic sound effects', *The New Soundtrack*, 2:2, 169–79
Eco, Umberto (1985) [1984], 'Casablanca: Cult movies and intertextual collage', reprinted in *SubStance*, 14:2, Issue 47: In Search of Eco's Roses, 3–12
Eco, Umberto (1992), 'Between author and text', in Stefan Collini (ed.), *Interpretation and Overinterpretation*, Cambridge: Cambridge University Press, 67–88
Eco, Umberto (1992), 'Overinterpreting texts', in Stefan Collini (ed.), *Interpretation and Overinterpretation*, Cambridge: Cambridge University Press, 45–66
Editors (2009), 'Introduction', *Velvet Light Trap*, 64 (Fall), 1–2
Egan, Kate and Sarah Thomas (2013), 'Introduction: Star-making, cult-making and forms of authenticity', in Kate Egan and Sarah Thomas (eds), *Cult Film Stardom: Offbeat Attractions and Processes of Cultification*, London: Palgrave Macmillan, 1–17
Fairservice, Douglas (2001), *Film Editing: History, Theory and Practice*, Manchester: Manchester University Press
Fawcett, Neil (2002), 'Tor Ramsey email – director of *Children of the Living Dead*', *Homepage of the Dead*. Available at: https://www.homepageofthedead.com/baps/cotld_email.html [Accessed 10 October 2020]
Flynn, Charles (1975), 'The schlock/kitsch/hack movies', in Todd McCarthy and

Charles Flynn (eds), *Kings of the Bs: Working Within the Hollywood System*, New York: E. P. Dutton, 3–12

Flynn, Charles and Todd McCarthy (1975), 'The economic imperative: Why was the B movie necessary?', in Todd McCarthy and Charles Flynn (eds), *Kings of the Bs: Working Within the Hollywood System*, New York: E. P, Dutton, 13–43

Gorfinkel, Elena (2000), 'The body as apparatus: Chesty Morgan takes on the academy', in Xavier Mendik and Graeme Harper (eds), *Unruly Pleasures: The Cult Film and its Critics*, Guildford: FAB Press, 157–69

Graham, Alison (1991), 'Journey to the center of the fifties: The cult of banality' in J. P. Telotte (ed.), *The Cult Film Experience: Beyond All Reason*, Texas: University of Texas Press, 107–21

Grey, Rudolph (1992), *Nightmare of Ecstasy: The Life and Art of Edward D Wood, Jr*, Los Angeles: Feral House

Hawkins, Joan (1999), 'Sleaze mania, Euro-trash, and high art: The place of European art films in American low culture', *Film Quarterly*, 53:2, 14–29

Heath, Stephen (1981), *Questions of Cinema*, London, New York: Macmillan

Hentzi, Gary (1993), 'Little cinema of horrors', *Film Quarterly* 46:3, 22–27

Hill, Rob (2017), *The Bad Movie Bible*, London: Art of Publishing

Hill, Rodney F. (2015), 'Science fiction and the cult of Ed Wood: Glen or Glenda?, Bride of the Monster, and Plan 9 From Outer Space', in J. P. Telotte and Gerald Duchovnay (eds), *Science Fiction Double Feature: The Science Fiction Film as Cult Text*, Liverpool: Liverpool University Press, 172–89

Hills, Matt (2013), 'Cult movies with and without cult stars: Differentiating discourses of stardom', in Kate Egan and Sarah Thomas (eds), *Cult Film Stardom: Offbeat Attractions and Processes of Cultification*, London: Palgrave Macmillan, 21–36

Hoberman, J. (1980), 'Bad movies', *Film Comment*, 16:4, 7–12

Hoberman, J. and Jonathan Rosenbaum (1991), *Midnight Movies*, New York: Da Capo Press

Hollows, Joanne (2003), 'The masculinity of cult', in Mark Jancovich et al. (eds), *Defining Cult Movies: The Cultural Politics of Oppositional Taste*, Manchester: Manchester University Press, 35–53

Hunter, I. Q. (2013), *British Trash Cinema*, London: Palgrave Macmillan

Hunter, I. Q. (2014), 'Trash horror and the cult of the bad film', in Harry Benshoff (ed.), *A Companion to the Horror Film*, Chichester: Wiley Blackwell, 483–500

Hunter, I. Q. (2019), 'Jaws: The revenge and the production of failure', *Continuum: Journal of Media & Cultural Studies*, 33:6, 677–91

Hutcheon, Linda (2013), *A Theory of Adaptation*, 2nd Edition, London, New York: Routledge

Jancovich, Mark (1996), *Rational Fears: American Horror in the 1950s*, Manchester: Manchester University Press

Jancovich, Mark (2002), 'Cult fictions: Cult movies, subcultural capital and the production of cultural distinctions', *Cultural Studies*, 16:2, 306–22

Jancovich, Mark, Antonio Lazaro Reboll, Julian Stringer and Andy Willis (2003), 'Introduction', in Mark Jancovich et al. (eds), *Defining Cult Movies: The Cultural Politics of Oppositional Taste*, Manchester; New York: Manchester University Press, 1–13

Jancovich, Mark and Shane Brown (2013), '"The screen's number one and number two bogeymen": The critical reception of Boris Karloff and Bela Lugosi in the 1930s and 1940s', in Kate Egan and Sarah Thomas (eds), *Cult Film Stardom: Offbeat Attractions and Processes of Cultification*, London: Palgrave Macmillan, 243–58

Jarosi, Susan (2012), 'Recycled cinema as material ecology: Raphael Montanez Ortiz's found-footage films and Computer-Laser-Videos', *Screen*, 53:3, 228–45

Jenkins, Steve (1981), 'I Led Two Lives', *Monthly Film Bulletin*, 48:564, 179
Johnson, John 'J. J.' (1996), *Cheap Tricks and Class Acts: Special Effects, Makeup and Stunts from the Films of the Fantastic Fifties*, Jefferson, NC: McFarland
Johnson, Nessa (2019), '"You made me look bad. And that's not good": The millennial cultification of *Fatal Deviation*, Ireland's only martial arts film', *Continuum: Journal of Media & Cultural Studies*, 33:6, 692–704
Juno, Andrea and V. Vale (eds) (1986), *RE/Search #10: Incredibly Strange Films*, San Francisco: RE/Search Publication
Juul, Jasper (2013), *The Art of Failure: An Essay on the Pain of Playing Video Games*, Cambridge, MA; London: MIT Press
Kael, Pauline (1994) [1969], 'Trash, art, and the movies', originally published in *Harper's Magazine*, reprinted in *Going Steady: Film Writings 1968–1969*, New York: Marion Boyars, 87–129
Klevan, Andrew (2005), *Film Performance: From Achievement to Appreciation*, London: Wallflower Press
Konow, David (1998), *Schlock-o-Rama: The Films of Al Adamson*, Los Angeles: Lone Eagle
Kozloff, Sarah (1984), 'Humanising the "voice of god": Narration in *The Naked City*', *Cinema Journal*, 23:4, 41–53
Kozloff, Sarah (1988), *Invisible Storytellers: Voice-Over Narrative in American Fiction Film*, Berkeley, Los Angeles: University of California Press
LoBrutto, Vincent (2009), '"Invisible" or "visible" editing: The development of editorial styles and strategies', *Cineaste*, 34:2, 43–47
Lucia, Cynthia and Richard Porton (2006), 'Focusing on the art and craft of acting', *Cineaste*, 31:4, 1
Luckhurst, Roger (2008), 'Found footage science fiction: Five films by Craig Baldwin, Jonathan Weiss, Werner Herzog and Patrick Keiller', *Science Fiction Film and Television*, 1:2, 193–214
MacDowell, James and James Zborowski (2013), 'The aesthetics of "so bad it's good": Value, intention and *The Room*', *Intensities: The Journal of Cult Media*, 6, 1–30
MacDowell, James and Richard McCulloch (2019), 'Introduction: "So bad it's good": Aesthetics, reception, and beyond', *Continuum: Journal of Media & Cultural Studies*, 33:6, 643–52
Mathijs, Ernest (2005), 'Bad reputations: The reception of "trash" cinema', *Screen*, 46:4, 451–72
Mathijs, Ernest (2013), 'Cronenberg connected: Cameo acting, cult stardom and supertexts', in Kate Egan and Sarah Thomas (eds), *Cult Film Stardom: Offbeat Attractions and Processes of Cultification*, London: Palgrave Macmillan, 144–62
Mathijs, Ernest and Xavier Mendik (2008), 'Editorial introduction: What is cult film?', in *The Cult Film Reader*, Maidenhead England: Open University Press, 1–11
McCulloch, Richard (2011), '"Most people bring their own spoons": *The Room*'s participatory audiences as comedy mediators', *Participations: Journal of Audience & Reception Studies*, 8:2, 189–218
McDonald, Paul (2004), 'Why study film acting? Some opening reflections', in Cynthia Baron, Diane Carson and Frank P. Tomasulo (eds), *More Than a Method: Trends and Traditions in Contemporary Film Performance*, Detroit: Wayne State University Press, 23–41
McGilligan, Patrick (2006), 'What is great acting?', *Cineaste*, 31:4, 36–29
Medved, Harry and Michael Medved (1978), *The Fifty Worst Films of All Time (And How They Got That Way)*, London: Angus & Robertson
Medved, Harry and Michael Medved (1980), *The Golden Turkey Awards: The Worst Achievements in Hollywood History*, London: Angus & Robertson

Medved, Harry and Michael Medved (1986), *Son of Golden Turkey Awards: The Best of the Worst from Hollywood*, London: Angus & Robertson
Mittell, Jason (2009), 'The aesthetics of failure', *Velvet Light Trap*, 64 (Fall), 76–77
Morton, Jim (1986), 'Film personalities', in Andrea Juno and V. Vale (eds), *RE/Search #10: Incredibly Strange Films*, San Francisco: RE/Search Publication, 186–204
Morton, Jim (1986), 'Herschell Gordon Lewis biography', in Andrea Juno and V. Vale (eds), *RE/Search #10: Incredibly Strange Films*, San Francisco: RE/Search Publication, 34–35
Morton, Jim (1986), 'Sexploitation films', in Andrea Juno and V. Vale (eds), *RE/Search #10: Incredibly Strange Films*, San Francisco, RE/Search Publications, 160–5
Muecke, D. C. (1970), *Irony*, London: Methuen
Mulvey, Laura (1975), 'Visual pleasure and narrative cinema', *Screen*, 16:3, 6–18
Naremore, James (1988), *Acting in the Cinema*, Berkeley, CA; London: University of California Press
Neal (1953), 'Robot Monster', *Variety*, 191:2, 16
Neyman-Jones, Jackey (2012a), 'Part II: The inside story of *Manos: The Hands of Fate*', *Debbie's Manos* (blog), 11 October 2012. Available at: http://debbiesmanos.blogspot.com/2012_10_11_archive.html [Accessed 15 March 2019]
Neyman-Jones, Jackey (2012b), 'John Reynolds/Torgo Story 1', *Debbie's Manos* (blog), 13 October 2012. Available at: http://debbiesmanos.blogspot.com/2012/10/john-reynoldstorgo-story-i.html [Accessed 15 March 2019]
Neyman-Jones, Jackey (2012c), '1966 world premiere of *Manos: The Hands of Fate*', *Debbie's Manos* (blog), 31 October 2012. Available at: http://debbiesmanos.blogspot.com/2012/10/1966-world-premire-of-manos-hands-of.html [Accessed 23 May 2019]
Neyman-Jones, Jackey (2012d), 'Dedicated to Hal', *Debbie's Manos* (blog), 26 December 2012. Available at: http://debbiesmanos.blogspot.com/2012/12/dedicated-to-hal.html [Accessed 15 March 2019]
Neyman-Jones, Jackey Raye (2013), 'Happy 47th Anniversary Manos!!', *Debbie's Manos* (blog), 15 November 2013. Available at: https://debbiesmanos.blogspot.com/2013/11/happy-47th-anniversary-manos.html [Accessed 15 March 2019]
Nichols, Bill (1983), 'The voice of documentary', *Film Quarterly*, Spring, 36:3, 17–30
Norden, Martin F (2002), 'A report on Bruce Conner's "Report"', in Xavier Mendik and Steven Jay Schneider (eds), *Underground U.S.A.: Filmmaking Beyond the Hollywood Canon*, London, New York: Wallflower Press, 76–85
O'Pray, Michael (1987), 'From Dada to junk: Bruce Conner and the found footage film', *Monthly Film Bulletin*, 54:645, 315–16
Orpen, Valerie (2003), *Film Editing: The Art of the Expressive*, London; New York: Wallflower Press
Pauletto, Sandra (2012), 'The sound design of cinematic voices', *The New Soundtrack*, 2:2, 127–42
Peary, Danny (1981), *Cult Movies: The Classics, the Sleepers, the Weird, and the Wonderful*, New York: Delacorte Press
Peary, Danny (1991), *Cult Movie Stars*, New York: Simon & Schuster
Pehl, Mary Jo (2011), 'Afterword', in Robert Weiner and Shelley E. Barba (eds), *In the Peanut Gallery with 'Mystery Science Theater 3000': Essays on Films, Fandom, Technology and the Culture of Riffing*, Jefferson NC: McFarland, 253–54
Pepperman, Richard (2004), *The Eye is Quicker: Film Editing, Making a Good Film Better*, Studio City, CA: Michael Wiess Productions
Perkins, Claire and Constantine Verevis (2014), 'Introduction: B is for bad cinema', in Claire Perkins and Constantine Verevis (eds), *B is For Bad Cinema: Aesthetics, Politics and Cultural Value*, Albany, NY: State University of New York Press, 1–18

Petersen, Sandy (2010), 'Monster A Go-Go', *Jabootu's Bad Movie Dimension*. Available at: http://jabootu.net/?p=2737 [Accessed 7 May 2019]
Rausch, Andrew J. and Charles E. Pratt (2015), *The Cinematic Misadventures of Ed Wood*, Albany, GA: Bear Manor Media
Rausch, Andrew J. and R. D. Riley (eds) (2015), *Trash Cinema: A Celebration of Overlooked Masterpieces*, Albany GA, BearManor Media
Rawle, Steven (2013), 'Hal Hartley's "Look-out-Martin-Donovan's-in-the-house!" shot: The transformative cult indie star-director relationship and performance "idiolect"', in Kate Egan and Sarah Thomas (eds), *Cult Film Stardom: Offbeat Attractions and Processes of Cultification*, London: Palgrave Macmillan, 126–43
Rebane, Bill (2010), Interviewed by Corey Udley, Madison, WI, October [DVD commentary]
Rorty, Richard (1992), 'The pragmatist's progress', in Stefan Collini (ed.), *Interpretation and Overinterpretation*, Cambridge: Cambridge University Press, 89–108
Routt, William (2001), 'Bad for good', *Intensities: The Journal of Cult Media*, 2. Available at: https://intensitiescultmedia.files.wordpress.com/2012/12/routt-bad-for-good.pdf [Accessed 10 July 2018]
Sarkhosh, Keyvan and Winfried Menninghaus (2015), 'Enjoying trash films: Underlying features, viewing stances, and experiential response dimensions', *Poetics* 57, 40–54
Sarris, Andrew (2000), 'Notes on the auteur theory in 1962', in P. Adams Sitney (ed.), *Film Culture Reader*, New York: Cooper Square Press, 121–35
Sauter, Michael (1999), *The Worst Movies of All Time, Or: What Were They Thinking?* Secaucus, NJ: Citadel Press
Schaefer, Eric (1999), *'Bold! Daring! Shocking! True!': A History of Exploitation Films, 1919–1959*, Durham; London: Duke University Press
Sconce, Jeffrey (1995), '"Trashing" the academy: Taste, excess and an emerging politics of cinematic style', *Screen*, 36:4, 371–93
Sconce, Jeffrey (2003), 'Esper, the renunciator: Teaching "bad" movies to good students', in Mark Jancovich et al. (eds), *Defining Cult Movies: The Cultural Politics of Oppositional Taste*, Manchester: Manchester University Press, 14–34
Sconce, Jeffrey (2019), 'The golden age of badness', *Continuum*, 33:6, 666–76
Sestero, Greg and Tom Bissell (2013), *The Disaster Artist: My Life Inside The Room, the Greatest Bad Movie Ever Made*, New York: Simon & Schuster
Sexton, Jamie and Ernest Mathijs (2011), *Cult Cinema: An Introduction*, Malden, MA; Oxford: Wiley-Blackwell
Shochat, Ella and Robert Stam (1985), 'The cinema after babel: Language, difference, power', *Screen*, 26:3–4, 35–58
Smith, Iain Robert (2019), 'So "foreign" it's good: The cultural politics of accented cult cinema', *Continuum: Journal of Media & Cultural Studies*, 33:6, 705–16
Smith, Justin (2013), 'Vincent Price and cult performance: The case of Witchfinder General', in Kate Egan and Sarah Thomas (eds), *Cult Film Stardom: Offbeat Attractions and Processes of Cultification*, London: Palgrave Macmillan, 109–24
Smoodin, Eric (1983), 'The image and the voice in the film with spoken narration', *Quarterly Review of Film Studies*, 8:4, 19–32
Sobock, Bryan (2009), 'Convergent consortia: Format battles in high definition', *Velvet Light Trap*, 64 (Fall), 34–49
Sontag, Susan (2009) [1964], 'Notes on "Camp"', in *Against Interpretation and Other Essays*, London: Penguin Classics, 275–92
Staiger, Janet (1985), 'The politics of film canons', *Cinema Journal*, 24:3, 4–23
Telotte, J. P. (2015), 'Robot Monster and the "watchable . . . terrible" cult/SF film', in J. P. Telotte and Gerald Duchovnay (eds), *Science Fiction Double Feature: The Science Fiction Film as Cult Text*, Liverpool: Liverpool University Press, 159–70

Tube (1961), 'The Beast of Yucca Flats', *Variety*, 222: 18, 6

Tucker, E. D. (2015), '*Monster-a-Go-Go* (1965)', in Andrew J. Rausch and R. D. Riley (eds), *Trash Cinema: A Celebration of Overlooked Masterpieces*, Albany GA, BearManor Media, 151–53

Tunc, Tanfer Emin and Nichole Prescott (2003), '*Glen or Glenda*: Psychiatry, sexuality, and the silver screen', *Bright Lights Film Journal*, 41. Available at: https://brightlightsfilm.com/glen-or-glenda-psychiatry-sexuality-and-the-silver-screen/#.XRyQdOhKiUl [Accessed 14 July 2019]

Turner, Graeme (2004), *Understanding Celebrity*, London: SAGE Publications

Vassilieva, Julia and Constantine Verevis (2010), 'After taste: Cultural value and the moving image', *Continuum: Journal of Media & Cultural Studies*, 24:5, 643–52

Verevis, Constantine (2006), *Film Remakes*, Edinburgh: Edinburgh University Press

Vernallis, Carol (2001), 'The kindest cut: Functions and meanings of music video editing', *Screen*, 42:1, 21–48

Vincendeau, Ginette (1988), 'Hollywood babel: The multiple language version', *Screen*, 29:2, 24–39

Vorel, Jim and Kenneth Lowe (2019), 'Bad movie diaries: *Ben & Arthur* (2002)', *Paste Magazine*. Available at: https://www.pastemagazine.com/movies/bad-movie-diaries/ben-and-arthur-2002-review/ [Accessed 10 October 2020]

Warren, Bill (2010), *Keep Watching the Skies! American Science Fiction Movies of the Fifties, 21st Century Edition*, Jefferson, NC: McFarland

Weaver, Tom (1988), *Interviews with B Science Fiction and Horror Movie Makers*, Jefferson, NC: McFarland

Weaver, Tom (1994), *Attack of the Monster Movie Makers: Interviews with 20 Genre Giants*, Jefferson, NC: McFarland

Weaver, Tom (1996), *It Came From Weaver Five: Interviews with Moviemakers in the SF and Horror Traditions*, Jefferson, NC: McFarland

Weaver, Tom (n. d.), 'Return to Yucca Flats: Anthony Cardoza's Tor of the Desert', (interview with Anthony Cardoza, part 1), *The Astounding B Monster*. Available at: http://www.bmonster.com/profile37.html [Accessed 14 May 2019]

Weaver, Tom (n. d.), 'The Grand Tor' (interview with Anthony Cardoza, part 2), *The Astounding B Monster*. Available at: http://www.bmonster.com/scifi37.html [Accessed 14 May 2019]

Wees, William C. (1993), *Recycled Images: The Art and Politics of Found Footage Films*, New York: Anthology Film Archives

Wees, William C. (2002), 'The ambiguous aura of Hollywood stars in avant-garde found-footage films', *Cinema Journal*, 41:2, 3–18

Weldon, Michael (1983), *The Psychotronic Encyclopedia of Film*, London: Plexus

Whit (1955), 'Review: *Bride of the Atom*', *Variety*, 198:13, 22

Wilson, John (2005), *The Official Razzie Movie Guide*, New York: Warner Books

Wolfe, Charles (1997), 'Historicising the "voice of god": The place of vocal narration in classical documentary", *Film History*, 9:2, 149–67

Wood Jr, Edward D (1998), *Hollywood Rat Race*, New York, London: Four Walls Eight Windows

Zyrd, Michael (2003), 'Found footage film as discursive metahistory: Craig Baldwin's Tribulation 99', *The Moving Image*, 3:2, 40–61

INDEX

Adamson, Al, 9, 24, 27, 38, 75–6, 78, 127
American Independent Pictures (AIP), 13, 18, 36–7
anti-pleasure experience, 134, 140, 155–60
Asylum Films, 171
asynchrony, 43, 56, 60, 61–3, 64–7, 168
   character, 58
Attack of the Killer Tomatoes, 29
auteurism, 15, 22, 26–8, 89, 90, 167
   auteur theory, 22
   cult, 37, 67, 130, 131, 136, 170
avant-garde, 3, 58, 71–3, 79–81, 83, 84, 86, 93, 139
   accidental, 84, 136
Azalea pictures, 137, 158–60

Baby Boomers, 9
badfilm
   canon, 5–10, 112, 162, 163–4, 167, 170, 172
   fans and fandom, 2, 6, 9, 11, 13–16, 18, 22, 24–5, 42, 84, 95, 107, 126, 127, 157, 160, 167, 171
badness
   golden age, 7, 9, 163, 164, 170
   just bad, 39, 160
   objective, 6, 15, 18, 19, 102–3, 110, 118, 133, 163
   subjective, 3
Barringer, Pat, 120–2
Beast of Yucca Flats, The, 8, 45–6, 48, 60–3, 65, 66, 68, 80, 127, 136, 147–9, 161
Bela Lugosi Meets a Brooklyn Gorilla, 80

Ben & Arthur, 8, 10, 165–6, 167, 168
Birdemic: Shock and Terror, 167, 171–2
Birdemic 2: The Resurrection, 171–2
bizarreness, 2, 16, 23, 28, 36, 39, 40, 141, 162
Black Dynamite, 29
Blamire, Larry, 29, 170
Blood of Ghastly Horror, 24, 78, 157
Bride and the Beast, The, 74–5, 76
Bride of the Monster, 8, 12, 25, 30, 33, 80, 86, 111–16
Bronson Canyon, 95
Buchanan, Larry, 18, 27, 36–8, 137, 158–60

camp, 12, 14, 34, 36, 40, 118
Chaney, Jr., Lon, 110, 111
Children of the Living Dead, 168–9
cinemasochism, 14
comedy, 34, 47, 172
   unintentional, 17, 25, 104, 146, 163
Conner, Bruce, 72, 79
continuity, 6, 37, 53, 58, 74, 140, 169
   classical continuity editing, 32, 134, 137–8, 151–2, 153, 156
   discontinuity, 43, 55, 84, 95, 146–7, 150–1, 154
counter-cinema, 21, 72, 139
Creeping Terror, The, 1, 45, 48–9, 61, 64–7, 127
Criswell, 44, 124–6, 150–1
cross-dressing, 23, 84, 105
cult film, 3, 6, 9, 13, 15, 20, 107–8, 123, 173
Curse of the Swamp Creature, 18, 30, 137, 158

Dracula Vs Frankenstein, 111, 157
dubbing *see* post-synchronisation
Duncan, Kenne, 110

Eve and the Handyman, 47
excess, 17, 20, 70
   and acting, 108–9, 118, 125, 132
   and editing, 155, 157, 158, 160
exploitation films, 7–9, 15, 25–6, 72, 83–4, 91, 92, 156
extratextual information, 27, 48, 54, 67–8, 104, 110–11, 116, 127, 128, 136
   absence of, 119, 123; *see also* trivia

failure studies, 4–5, 172
Famous Monsters of Filmland, 12
Flagg, Cash *see* Steckler, Ray Dennis
found footage films, 72, 79, 80, 81–2
Francis, Coleman, 8, 27, 60, 127, 136

Glen or Glenda, 21, 26, 29, 44, 82–91, 92, 105, 128, 136–7, 156, 165
Godard, Jean-Luc, 59, 138–9
Golden Raspberry Awards, The, 104
Golden Turkey Awards, The, 12, 13
good-bad art, 16, 23, 29, 36, 39
gorilla suit, 1, 35–6, 127

Hall, Sr., Arch, 127
has-been, 109–11
Hewitt, David L., 27
horror films, 7, 8, 17, 25, 30, 106, 112
Horror of the Blood Monsters, 74–5

Incredibly Strange Creatures Who Stopped Living and Became Mixed Up Zombies!!?, The, 29, 35, 130–1, 156
Incredibly Strange Films, 14, 126
independence, 8
intertextuality, 22, 32–3, 34, 72, 78, 94, 95, 100, 107, 110, 111, 119, 124, 127, 147, 167
ironic decontextualization, 81, 97
irony
   and intention, 29, 30, 32, 34, 39, 59
   as a reading strategy, 14, 146
   in voice-over narration, 47–9, 51, 52, 53, 55, 82

Jail Bait, 1
Johnson, Tor, 60, 113

Karloff, Boris, 110
Keep Watching the Skies, 25

Lewis, Herschell Gordon, 50–1, 53, 55
Love Feast, 128
Lugosi, Bela, 77, 111–18

Madmen of Mandoras see They Saved Hitler's Brain
Mahon, Barry, 27
mainstream, opposition to, 3, 15, 20, 72
Maniac, 19, 83
Manos: The Hands of Fate, 17, 37, 58, 106–7, 108, 129, 141–6
Mars Needs Women, 37
Mason, Tom, 118, 150
material poverty, 3, 21, 70, 134, 158
Medved, Harry and Michael, 7, 12, 13
Mesa of Lost Women, 8, 25, 46, 50
Meyer, Russ, 47–8
Mighty Gorga, The, 1, 127
Monster A-go Go, 50–5, 118, 135, 139
Monster from Green Hell, 74
Monster of Camp Sunshine, The, 91–2
Morley, David, 25
Motion Picture Association of America, 7
Mystery Science Theater 3000 (MST3K), 13–14, 35, 141, 146

Necromania: A Tale of Weird Love, 156
Night of the Ghouls, 32–4, 44, 77, 119, 124, 127
Night Train to Mundo Fine, 1, 127
nudie-cutie, 156

One Million AC/DC, 1, 94, 118
One Million B.C., 94, 95, 96, 100
Orgy of the Dead, 119–23, 124–6, 157

paracinema, 14–15, 18, 21, 42, 109, 150, 159
pedagogical value, 5, 19, 173
plagiarism, 73, 74, 76–7, 78–9
   self-plagiarism, 77–8
Plan 9 From Outer Space, 10, 12, 31–2, 33–4, 39, 77, 92, 124, 127, 136, 149–55
pornography, 3, 79, 106, 156, 170

post-synchronisation, 56–7, 58, 60, 64–5, 75, 141
Poverty Row, 112
psychotronic films, 13, 35

queer film, 84, 165

recycled footage
  atomic bomb, 79–80, 91, 96
  hunting, 74
  military, 91–2
  stock footage, 30, 54, 70, 74, 78–9, 80, 82, 85–9, 150, 152
  war, 91–2
  see also spectacle
Red Zone Cuba see *Night Train to Mundo Fine*
Reefer Madness, 25, 83
Reynolds, John, 108
Robot Monster, 17, 35–6, 38, 58, 93–100
Room, The, 8, 10, 25, 39, 164–5, 167

Savage, Vic *see* White, Arthur Nelson
Savini, Tom, 168
schadenfreude, 5, 23–4, 35, 172
Schelling, 'Bud', 89, 137
science-fiction films, 7, 9, 25, 50, 60, 94
  recycled, 72, 93
seriousness, 8, 12, 34–6, 50, 53, 93–4, 172
sexploitation, 119–20
Sharknado, 171
Sherman, Sam, 24, 78, 110, 137
sincerity, 5, 35, 36, 93, 171
  in performance, 104, 111, 114, 116, 128
Sinister Urge, The, 77
Skydivers, The, 74, 139, 157
so bad it's good, 8, 10, 16–18, 39–40, 107, 133, 140, 145, 158–60, 169
special effects, 9, 33, 99, 164
spectacle, 9, 11, 37, 53, 98, 156, 171
  erotic, 122–3
  recycled, 70, 75, 80, 83, 91–3, 94–7, 99

stardom, 103, 107
  cult, 107–8, 109, 110, 118, 123–4, 132
  death, 108
Steckler, Ray Dennis, 130–2
stock footage *see* recycled footage
surrealism, 29, 89, 145, 148
  Surrealists, 12

Tagani, 75
Take it Out in Trade, 170
Talbot, Lyle, 110
taste, 3, 9, 10, 13, 15, 39–40, 163, 173
television, 7, 9, 36–7, 77, 124
They Saved Hitler's Brain, 9, 76–7
trash
  criticism, 31, 145
  films, 3, 13, 14, 35, 72
  trivia, 136, 145; *see also* extratextual information
Tucker, Phil, 8, 24, 35, 38

voice-off, 44, 61–2, 87
voice-over narration
  and recycled footage, 82, 87
  first-person, 44
  theories of, 43–6
  third-person, 44, 48, 50–5, 60, 61, 65, 67, 75, 80, 92, 151
  see also irony

Warren, Harold, 37, 106, 127, 129, 141
Weiss, George, 89–90
White, Arthur Nelson, 48, 126
Wiseau, Tommy, 25, 164–5, 167
Wishman, Doris, 59, 66
Wood, Jr., Edward D., 4, 10, 16, 20, 21, 22, 23, 27, 32, 37, 38, 77, 83, 84–5, 105, 111–2, 127–8, 136, 156
  Ed Wood films, 23, 78, 119, 170
  see also *Bride of the Monster*, *Glen or Glenda*, *Plan 9 From Outer Space*

Zontar: The Magazine from Venus, 3, 18, 159, 160
Zontar: The Thing from Venus, 18, 36, 137, 158

EU representative:
Easy Access System Europe
Mustamäe tee 50, 10621 Tallinn, Estonia
Gpsr.requests@easproject.com

www.ingramcontent.com/pod-product-compliance
Lightning Source LLC
Chambersburg PA
CBHW070825250426
43671CB00036B/2069